Visiting 'Abdu'l-Bahá

This book is dedicated to

early pilgrims

*who recorded their impressions, thoughts and emotions
when meeting the Centre of the Covenant,
thus allowing us in this day to feel at least a little
of what it was like to be face to face with
'Abdu'l-Bahá*

Visiting 'Abdu'l-Bahá

Volume 1
The West Discovers the Master, 1897–1911

Earl Redman

GEORGE RONALD
OXFORD

George Ronald, Publisher
Oxford
www.grbooks.com

©Earl Redman 2019
Reprinted 2021

All Rights Reserved

A catalogue record for this book is available from the British Library

ISBN 978-0-85398-617-1

Cover design: Steiner Graphics

CONTENTS

Preface   vii
Acknowledgements   xv

Who is 'Abdu'l-Bahá?   1

1897–1898   3
    Mírzá Habíbu'lláh Afnán – Anton Haddad – Arrival of the first Western pilgrims – Ibrahim Kheiralla and his march to oblivion – Lua and Edward Getsinger – Phoebe Hearst and Maryam Thornburgh-Cropper

1899   17
    May Bolles and Harriet Thornburgh – Anne Apperson, Julia Pearson and Robert Turner – Margaret Peeke – Ella Goodall and Helen Hillyer – Naw-Rúz 1899 – Ali-Kuli Khan – Anton Haddad

1900   36
    Sarah Farmer and Maria Wilson – Arthur and Elizabeth Dodge, and Anna Hoar – Charlotte, Louise and Eleanor Dixon – Laura Barney, Ellen Goin and Emma Tronvé – Emogene Hoagg, Helen Ellis Cole and Alma Albertson – Reverend Henry Jessup turns against the Faith

1901   52
    Edith and Marie-Louise McKay – Edith Jackson and Sigurd Russell – Starting the Shrine of the Báb – Mírzá Habíbu'lláh Afnán – Laura Barney and Mason Remey – Yúnis Khán and William Hoar – Confined to 'Akká – Thomas Breakwell, Herbert Hopper and Isabella Brittingham – William and Wendell Dodge

1902–1903   80
    The Mashriqu'l-Adhkár in Ashkabat – Madame de Canavarro and Myron Phelps – Hippolyte Dreyfus and Edith Sanderson – Contacts and enemies

1904   89
George and Rosa Winterburn – Frank Frank and his guide – Azíz'u'lláh Azízí – Investigation and Interrogation of 'Abdu'l-Bahá – Edith Jackson and Sigurd Russell – Ethel Rosenberg, Laura Barney and Some Answered Questions – Sydney Sprague – Other visitors

1905   110
Howard and Mary MacNutt, and Julia Grundy – Mary Lucas – Josephine Cowles de Lagnel – The Ottoman Commission of Enquiry

1906   132
Jane Whyte – William Jennings Bryan – Florence and Ali-Kuli Khan – Azíz'u'lláh Azízí returns – Hooper Harris and Harlan Ober, and others

1907   149
Edwin Woodcock, and Edith and Joseph de Bons – Corinne and Arna True, and Mary Scaramucci – Thornton Chase, Arthur and Mary Agnew, and Carl Scheffler – Wellesca (Aseyeh) Allen-Dyar – Roy and Laurie Wilhelm – Mason Remey and Frances Phelps – Mary Hanford Ford – Other visitors – Troubles and the threat of exile

1908   187
Helen Goodall, Ella Cooper and Marion Jack – Jean Stannard – Stanwood Cobb – Mason Remey and the Revolution – The Knobloch sisters

1909   208
May and Sutherland Maxwell – Joseph and Pauline Hannen – Placing the Báb's remains in His Shrine – Juliet Thompson, and Edward and Carrie Kinney – Valíyu'lláh Varqá – Susan Moody and Louise Waite – Other pilgrims and visitors

1910–1911   239
Howard Struven and Mason Remey – Grace Crockett – Stanwood Cobb returns – The mouse and the sugar – Agnes Parsons – Sydney Sprague gets married and sets the stage for conflict – The future Guardian through the eyes of a Westerner – Ethel Stefana Stevens – The Master's departure for the West – Egypt – The Master's Western journey

Bibliography	259
Notes and References	267
Index	283
About the Author	288

PREFACE

> Among those who visit 'Akká, some have made great forward strides. Lightless candles, they were set alight; withered, they began to bloom; dead, they were recalled to life and went home with tidings of great joy. But others, in truth, have simply passed through; they have only taken a tour.[1]
>
> 'Abdu'l-Bahá

The book *'Abdu'l-Bahá in Their Midst*, about 'Abdu'l-Bahá's three-year journey to Egypt, Europe and North America, had sprung upon me unasked and unexpected, inspired in 2007 by 45 mysterious minutes lost in prayer in 'Abdu'l-Bahá's room in His house in Haifa and triggered by a Bahá'í World News Service story in 2010[2] about the Master's three-year journey to spread His Father's Faith through Europe and America. While working on the book, the idea of another book kept popping into my mind, only to be rejected by the apparent reality of having absolutely no idea what else to write about.

May Hofman and I had almost finished editing the manuscript for *'Abdu'l-Bahá in Their Midst* and I was chasing an elusive reference in a *Star of the West* volume. *Star of the West* was at that time unindexed and unavailable in a searchable electronic format so I was having to go through the volumes page by page. That is how I encountered an article written by a pilgrim in 'Akká in 1907 and read about how the Master answered the unasked questions of His visitor. I was struck by the feeling that the story should be shared with others. I had also just finished reading *Lighting the Western Sky* by Kathryn Jewett Hogenson, a beautiful description of the first pilgrimage of Westerners to 'Abdu'l-Bahá in 'Akká, and it suddenly appeared possible that the primary concept behind *'Abdu'l-Bahá in Their Midst*, of how people reacted to meeting the Master, could be extended into a book about His interactions with pilgrims and other visitors in 'Akká and Haifa.

I had only just begun returning the stacks of books used to research and write *'Abdu'l-Bahá in Their Midst* to the bookshelf, when they began to return to my desk. These books had the same amazing stories about people on spiritual quests encountering 'Abdu'l-Bahá, this time in 'Akká and Haifa instead of Europe and America, and being transformed by the experience. Yúnis Khán (Dr Youness Afroukhteh), who spent a year working as 'Abdu'l-Bahá's secretary, described the effect 'Abdu'l-Bahá had on pilgrims:

> The talents and capacities of all those who entered the shores of this Most Great Ocean differed, of course, each profiting according to his own potential. For example, one who was devoid of any depth of spiritual understanding would find it sufficient to merely behold the boundless Ocean and marvel at its beauty. Another, who came with a small cup, would receive his cupful; while he who possessed a chalice would partake of a larger share. But true contentment and joy belonged to the one who ventured further, who was able to tread the deeper waters and acquire the hidden and priceless pearls and precious gems. It is then clear that capacity, worthiness, volition and effort were the first requirements. And so these were the conditions of those who besought 'Abdu'l-Bahá's heavenly blessings.
>
> But the blessings of this Most Great Ocean, as ordained by its very nature, did not emanate with any uniform or predictable consistency. This boundless Ocean was sometimes calm; at other times it would surge; and at yet other times it was turbulent, leaving a variety of impressions in the minds of His listeners.
>
> When calm and tranquil, He filled every observer's heart and soul with joy, breathed into them the spirit of faith, and bestowed upon them visions of the world of spirit. At other times, He brought out in them feelings of wonder and astonishment. Sometimes the wine of the love of God was so intoxicating that, utterly unaware of self, a person's entire being was transformed into a pair of eyes fixed on the exalted beauty of the Beloved.[3]

Eastern pilgrims had been going on pilgrimage to visit first Bahá'u'lláh and then 'Abdu'l-Bahá since They were first exiled. These pilgrims seldom wrote down their experiences or, if they did, their narratives were not available in a Western language. The first Western pilgrims didn't seek out the Centre of the Covenant until 1898, but they tended to be prolific writers who shared what they had written. Because of this, the present account is dominantly by and about Western pilgrims. Many people who were not Bahá'ís went to see 'Abdu'l-Bahá as well, either because of a desire to learn who He was or as tourists in the area who wanted to meet the most talked about person in Haifa and 'Akká.

Because of the dramatic increase in written accounts of visits to 'Abdu'l-Bahá that began in 1898 following the return of the members of that first American pilgrimage organized and led by Phoebe Hearst, it became possible to learn about the history and people of 'Akká and Haifa through their remembrances. This two-volume account, along with the previously published *Abdu'l-Bahá in Their Midst*, is therefore both a history of the time starting with the pilgrimage of Mírzá Habíbu'lláh Afnán in 1897 and ending with the passing of 'Abdu'l-Bahá in late 1921, and a recounting of the experiences of those who met the Master, using their own words as much as possible.

Initially conceived as a single book stretching from 1897 to 1921, the number of fascinating accounts by pilgrims rapidly increased the book's size until it was decided to break it into two volumes which would sandwich *Abdu'l-Bahá in Their Midst*, making the three books a trilogy about the Master. This volume covers the time from 1897 until the Master's departure on His three-year journey to the West. The second volume follows on from *Abdu'l-Bahá in Their Midst* with His return to Haifa at the end of 1913 and covers the time until His passing in 1921.

Virtually all pilgrims and many other visitors wrote down what 'Abdu'l-Bahá said, including many of His talks, both formal and informal. The talks were translated from Persian to English by a series of interpreters including Ibrahim Kheiralla, Ali-Kuli Khan, Yúnis Khán, Amin Fareed, Ahmad Sohrab, Shoghi Effendi, Lotfullah Hakim and others. Sometimes, 'Abdu'l-Bahá Himself would correct the Persian versions from which the translations were made. But, in the end, almost everything that 'Abdu'l-Bahá is reported to have said within this book is pilgrims' notes, unauthenticated remembrances which the pilgrims wrote down as the translators converted the Master's musical Persian into English. A few of the translators, especially Ibrahim Kheiralla, translated 'Abdu'l-Bahá's words to fit their own beliefs, leaving out some things and changing others. It is very important, therefore, to remember that pilgrims' notes are simply remembrances by the pilgrims of what 'Abdu'l-Bahá said. Edward Getsinger specifically refers to this matter of authenticity in a letter:

> When a question comes up regarding meetings, feasts, explanations, it was said by 'Abdu'l-Bahá in my presence that the written word or tablet must be taken as guidance, and not the spoken word, for 'have I not said on the steamer in [New York] that they will say he said so and so, but pay only attention to the Tablets written with my signature and seal', He said . . . so it is with all matters, those who claim authority for this and that he said 'have they a Tablet to that effect?'[4]

Rather ironically, this quotation is itself a pilgrim's note, but it gets the point across. Shoghi Effendi, Guardian of the Bahá'í Faith, stated:

> Much of the confusion that has obscured the understanding of the believers should be attributed to this double error involved in the inexact rendering of an only partially understood statement. Not infrequently has the interpreter even failed to convey the exact purport of the inquirer's specific questions, and, by his deficiency of understanding and expression in conveying the answer of 'Abdu'l-Bahá, has been responsible for reports wholly at variance with the true spirit and purpose of the Cause. It was chiefly in view of the misleading nature of the reports of the informal conversations of 'Abdu'l-Bahá with visiting pilgrims, that I have insistently urged the believers of the West to regard such statements as merely personal impressions of the sayings of their Master, and to quote and consider as authentic only such translations as are based upon the authenticated text of His recorded utterances in the original tongue.[5]

Though they must be viewed as 'personal impressions', a letter written on behalf of the Guardian clarified how pilgrim notes could be used: 'On the other hand, each pilgrim brings back information and suggestions of a most precious character, and it is the privilege of all the friends to share in the spiritual results of these visits.'[6]

Here you have a great wealth of stories that can be told to help illustrate who 'Abdu'l-Bahá was in the context of history and how he taught and interacted with others, nothing more.

PREFACE

This book is filled with quotations extracted from what people wrote while visiting 'Abdu'l-Bahá. Most come from personal diaries and letters initially written in longhand, though many were later typed. Since the pilgrims were primarily writing for themselves and not for publication, their writings not uncommonly contain typographical errors and grammatical stumbles, as well as missing punctuation, apostrophes and accents. Quoted text throughout this book has been left exactly as it was written by the pilgrims in order not to change their meaning or emotion or, on occasion, their confusion.

Many different types of people visited 'Abdu'l-Bahá. Dr John Esslemont, author of *Bahá'u'lláh and the New Era*, noted a difference between Eastern and Western pilgrims:

> When they [Americans] were here there was always bustle. At meal times there were always many questions put to the Master. Generally two or three were taking notes. Afterwards they were very busy transcribing and completing their notes and discussing what the Master said or meant about this or that.
>
> At the meeting last night [with Eastern pilgrims] the initiative was left entirely to the Master. If a silence occurred . . . no one seemed to feel the slightest awkwardness. The Persian believers seem to be quite happy to be in the Presence of their Lord even when nothing is being said.[7]

Among the Western pilgrims there were differences as well. Those who were on their first pilgrimage, particularly those who had not met 'Abdu'l-Bahá before, tended to try to write about their spiritual experiences. Many would say that their experiences could not be put into words, but then they would try to do so with greater or lesser success. First-time pilgrims very commonly wrote about four aspects of their journey: the arrival at Haifa's harbour and the rowboat trip to shore; the wagon trip along the wave-washed sandy beach to 'Akká; how they reacted to their first meeting of the Centre of the Covenant; and lastly a physical description of 'Abdu'l-Bahá. And many were mesmerized by the Master's ever-changing, all-seeing eyes. Pilgrims on their second or third pilgrimage, or who had met 'Abdu'l-Bahá on His travels to the West, tended to record mostly their questions and the Master's answers.

People came to meet 'Abdu'l-Bahá for many different reasons. Edwin Woodcock noted that

> Acca, at the present time, is the mecca of many pilgrims from all parts of the world, who go there to see and hear Abbas Effendi, whom they lovingly call 'The Master,' explain his teachings of divine love. Being a prisoner, and subject to many physical restrictions and conditions, it can be readily understood how difficult it is for him to serve all. Yet, strange as it may appear, none are turned away empty handed. It seems to be another case of the loaves and fishes.[8]

Corinne True quotes 'Abdu'l-Bahá as saying that 'There are two kinds of visits, – one the person comes very thirsty and the water will taste very sweet to him; the other will be that the person is not thirsty and the water will be bitter.'[9] Louise Waite records the Master as saying that some people do not 'see' the spiritual side of the visit while others do:

> Some souls come here and return unaltered. It is precisely like one who comes to a fountain and not being thirsty, returns exactly as he came, or like a blind man who goes into a rose-garden; he perceives not, and being questioned as to what he has seen in the rose-garden, replies: 'Nothing.' But some souls who come here are resuscitated. They come dead; they return alive. They come frail in body; they returned healed. They come athirst; they return satisfied. They come sorrowing; they return joyous . . . These souls have in reality done justice to their visit.[10]

Isabella Brittingham noted that each person received what they were prepared to receive:

> Each one receives according to the measure of the cup that he takes. If the cup is full of something else, or some other things, only a little will be placed in that cup and that will mix with the other things and be lost. The fragrance will depart . . . The length of the visit has nothing to do with the absolute blessing, but it is the condition of the heart. You may go and stay there ten years in the presence of our Lord and receive a very small bit, and you may go and be filled in an hour. That is with your soul and mine.[11]

Aseyeh Allen-Dyar noted an interesting dual nature in 'Abdu'l-Bahá: when she and her companions didn't ask questions and just enjoyed being with Him; and when they asked a question:

> He was able to be to us a loving father, a companion and friend, and we could enjoy ourselves socially because we did not continually keep Him answering questions, at which time He would at once assume a different attitude and a distance would come between us and one would feel His Kingship, His Greatness, the unlimited depths of His Wisdom.[12]

The Western Bahá'ís, and particularly the Americans, were full of questions to which they wanted answers. Many came with lists of questions they wanted to ask. George Latimer, however, voiced a common problem: the pilgrims kept forgetting those questions when they came into the presence of 'Abdu'l-Bahá. George remembered that at the end of a question and answer session 'the Master asked for further questions and I replied it was most difficult to remember questions in His Presence and He answered that there was a wisdom therein for He had a great deal to do.'[13] It appears that 'Abdu'l-Bahá allowed people to ask questions as long as He had time and the questions would help them understand. But sometimes, it seemed that answers to questions were not what they needed to understand.

ACKNOWLEDGEMENTS

I have discovered that there is a wealth of information about various aspects of the Bahá'í Faith, but it is scattered in many places. Two people in particular gave me a great deal of help for this book: Lewis Walker and Dr Duane K. Troxel. Lewis Walker, at the United States National Bahá'í Archives, initially supplied me with over 2,500 pages of pilgrim notes which contained amazing stories, numerous historical facts and vivid descriptions of the life and times of those who lived in or visited Haifa and 'Akká. He also continually sent me materials from the Archives that improved the book. Lewis's selfless efforts at uncovering and copying all that information are what fill the bulk of this book.

Dr Duane K. Troxel, of The Heritage Project of the National Spiritual Assembly of the United States, supplied me with little-known publications, audio files, and searchable electronic versions of many books, all of which greatly aided my work. His contributions filled in gaps and added inspiring new stories.

Judy Hannen Moe shared some of her research on the Knobloch sisters and provided me with a colourful note about their arrival in Haifa. Maurice Sabour-Pickett, who is an accountant, put his nit-picking skills to good use in searching out and eradicating typos, grammatical errors and other unwanted bits that always end up scattered throughout a long book. Byron McCord also read through the text and offered some very good suggestions. All of their help is greatly appreciated.

Karl Schoeppe, whose continuous gifts of corn tortillas, mailed expensively from Alaska to Ireland, also deserves my grateful thanks. The enchiladas those tortillas created were a necessary staple for this former New Mexican.

My wife, Sharon O'Toole, must also be acknowledged for her constant support and encouragement. And for permitting me to work on the book when she probably would have rather I'd been out working in the gardens or painting something.

This book, though it is just now being published, has been the source of most of the stories that Sharon and I have been sharing across the world for the last several years. Between the beginning of 2014 and late 2017, we slept in 160 different beds in Tunisia, Poland, Ireland, Northern Ireland, Iceland, Israel, Alaska, the United States, Canada, Hawaii, Fiji, Samoa, New Zealand, Australia and Tasmania. We greatly appreciate all those who graciously provided them. Without all of you, our trips would have been financially prohibitive.

In addition, a number of people made our trips much easier by organizing multiple events for us. Chris Cholas and Pearl and Kevin Trick organized most of our Hawaiian tour, Carol Hitti set up our visit in the Navajo and Ute region of the American Southwest, Anne Perry organized things in the Dallas area, Sid and Nancy Korn were a great help in Madison, Wisconsin, and Marvel Guhrke put together several meetings in Albuquerque, New Mexico. Erica Toussaint-Brock, Laurie King, John Kolstoe, Doug and Tania Stevens, Carol Hudson, and Kurt and Leslie Asplund put together story-tellings in the Pacific Northwest of America and John Craig and Alfred Fox set us up in Roanoke, Virginia. Chad Jones organized our events in the Sacramento, California area, and Gavin Reed helped us get into contact with many of the Alaska communities. In Alaska, Karina Rawhani, Georgia Haisler and Keith Hermann helped set up events.

Internationally, Chris Anderson aided us up in the Yukon, John Davidson was our organizer in Tasmania, Rowshan Mustapha put us to work in Tunisia, and Bee McEvoy set us up with 11 story-tellings in 12 days in Iceland. Thanks also go to Shahin Ansari, John Kirsch and David Young and Brian Ashton for their special contributions to our story-telling efforts.

We have shared the stories with many people and are very grateful to those who managed to stay awake.

WHO IS 'ABDU'L-BAHÁ?

Who was this man who attracted people from all over the world, whose magnetism was powerful enough to cause Persians, Russians and Indians to walk for months just to be in His presence? Who was this man who caused people from Europe and America to take long, expensive sea voyages in order to ask Him questions? Who was this man who was knighted for his humanitarian services during the First World War and whom every high military commander and governor in post-war Palestine came to meet and from whom they asked advice?

One of those who visited Him struggled to understand how a simple man, a prisoner of the Turks, could have such a power that He didn't wield, but just seemed to exude:

> What is it in this Man that conquers all who come in contact with Him? This man to whom all about Him go in their troubles, but who Himself, if He has any troubles never mentions them, except to rejoice over them as victories . . .
>
> . . . What, I repeat, is the strange Power of this Man, so simple, so natural, so unassuming, who asks for himself no special consideration, or reverence whatever, but continually points us to the things of the Spirit and to God . . .[1]

By His own admission, He was 'Abdu'l-Bahá, a servant; a servant of Bahá'u'lláh, His father, Who was the Manifestation of God for this time. When Bahá'u'lláh ascended from this material world, He, in His own hand, wrote a will in which He 'bequeathed to Our heirs an excellent and priceless heritage. Earthly treasures We have not bequeathed, nor have We added such cares as they entail.' Bahá'u'lláh then wrote that 'It is incumbent upon the Aghsán, the Afnán and My kindred to turn, one and all, their faces towards the Most Mighty Branch.'[2] The

Most Mighty Branch is 'Abdu'l-Bahá. The 'Aghsán, the Afnán and My kindred' are all of His relatives and the relatives of the Báb. Bahá'u'lláh plainly stated:

> Whoso turneth towards Him hath turned towards God, and whoso turneth away from Him hath turned away from My Beauty, hath repudiated My Proof, and transgressed against Me. He is the Trust of God amongst you, His charge within you, His manifestation unto you and His appearance among His favoured servants . . . They who deprive themselves of the shadow of the Branch, are lost in the wilderness of error . . .'[3]

Bahá'u'lláh explicitly stated that 'When the Mystic Dove will have winged its flight from its Sanctuary of Praise and sought its far-off goal, its hidden habitation, refer ye whatsoever ye understand not in the Book to Him Who hath branched from this mighty Stock.'[4] 'Abdu'l-Bahá was therefore the infallible Interpreter of Bahá'u'lláh's Word.

'Abdu'l-Bahá considered Himself to be nothing more than the pure channel for Bahá'u'lláh's will. This was probably why He could be sociable one moment, but would withdraw and become kingly when asked a question. At those moments, He became that pure channel for Bahá'u'lláh's Word, the mirror to the Mirror of God.

For the first time in religious history, a Manifestation of God had unambiguously named a successor and bestowed upon Him the ability to infallibly interpret His Word and desires. In the words of Shoghi Effendi, the Guardian of the Cause of God, 'Abdu'l-Bahá is

> the 'Mystery of God' – an expression by which Bahá'u'lláh Himself has chosen to designate Him, and which, while it does not by any means justify us to assign to Him the station of Prophethood, indicates how in the person of 'Abdu'l-Bahá the incompatible characteristics of a human nature and superhuman knowledge and perfection have been blended and are completely harmonized.[5]

1897–1898

Mírzá Habíbu'lláh Afnán

Pilgrims from the East had been making the long journey to meet Bahá'u'lláh since His arrival in 'Akká in 1868. After His passing, the pilgrims continued to make the arduous trek from Iraq, Persia and India to gain spiritual guidance from Bahá'u'lláh's son, 'Abdu'l-Bahá. Most of those early pilgrimages remain unavailable to those not familiar with Farsí or Arabic, but one man's experiences were translated into English. Sometime in the first half of 1897, Mírzá Habíbu'lláh Afnán made his first pilgrimage from his home in Cairo to meet 'Abdu'l-Bahá.[1] He had been able to be with Bahá'u'lláh in 1891 and had first met 'Abdu'l-Bahá at that time.

Now he returned to meet the Centre of the Covenant, and during his pilgrimage heard about a dream 'Abdu'l-Bahá had and which He had earlier recounted to Mírzá Aqay-i-Afnán (Núri'd-Dín), the father of this young pilgrim. 'Abdu'l-Bahá had said:

> 'Last night the Ancient Beauty appeared in my dream and said, "I have guests that have never been here before. I want you to receive them most befittingly." I related Bahá'u'lláh's command to the Greatest Holy Leaf. Together, we went to the storage [area] and retrieved the set of fine china that the Khal's son (that is, the honored Hájí Mírzá Muhammad-'Alíy-i-Afnán) had sent from China and got it ready' . . . 'Abdu'l-Bahá explained the meaning of the vision: 'The standard of the Faith has been raised in America. A number in that country have embraced the Faith and will come here soon for pilgrimage to the Sacred Shrine of Bahá'u'lláh. These friends have never outwardly been here and will now come and share in this blessing.'[2]

This was the first intimation of the impending flood of pilgrims from Europe and North America that Bahá'u'lláh Himself had predicted:

We, in truth, have sent Him Whom We aided with the Holy Spirit that He may announce unto you this Light that hath shone forth from the horizon of the Will of your Lord, the Most Exalted, the All-Glorious, and Whose signs have been revealed in the West.³

In the East the light of His Revelation hath broken; in the West the signs of His dominion have appeared.⁴

It was a very bittersweet pilgrimage, because the Master was surrounded by the nefarious activities of his Covenant-breaking half-brothers, Mírzá Muḥammad-'Alí and Badí'u'lláh, and their cohorts, including Majdu'd-Dín and Mírzá Áqá Jan (who had served Bahá'u'lláh as his amanuensis for 40 years, but then rejected His testament in the Kitáb-i-'Ahd and joined those who were unfaithful).

Immediately after the passing of Bahá'u'lláh, this group turned against 'Abdu'l-Bahá in spite of the unambiguous declarations by Bahá'u'lláh in the Kitáb-i-'Ahd that all the Bahá'ís should turn to 'Abdu'l-Bahá and follow His guidance. Bahá'u'lláh wrote that 'whoso turneth away from Him hath turned away from My Beauty, hath repudiated My Proof, and transgressed against Me',⁵ but the group rejected that clear statement and occupied the Mansion at Bahjí, where Bahá'u'lláh had spent His final years and from which He ascended. They held the Mansion until 1927, when they finally abandoned it due to its dire state of disrepair. Because they turned against 'Abdu'l-Bahá in the face of Bahá'u'lláh's specific statements, they were declared to be breakers of Bahá'u'lláh's Covenant.

Mírzá Habíbu'lláh arrived in 'Akká about the same time as Dr Youness Afroukhteh (better known as Yúnis Khán) and Áqá Mírzá Faḍlu'lláh Kandí, Mírzá 'Abdu'lláh Khán-i-Varqá and Mírzá 'Azízu'lláh Khán, father and eldest son of the Hand of the Cause of God Mírzá 'Alí-Muḥammad Varqá, who had been martyred in Iran just the year before. Mírzá Habíbu'lláh wrote that 'Abdu'l-Bahá

> showered us with His measureless favors and infinite bounties and asked after the friends in Cairo. He then warned, 'This region is beset with turmoil. The gale of tests from the Blessed Beauty blows in every direction. Calamity's tempest has agitated the sea of the world of being. You must exert yourself and be vigilant lest, God

forbid, the dust of rancor, enmity and infidelity to the divine Covenant should sully your pure hearts.⁶

That warning, Mírzá Habíbu'lláh wrote, 'profoundly saddened my heart, withered my spirit and paralyzed my whole being'. He remembered 'Abdu'l-Bahá's youthful vibrant personality in 1891, but 'Now', he wrote, 'I wondered: what had robbed Him of His strength and vitality? What had diminished His radiance and those heavenly smiles? His hair and beard had turned white; His luminous cheeks were now full of lines; and His blessed eyes, which at the time of the Ancient Beauty were full of life and brilliance, now looked bitterly tired. He seemed very sad and grief-stricken.'⁷

The pilgrims were cautioned to not disclose what was happening in 'Akká when they returned home.⁸ Officials from Istanbul were investigating 'the constant barrage of false and calumnious reports that Mírzá Muhammad-'Alí had sent to the Sublime Court and the string of lies and deceptions that he had woven'. 'Akká's Chief of Police was a close companion of Mírzá Muhammad-'Alí. 'Abdu'l-Bahá told the pilgrims that the Covenant-breakers had

> sent a report to the Commission of Inquiry, which has resulted in the Commission's head moving with a vengeance to eradicate the Cause of God. He is now raising a tumult by saying, 'The claims of Your Father and Yourself vary with Your deeds and the objections of Your brother. We have a Hadith that states: 'The Messengers and Prophets do not inherit and have no heir.' Your Father claimed the station of Prophethood and gave You His successorship. Your brother states that You have confiscated the estate of the Shaykh-i-Kabir [Bahá'u'lláh] and deprived them of their inheritance.
>
> I realized that, with such slanders, they sought to shatter the foundation of the Cause . . . I said to him, 'The Shaykh-i- Kabir has left a Will and Testament in His own hand and seal, and defined in it the inheritance of His heir: 'Although the Realm of Glory hath none of the vanities of the world, yet within the treasury of trust and resignation We have bequeathed to Our heirs an excellent and priceless heritage. Earthly treasures We have not bequeathed, nor have We added such cares as they entail. By God! In earthly riches fear is hidden and peril is concealed'. . . I said this to him and the words choked his breath!

Those attacking 'Abdu'l-Bahá would befriend newly arrived pilgrims, saying they were devoted to the Master, but then would 'plant seeds of discord in the heart of their victims, poison their soul and undermine their faith'. This was why 'Abdu'l-Bahá looked so aged, sad and tired to Mírzá Habíbu'lláh.

In the days before the Commemoration of the Ascension of Bahá'u'lláh in May 1897, 'Abdu'l-Bahá's grief and sorrow were apparent and those believers who had served the Master for years in the Holy Land, such as Mishkín-Qalam, said that they had 'never seen so much despondency on His face'. On the day, 'Abdu'l-Bahá

> summoned all the believers and gave each a candle and a bottle of rosewater. With unreserved grief and sorrow, we proceeded towards the Mansion of Bahjí and Bahá'u'lláh's Shrine, following His blessed Figure.
>
> 'Abdu'l-Bahá called on several of the friends to chant prayers . . . and, in such a meditative atmosphere, we arrived at the Shrine. 'Abdu'l-Bahá instructed us to pour the rosewater on the inner garden of the Shrine and to plant the candles in the same soil. With His heavenly and soul-stirring tone, 'Abdu'l-Bahá chanted the Tablet of Visitation. Tears were streaming from His eyes and the mourning of the friends soared heavenwards. The sound of sobbing and yearning filled the court of the Shrine of Bahá'u'lláh. Until morning, each person was occupied offering prayers and supplications to the Threshold of the Beloved, oblivious of his surroundings.

The next afternoon, Mírzá Áqá Jan went to the pilgrim house at Bahjí, where most of the pilgrims were napping, climbed onto a stool and according to Mírzá Habíbu'lláh, declared that

> because of countless favors bestowed on him by Bahá'u'lláh, [he] had attained a great station and possessed unequalled prestige in the Faith, to the point where the most prominent believers were humbled before him. He spoke like this: 'In a dream, the Ancient Beauty bequeathed the station of divine revelation upon me,' and then proceeded to belittle, and speak disparagingly of the sacred station of 'Abdu'l-Bahá.

Mírzá Áqá Jan had a plan, conceived by Mírzá Muḥammad-'Alí, which was to create a commotion and cause the Bahá'ís to attack him, which would enable the Chief of Police to intervene, thus making the Bahá'ís appear as the aggressors. It almost worked, with some of the Bahá'ís pulling Mírzá Áqá Jan from his stool and beginning to beat him. But at that moment, 'Abdu'l-Bahá arrived. He took Mírzá Áqá Jan into the Shrine of Bahá'u'lláh and locked the door. 'There', wrote Mírzá Habíbu'lláh,

> this abominable man, who had been freed from the grasp of the friends [by 'Abdu'l-Bahá], made an attempt on the Master's life. Furious and deeply upset, the friends stood outside the Shrine . . . We were truly distressed and agitated, until the Master opened the Shrine's entrance. He instructed Mírzá Habíb and Taraz to take Mírzá Áqá Ján to a stable near the Mansion. He confiscated all the papers he had hidden inside his pockets and returned only his seal to him.

The papers 'were found to be all written in the style of Revelation Writing and addressed to different friends, particularly prominent believers throughout the Bahá'í world. Each was given a mission and a [new] title.' Mírzá Muḥammad-'Alí and Majdu'd-Dín 'hoped that the letters would confuse the friends and undermine their confidence [in 'Abdu'l-Bahá]'.[9]

Anton Haddad

Anton Haddad, from Lebanon, was the first Bahá'í who had been in America to set foot in 'Akká when he arrived later in 1897. He saw things much differently than had Mírzá Habíbu'lláh. Anton Haddad had gone to America in 1892, arriving just before his business partner, Ibrahim Kheiralla. In 1894, he returned to Lebanon after which, in 1897, he was able to go on pilgrimage to see 'Abdu'l-Bahá in 'Akká. Upon his return to America in mid-December 1897, his description of his pilgrimage sparked the interest of many others:

> Oh my dear brother heaven is there & the paridise [sic] of God. Every body would desire to be a servant in that place. I can not

explain to you the dignity & respect appearing on the faces of the favorites. The appearance of glory & besides these attributes the signs of kindness & generosity, love & happiness for the human race. On account of this he ['Abdu'l-Bahá] cannot sleep nights, people not leaving him a minute. Everybody goes to him for help & he never rejects them. His time is spent enlightening all – rich as well as poor, it makes no difference to him. His knowledge, understanding & high attributes are his characteristics & he is really the spirit & son of God . . . There is paradise & happiness . . . He said great blessings were coming to the U.S. He said 'If God wished it will be the happiest country in the world.'[10]

Arrival of the first Western pilgrims

Anton Haddad was just the first drop in a flood that was about to be unleashed. His descriptions of 'Abdu'l-Bahá excited the interest of those in the nascent American Bahá'í community. In August 1898, Phoebe Hearst, the wealthy American heiress and mother of newspaperman William Randall Hearst, was planning to spend the winter on the Nile in Egypt and then cruise the eastern Mediterranean. Between then and her departure, she decided to add a stop in 'Akká to meet the Master.

In October, before the first American pilgrim arrived to meet 'Abdu'l-Bahá, Kaiser Wilhelm II of Germany visited Haifa, landing 'with much fanfare and ceremony'.[11] He, however, chose not to go to 'Akká where 'Abdu'l-Bahá lived. 'Abdu'l-Bahá said He did not go to see the Kaiser because the latter 'was proud. He was the embodiment of pride.'[12]

A month before the first Western pilgrims arrived in Port Said, Egypt, on their way to 'Akká, 'Abdu'l-Bahá sent a cable to Mírzá Aqay-i-Afnán (Núri'd-Dín) telling him to look after coming pilgrims. When the ship arrived, Núri'd-Dín sent his two sons and another Bahá'í to find them. One of his sons, Mírzá Habíbu'lláh Afnán, recalled that:

> When [they arrived and] we saw each other, the sound of 'Allah-u-Abha' was raised all throughout the Custom Office. And as we tenderly embraced and kissed one another, tears of joy streamed from our eyes because this was the first time that we had met Bahá'ís from the western countries. They numbered fifteen and came to our home.

Without delay, my father telegraphed the Master informing Him of the arrival of the [western] friends. 'Abdu'l-Bahá instructed that they be divided in three groups of five. Each group was to leave for the Holy Land only after the previous one had arrived back in Port Said.[13]

For the Westerners, it was a very emotional beginning. Lua Getsinger broke down loudly into tears, to the amazement of the Persians. She explained her emotions by saying:

> If, at every moment, we were to offer a thousand thanks at the threshold of the Blessed Beauty, it would not suffice. See how the promises of the Bible and the prophecies of the New Testament and all other Holy Books of the Divine Messengers have come to pass . . . Consider how each of us is from a different race, religious background or nationality. And yet, with utmost peace and affection, we have come together under the shadow of God's Sacred Tree, dwell within the tabernacle of unity raised by the Blessed Beauty and sit at the same table spread in the name of oneness. I am from America and of Christian background, while you are Iranian and of Jewish, Zoroastrian or Shi'ah backgrounds . . . This is none other than the miracle of the teachings of Bahá'u'lláh and the result of His regenerative and life-giving revelation.[14]

By the time Phoebe Hearst's group arrived in 'Akká, the group included her black butler, Robert Turner, Lua and Edward Getsinger, Ibrahim and Marian Kheiralla, Anne Apperson, Julia Pearson, May Bolles, Helen Hillyer, Ella Goodall and Harriet Thornburgh and her daughter, Mary Virginia (Maryam) Thornburgh-Cropper.[15] 'Abdu'l-Bahá was closely watched by Turkish spies so it was not wise for the whole group to visit at one time. Therefore, the pilgrims came in small groups and spread out their arrivals between November 1898 and March 1899.

Ibrahim Kheiralla and his march to oblivion

Ibrahim Kheiralla, a Syrian doctor, learned of the Faith in Cairo and had received a Tablet from Bahá'u'lláh. After corresponding with 'Abdu'l-Bahá, Kheiralla went to New York in December 1892, then moved on to Chicago. Over the next several years, he was very successful in attracting Americans to the Bahá'í Cause, including such illustrious people as Thornton Chase, Louisa Moore (better known as Lua Getsinger), Edward Getsinger, Howard MacNutt, Arthur Dodge, Isabella Brittingham and Helen Goodall. By 1898, hundreds of Americans had accepted the Bahá'í Faith because of Kheiralla's efforts. When Lua Getsinger brought Phoebe Hearst into the Faith, her desire to meet 'Abdu'l-Bahá resulted in the first pilgrimage of American Bahá'ís to 'Akká. Kheiralla was invited on the journey.

Kheiralla was the first of the party to arrive, reaching 'Akká on 11 November 1898. 'Abdu'l-Bahá's welcome was effusive for this man who had raised up the American Bahá'í community. He gave Kheiralla titles such as 'Bahá's Peter', 'The Second Columbus' and 'Conqueror of America'. In light of what was to come, Kheiralla's reaction was illuminating; he had reached the edge of a high cliff and was about to step off into the void:

> ... the Master (May my soul be a ransom to the dust of His feet!) has shown me so much kindness and benevolence that it is beyond my power to express them either in writing or in speech. Not only the Master, but all the believers and the prominent and distinguished guides and grandees have paid me more deference than I am worthy of. This was no other than a Divine gift and a heavenly mercy. Exalted be He who gives to whom He pleaseth without merit.
>
> I now have thoroughly have [sic] realized the great station to which I have attained, and the Master has imbued my mind with a spirit of knowledge which I never expected to attain in this world.[16]

But then the other members of the Hearst pilgrimage began to arrive and only he and one other resident Bahá'í were capable of translating between them and the Master. Kheiralla suddenly found himself having to translate words of 'Abdu'l-Bahá that flatly contradicted some of what he himself had been teaching, so he translated to conform with what he had taught in America. The Getsingers wrote to the Bahá'ís in Chicago on 19 October 1900:

> We have found since we are here this time that our dear Master ... explained many things to Dr K. during our first visit, which he (Dr K.) never translated to us, as the teachings of our Lord conflicted

with his own ideas – thus he translated to us, if at all, everything that would substantiate his book.¹⁷

Kheiralla's pilgrimage was very different from the rest. Whereas the other pilgrims were awed by 'Abdu'l-Bahá's wisdom and hung on His every word, Kheiralla disputed with the Eastern Bahá'ís so much that 'Abdu'l-Bahá had to intervene. The Master ultimately instructed them not to discuss controversial subjects with Kheiralla. Unity played no part in Kheiralla's pilgrimage: he disputed with the Eastern Bahá'ís, he disputed with Hand of the Cause Ibn-i-Abhar, he disputed with Edward Getsinger and he even disputed with 'Abdu'l-Bahá.¹⁸

Kheiralla had written a book about the Faith and had left the book with Anton Haddad in New York to translate into Arabic. Realizing that his book had too many differences from what 'Abdu'l-Bahá was teaching, he wrote Anton Haddad a letter telling him not to send it to 'Akká. Unfortunately for him, the manuscript was already on its way with Ella Cooper and Helen Hillyer. His initial plan had been to give it to 'Abdu'l-Bahá for correction, but Kheiralla didn't want anything changed so now he didn't want the Master to see it.¹⁹ Later, Kheiralla claimed that 'Abdu'l-Bahá had reviewed at least part of the book and approved it, but other pilgrims returned with strong cautions that the book should not be published because parts of it were not accurate.²⁰

Kheiralla ended up in trouble with just about everyone. He apparently had somehow forgotten to tell his Egyptian wife, with whom he had two adult daughters, that he had divorced her when he married Marian Miller in America, and had forgotten to tell Marian about his Egyptian wife and daughters. So Marian was a bit surprised to meet his equally surprised former wife and two grown-up daughters when they arrived in Egypt. The culmination of it all was that when Marian left Haifa, she also left Kheiralla, eventually divorcing him.²¹

Edward Getsinger had long been suspicious of Kheiralla and a conversation they had while walking on the beach in Haifa didn't help. Kheiralla wanted Edward to get him a sum of money from Phoebe Hearst. When Edward told him that a plan had already been advanced to set up a trust fund to help teachers of the Faith, Kheiralla said no, that he wanted a lump sum. Then he suggested that Mrs Hearst buy the rights to his book, the same one he didn't want 'Abdu'l-Bahá to see and which 'Abdu'l-Bahá wouldn't approve without significant changes. That made Edward and Phoebe Hearst unhappy with Kheiralla.[22]

'Abdu'l-Bahá later said that He sent Kheiralla:

> to America and assured him that he would be confirmed. In America, he found that all the doors were open before his face. Then he became arrogant, and thought he was great. When he first came here, he praised Lua Getsinger and her husband and he requested me to appoint them as leaders in America. I did not heed his request. He sent Lua to Mrs. Hearst and she gave her twelve hundred dollars and sent two hundred to Ibrahim Khairallah through Abdul Karim. Khairallah came to me, weeping and complaining. He said, 'Is this right, that Mrs. Getsinger should receive twelve hundred dollars, and for me only two hundred dollars . . .'
>
> Finally, he asked me to make him the leader in America. I told him to drop the thought of leadership and to be severed and sanctified. He became very angry: Then the violators deceived him and agitated him. Their custom is that as soon as they learn that someone is angry they go to him and show him their sympathy, and to agitate him and plant in him the seeds of hatred. Thus Ibrahim Khairallah became an enemy . . .
>
> If Ibrahim Khairallah had not violated the Covenant, the growth of the cause in America would have been astonishing . . .[23]

Lua and Edward Getsinger

Lua and Edward Getsinger were the first of the American pilgrims to land in Haifa, arriving at 10:30 p.m. on 8 December 1898. The Getsingers had become Bahá'ís in 1897 and had introduced Phoebe Hearst to the Faith that same year.

Kheiralla met them at the dock in Haifa and took them to a coffee house where they met a few other believers. They finally left for their hotel at midnight and because the 'streets are very narrow and dark . . . the hotel keeper walked ahead of us with a lantern to light the way'. The next morning, the first American pilgrims were up early, but there was no word from 'Akká. The day was spent in waiting until they were invited to the home of a local Bahá'í. When they arrived, the eagerly awaited summons was awaiting them. It said that 'Abdu'l-Bahá's 'heart longed to see the first American pilgrims'.[24]

1897–1898

There was no sleep that night for the Getsingers, the first American Bahá'ís to be able to meet 'Abdu'l-Bahá, and they spent the slowly passing hours talking about their amazing good fortune. At 8 a.m. a carriage arrived and they were on their way. Lua wrote of their anticipation:

> It is about five miles from Haifa to Acca the road close to the sea – indeed in the sea, for the horses were walking in the water and at times the waves dashed nearly to the top of the wheels. After riding for about a quarter of an hour we could see the City in the distance. It was a beautiful morning and as we looked we could but think of the description in the Bible, 'a city all of gold beside the crystal sea'. It was bathed in a flood of golden sunshine and the sea splashing up against its walls sparkled with splendor! We gradually approached nearer and nearer until at last we passed 'the shed which serves as a coffee house outside the wall,' and entered the city by its solitary gate and drove straight to the house of Abbas Effendi. We entered the garden, ascended one flight of stairs, and were shown into a hall, or reception room, where we removed our wraps, and were welcomed by the uncle who told us to pass into the next room. Dr K. went ahead, and by the violent beating of my heart, I knew we were soon to behold the Blessed Face of the Prince of the House of David, the King of the whole world. We reached the door and stopped – before us, in the center of the room, stood a man clad in a long raiment, with a white turban upon His head; stretching out one hand to us, while His face, which I cannot describe, was lighted by a rare, sweet smile of joy and welcome! We stood thus for a moment, unable to move; then my heart gave a great throb, and, scarcely knowing what I was doing, I held out my arms, crying, 'my Lord, my Lord!' and rushed to Him, kneeling at His blessed feet, sobbing like a child. In an instant my husband was beside me, crying as only men can cry! He put His dear hands upon our bowed heads and said, in a voice that seemed to our ears like a strain of sweet music, 'Welcome, welcome, my dear children, you are welcome; arise and be of good cheer.' Then He sat down upon a low divan and we sat on one side almost facing Him, Dr K. and his daughter on the other side, and He began to talk to us. To my husband He said that he would prosper in his scientific work and God would bless him and enable him to do good in many directions; and as the vibrations of

light emanating from the sun magnetized the earth, so would the Word of God magnetize the hearts and draw them from the west to mingle in love with the hearts in the east. He remained with us but a few moments . . . when He arose, and again bidding us welcome, went into another room where He writes and meets those who come to Him for help and counsel.[25]

When Lua had climbed the stairs at the House of 'Abdu'lláh Páshá, the daughters of 'Abdu'l-Bahá thought that they had seen an angel. They thought that Lua was so beautiful with her blond hair and her amazingly beautiful clothes. The Master's daughters quickly fell in love with her. At night, they could hardly wait for Lua to go to bed because then they could try on those beautiful clothes. They had never seen a Western woman's undergarments and they had great fun modelling them for each other. But meeting 'Abdu'l-Bahá caused Lua to change her dressing style to something much more simple.[26]

After 'Abdu'l-Bahá's departure from that first meeting, the Getsingers were taken to meet the Greatest Holy Leaf, with whom they spent most of the rest of the day, listening to her talk about the early history of the Faith. That evening, they found themselves seated on either side of 'Abdu'l-Bahá for supper. Turning to Lua, He said, 'The Love of God burning in your heart is manifest upon your face and it gives us joy to look upon you.'[27]

The next day, the Getsingers visited the Garden of Riḍván and the Shrine of Bahá'u'lláh. 'Abdu'l-Bahá Himself conducted them to the Shrine. Lua was left without words when she tried to summarize the day's events: 'you must excuse me if I do not enter into detail about this – I cannot find words to express myself . . . I will try to tell you more when I see you, but I cannot write it.' Before leaving, the Master gathered flowers which He gave them to share with the believers in America. At supper that night, 'Abdu'l-Bahá served His guests with His Own hands. The next day they returned to Haifa.[28]

A couple of months later, when Lua was studying Persian at 'Abdu'l-Bahá's request, she wrote Thornton Chase, to describe what it was like living in 'Akká:

> I feel like one in a dream, and now can scarcely collect my senses enough to write anything about this most wonderful and Holy

Household. For the past two weeks I have been staying at Acca for the purpose of studying the Persian language, which Our Lord commanded both myself and my husband to learn as soon as possible. One of His daughters is my teacher and though I have studied such a short time, I am now able to read easy words and know one prayer by heart. The atmosphere of the place is wondrous, knowledge and understanding seem to float in the air! I am simply benumbed by the great privileges and blessings showered upon me daily, and so much so, that I feel myself to be a miserable worm of the dust unable even to crawl. One can't imagine such love and kindness as they continually show to be manifest upon this earth but it is true, and now I know that we Americans have only the <u>semblance</u> while they have the <u>real</u> thing.[29]

Phoebe Hearst and Maryam Thornburgh-Cropper

Phoebe Hearst, her maid Amelia (Emily) Bachrodt, and Maryam Thornburgh-Cropper arrived about a week after the Getsingers, possibly escorted from Egypt by Edward.[30] Mary Virginia Thornburgh-Cropper (given the name 'Maryam' by 'Abdu'l-Bahá) was an American who had married an Englishman and become one of the first Bahá'ís in the United Kingdom. Years later she described her arrival and her reaction:

> We . . . took a small, miserable boat [from Egypt] to Haifa. There was a storm here also, and we were beaten about unmercifully in our all too inadequate steamer. Upon arrival we went to an hotel, where we remained until nightfall as it was too dangerous for us, and for 'Abdu'l-Bahá, Whom we were to visit, for strangers to be seen entering the city of sorrow.
>
> We took a carriage after the night had fallen, and drove along the hard sand by 'way of the sea beyond Jordan', which led us to the gates of the prison city. There our trusted driver arranged for us to enter. Once inside we found the friends who were awaiting us, and we started up the uneven stairs that led to Him. Someone went before us with a small piece of candle, which cast strange shadows on the walls of this silent place.
>
> Suddenly the light caught a form that at first seemed a vision of mist and light. It was the Master which the candle-light had revealed

to us. His white robe, and silver, flowing hair, and shining blue eyes gave the impression of a spirit, rather than of a human being. We tried to tell Him how deeply grateful we were at His receiving us. 'No,' He answered, 'you are kind to come.' This was spoken in a very careful English.

Then He smiled, and we recognized the Light which He possessed in the radiance which moved over His fine and noble face. It was an amazing experience. We four visitors from the Western world felt that our voyage, with all its accompanying inconvenience was a small price to pay for such treasure as we received from the spirit and words of the Master, Whom we had crossed mountain and seas and nations to meet.[31]

Phoebe Hearst's reaction is not well recorded because, as she wrote later:

> . . . I was there only three days, yet I assure you those three days were the most memorable days of my life. Still I feel incapable of describing them in the slightest degree . . .
>
> The Master, – I will not attempt to describe. I will only state that I believe with all my heart that <u>He is the Master</u> – and that my greatest blessing in this world is – that I have been privileged to be in His Presence, and look upon His sanctified and Glorious Face.[32]
>
> It seems to me a real Truthseeker would know at a glance that He is the Master! Withal, I must say He is the Most Wonderful Being I have ever met or ever expect to meet in this world. Tho He does not seek to impress one at all, strength, power, purity, love and holiness are radiated from His majestic, yet humble, personality, and the spiritual atmosphere which surrounds Him and most powerfully affects all those who are blest by being near Him, is indescribable . . .[33]

Marian Kheiralla arrived in late December. She, too, succumbed to the spiritual power of 'Abdu'l-Bahá and, when she met him in His own room, immediately fell at His feet, 'sobbing and kissing His delicate hands.'[34]

1899

May Bolles and Harriet Thornburgh

The next members of the Hearst group to arrive were May Bolles, a young American living in Paris and the god-daughter of Phoebe Hearst, and Harriet Thornburgh, a close friend of Phoebe.[1] When May and Harriet arrived in Port Said on 13 February 1899, they were taken in hand by Aḥmad Yazdí and Núru'lláh Effendi, who arranged for their hotel rooms and for the transport of their baggage. Mr Yazdí and his brother Muḥammad, who lived in Alexandria, would become very well known by Western pilgrims travelling through Egypt because of their true Bahá'í spirit and helpfulness. The attention and care the travellers received amazed them, and May wrote: 'At the time we could not understand the spirit which animated them, but afterwards we knew that we were dead and they were living and were quickened with the love of God.' The afternoon of their arrival, Núru'lláh Effendi took them to his home and introduced them to his wife and daughters. Then he floored them by bringing out a photograph of 'Abdu'l-Bahá and May said she could not remove her eyes from the picture. To further astound the two Americans, Núru'lláh Effendi gave each of them a copy of the photo and a lock of Bahá'u'lláh's hair.[2]

On 16 February, May and Harriet, along with two Russian pilgrims who had been standing 'motionless at the ship's rail facing the east' with 'their steadfast gaze . . . on 'Akká', arrived at Haifa. They were met at the dock by some of the American pilgrims and driven directly to the house the Master had prepared for them. They joined the others in the pilgrim house and spent a restless night 'between waking and sleeping'.[3]

May was awakened at seven the next morning with the news that 'Abdu'l-Bahá was coming. She barely had time to dress before He arrived. Following the other pilgrims, May entered last and

> In a moment I stood on the threshold and dimly saw a room full of people sitting quietly about the walls, and then I beheld my Beloved. I found myself at His feet, and He gently raised me and seated me beside Him, all the while saying some loving words in Persian in a voice that shook my heart. Of that first meeting I can remember neither joy nor pain nor anything that I can name. I had been carried suddenly to too great a height; my soul had come in contact with the Divine Spirit; and this force so pure, so holy, so mighty, had overwhelmed me. He spoke to each one of us in turn of ourselves and our lives and those whom we loved, and although His Words were so few and so simple they breathed the Spirit of Life to our souls . . .
>
> The Russian Jews who had been on the boat the night before now arrived, their faces shining with a great light as they entered His Presence. We could not remove our eyes from His glorious face: we heard all He said; we drank tea with Him at His bidding; but existence seemed suspended, and when He arose and suddenly left us we came back with a start to life: but never again, thank God, to the same life on this earth! We had 'beheld the King in His beauty. We had seen the land which is very far off.'[4]

The next day, the pilgrims were to ascend Mount Carmel to the future site of the Shrine of the Báb, but May was ill and 'Abdu'l-Bahá cancelled the trip, much to May's amazement:

> That anything so important as this meeting in that blessed spot should be cancelled because one person was ill and could not go seemed incredible. It was so contrary to all ordinary habits of thought and action, so different from the life of the world where daily events and material circumstances are supreme in importance that it gave us a genuine shock of surprise, and in that shock the foundations of the old order began to totter and fall. The Master's words had opened wide the door of God's Kingdom and given us a vision of that infinite world whose only law is love.[5]

1899

Anne Apperson, Julia Pearson and Robert Turner

On 20 February, Anne Apperson, Julia Pearson and Robert Turner joined May Bolles and Harriet Thornburgh in Haifa. Robert was Phoebe's African-American butler who had probably first heard about the Faith when the Getsingers began teaching it to Phoebe and is recognized as the first American believer of African descent.[6]

The new pilgrims had a very brief meeting with 'Abdu'l-Bahá that day, but He then had to leave for 'Akká. He instructed them to go to 'Akká themselves two days later, on Wednesday. May was still quite ill Tuesday night and bewailed that 'the Master evidently did not realize how ill and weak I was or He would never have expected me to leave with the others on Wednesday morning.' Lua just smiled and said, 'You will soon realize something of the power of 'Abdu'l-Bahá.'

At dawn the next day, May awoke,

> feeling myself stirred by a breeze. I cannot describe what followed, but through my soul was flowing an essence; a mighty, unseen force was penetrating all my being, expanding it with boundless life and love and happiness, lifting and enfolding me in its mighty strength and peace. I knew then it was the Holy Spirit of God and that our Lord was praying for His servants in that blessed dawn, and I arose and prayed and was quite well.[7]

A short while later, the pilgrims, including May, set out for 'Akká. When they arrived at what is now called the House of 'Abdu'lláh Páshá, they were met by 'Abdu'l-Bahá. The Greatest Holy Leaf and Munírih Khánum then showed them to their rooms, which the two selfless members of the Holy Household had vacated especially for the pilgrims. A little later, the American pilgrims were seated with 'Abdu'l-Bahá. Suddenly, He said, 'Where is Robert?' Phoebe Hearst's black butler soon arrived and was greeted by 'Abdu'l-Bahá with, 'Robert, your Lord loves you. God gave you a black skin, but a heart white as snow.' He followed this greeting by telling all present: 'We can all serve in the Cause of God no matter what our occupation is. No occupation can prevent the soul coming to God. Peter was a fisherman, yet he accomplished most wonderful things; but the heart must be turned always toward God, no matter what the work is.'[8]

The pilgrims soon learned that although being in the Master's presence was 'all life, joy and blessedness', they also learned that the 'pilgrimage to the Holy City is naught but a crucible in which the souls are tried; where the gold is purified and the dross is consumed'. May learned that lesson very quickly. That very afternoon, she spoke against another Bahá'í. 'Abdu'l-Bahá at almost that moment, returned from visiting the poor and called for Lua, who was with May and the others. The Master bluntly told her that 'in His absence one of His servants had spoken unkindly of another and it grieved His heart that the believers should speak against any soul'. He told Lua to go and pray, but not to tell anyone why. That evening at dinner, May sat unknowingly at the table, happy and content; until, that is, she looked at 'Abdu'l-Bahá and 'in that pure and perfect mirror I saw my wretched self and burst into tears'. 'Abdu'l-Bahá took no notice of her and the meal continued with everyone ignoring her tears. Finally, He looked at May, smiled and called her name several times whereupon 'in an instant such sweet happiness pervaded my soul, my heart was comforted with such infinite hope, that I knew He would cleanse me of all my sins'.[9]

Towards the end of the evening, Harriet Thornburgh asked if she could tell a story about a little boy who had stolen an egg. With the Master's permission, she said that the little boy had taken a nest full of eggs. While carrying his prize, he encountered a lady who chastised him saying, 'Don't you know that it is very cruel to steal that nest? What will the poor mother bird do when she comes home to the tree and finds her eggs all gone?' The sharp little fellow quickly retorted: 'Maybe that is the mother you have got on your hat.' The Master laughed heartily and commented, 'That is a good story and a clever little boy.'[10]

On 25 February, the American pilgrims went to the Shrine of Bahá'u'lláh. On the way, they visited the Garden of Riḍván, then continued to Bahjí where they found about a hundred Eastern believers awaiting them. May wrote: 'Knowing that we were among the first American pilgrims to that Holy Spot they had come from all directions to see our faces, and their own shone with a love and joy which amazed us . . .'[11] The Mansion of Bahjí itself was at that time occupied by Mírzá Muḥammad-'Alí, the Archbreaker of Bahá'u'lláh's Covenant and 'Abdu'l-Bahá's half-brother, so the pilgrims stopped at the Tea House, south of the Mansion, and went to a small room on its roof where 'Abdu'l-Bahá would sometimes stay, and which was surrounded by a roof terrace.

1899

After the passing of Bahá'u'lláh in 1892, Mírzá Muḥammad-'Alí broke the Covenant and occupied the Mansion, leaving 'Abdu'l-Bahá with only the small Tea House at the southern edge of the gardens and the Pilgrim House which He had rented. In spite of the nearness of the Covenant-breakers, 'Abdu'l-Bahá continued to bring pilgrims to Bahá'u'lláh's tomb. Since the Covenant-breakers were bereft of any spiritual vision, the Mansion soon began to fall into disrepair, mirroring the spiritual state of its occupiers. 'Abdu'l-Bahá passed away with the Mansion still in the hands of the Covenant-breakers and in January 1922, the Covenant-breakers forcibly took the keys to the Shrine of Bahá'u'lláh. Within a year, the British authorities had determined that the Shrine of Bahá'u'lláh was, indeed, rightfully the property of the Bahá'ís and the keys were returned. The Covenant-breakers continued their occupation of the Mansion until it fell into such a state of disrepair that they began to drift away. The end for the Covenant-breakers began in 1927, when one of their members wrote to Shoghi Effendi, the Guardian of the Faith appointed by 'Abdu'l-Bahá, that the Mansion roof was about to collapse and needed immediate repairs. Shoghi Effendi replied that no work would be done until all the Covenant-breakers had left. Two years later, they were all gone and Shoghi Effendi was able to begin restoration work.[12]

As recounted later by May Bolles, the Americans were given tea and while they were drinking it, 'Abdu'l-Bahá abruptly left them and went out onto the terrace where He paced back and forth. The pilgrims by this time knew that no action of the Master's was without a reason and they soon realized that He was on the terrace so that the Eastern believers could see Him. When they looked, they saw all the Bahá'ís on the grass 'perfectly motionless and silent, gazing in rapt love and devotion . . .'

Soon, 'Abdu'l-Bahá led them to the Tomb itself where they removed their shoes and entered the glass-roofed court with its central garden. As they entered, the ladies of the Holy Family, completely veiled, joined them. May wrote:

> The blessed Master was calm and radiant and led us to the open space at the end of the court beside the Tomb, where, in the mellow light of a stained glass window, we all stood in silence until He bade one of our group to sing *The Holy City*. No pen could describe the solemn beauty of that moment, as, in a broken voice, this young

girl sang the praise and glory of God, while all were immersed in the ocean of the Divine Presence. The tears of the pilgrims flowed and strong men wept aloud. Then 'Abdu'l-Bahá led us to the door of the Tomb where we knelt for a moment, then He opened the door and led us in. Those who have passed that threshold have been for a brief moment in the presence of God, their Creator, and no thoughts can follow them. The Tablet of the Holy Tomb was chanted by a young Persian, and when we left that blessed spot the oriental pilgrims entered slowly, until all had been within; then our Beloved closed the door, and after singing *Nearer, my God to Thee* at His request, we quietly withdrew.[13]

Later, May wrote, '. . . a great peace descended upon us, and in the heavenly calm and beauty of that last night in 'Akká, we were girded with strength for the future.' The Americans did not know it at the time, but they were the first pilgrims to be allowed to go into the inner room under which the Manifestation had lain since His passing.[14]

The next morning they were to leave for Haifa, but they had one last meeting with 'Abdu'l-Bahá. He told them to 'Pray that your hearts may be cut from yourselves and from the world, that you may be confirmed by the Holy Spirit and filled with the fire of the love of God.' He then led them into the next room where, resting on a divan, was the portrait of Bahá'u'lláh.

> We fell on our knees before it, and the tears that flowed were of pure love and adoration. We could have remained thus for ever with our eyes fastened on that wonderful face, but the Master touched us on the shoulder, that we might see also the picture of His Highness the Báb. His was a beautiful young face, but I could not keep my eyes from the eyes of Bahá'u'lláh, until 'Abdu'l-Bahá turned suddenly to us, and raising His voice in a tone so poignant that it pierced every heart, He stretched His hands above us and said:
>
> 'Now the time has come when we must part, but the separation is only of our bodies, in spirit we are united. Ye are the lights which shall be diffused; ye are the waves of that sea which shall spread and overflow the world. Each wave is precious to Me and My nostrils shall be gladdened by your fragrance. Another commandment I give unto you, that ye love one another even as I love you. Great

mercy and blessings are promised to the people of your land, but on one condition: that their hearts are filled with the fire of love, that they live in perfect kindness and harmony like one soul in different bodies. If they fail in this condition the great blessings will be deferred. Never forget this; look at one another with the eye of perfection; look at Me, follow Me, be as I am . . . Behold a candle how it gives its light. It weeps its life away drop by drop in order to give forth its flame of light.[15]

Members of the Holy Family gently led them away and they returned to Haifa and the other world.

Margaret Peeke

On 12 March 1899, 'Abdu'l-Bahá received a note from an unexpected American visitor. She was camped in a tent outside the walls of 'Akká and she wanted to meet Him. Less than four hours later she found herself following her guide and her interpreter, a soldier and a man with a lantern through the dark streets of the ancient city, passing many soldiers and groups of men who watched them pass.

Margaret Peeke hadn't initially planned to seek out 'Abdu'l-Bahá. She was going on a Mediterranean cruise and a friend had asked her to go see if 'Abdu'l-Bahá was real, but at first it wasn't on her list of things to do. As the ship crossed the Atlantic from America, her mind couldn't get rid of the idea: 'indifference gave place to curiosity; curiosity ended in interest; the impossible grew into the possible and possible became probable, until, by the time we reached Gibraltar, I had made a change of route that took in Acca and Abbas-Effendi.'[16] Upon reaching Egypt, she wrote for letters of introduction to the Bahá'ís of Cairo, though she never thought of asking 'Abdu'l-Bahá if it was alright to drop by.

On 12 March, Margaret and her companion pitched their tents outside the walls of 'Akká and she sent the note asking to see the Master. After half an hour of suspense, the messenger returned giving them an appointment at eight o'clock that evening. So, at eight o'clock they prepared to climb the long flight of stairs. A soldier stopped her interpreter, Joseph, saying he could not enter. Margaret and her companion entered a long, bare room to find a few Americans and others already there. Then a figure rose to meet them:

The motion was almost like gliding, so smooth was it, and as he drew nearer, we noticed the mouse-colored gown he wore with a turban to match, and there stood before us One who was the personification of all gentleness and meekness, and yet a sublime dignity rested upon him which we had never seen in others of the same faith, unusual in type as they were. He approached with extended hands, as if meeting friends and followers and then led us to seats at the upper end of the long room, motioning us to sit at his right hand.[17]

The new guests were given tea. Margaret, not being a Bahá'í, expected a talk all about the Bahá'í Faith, so she was bewildered to hear 'Abdu'l-Bahá begin to talk about the 'Grand Architect of the Universe, about the Laws of Creation and Preservation'. Try as she could, Margaret could think of no question to ask. Then she noticed that Joseph, her interpreter, was sitting near the door. No sooner did she see him than 'Abdu'l-Bahá motioned Joseph to sit next to Him, giving him a cup of tea. He continued to explain the Divine Being and His plan. It was a great historical lesson with civilization and centuries passing in review. Then followed a review of the Manifestations of God, beginning with Moses, and how each had made clearer man's relationship to God. He explained this progressive revelation, saying that

> [w]hen the rim of a new moon comes into view, if we had never seen it before, we would think it could be no greater, but night after night it grows from the crescent to the gibbous, and from that to the full moon, so also the Light of Truth had come by degrees, and when the fullness of the whole could be seen, it would be the same Light that had shown in the crescent, in the gibbous, and in the full moon, but differing only in degree.[18]

Finally, at ten o'clock, Margaret and her group prepared to leave for their tents. As they thanked the Master, He

> said in that soft, but commanding voice, which no one would think of resisting, 'I shall be glad to see you again tomorrow morning at nine o'clock.' Could we be dreaming? Were we to be so favored as to have another interview? Going forth into the darkness, to be escorted back to our tents, we felt a great interest awaken in this

wonderful personality, so meek, yet so majestic; commanding, and yet so humble.

When they reached their tents, watched over by flute-playing soldiers, Margaret said to her companion,

> I am surprised and very much impressed; who ever could think that Abbas-Effendi would be like that? Think of it! We have talked fully two hours and he never once spoke of those things one would expect to be uppermost in his mind. Where could we find, in the length and breadth of America, a man devoted to one pursuit and when meeting a stranger, would talk for hours and make no mention of it? He did not even ask whether or not the Movement was progressing in our own land; he made no inquiry as to the teacher who had first brought it into notice there; most astonishing of all is the fact that he did not try to tell us of how superior it was to all other Religions, nor did he speak of his Father, the Great Manifestation or of himself as his Father's representative. One cannot but marvel at the greatness of his universal knowledge; the meekness of his character; the majesty of his humility.[19]

The next morning, Margaret returned to the same room. When 'Abdu'l-Bahá arrived, He picked up exactly where He had left off the night before and continued until noon. Though the Master had not spoken a word about what they had expected, 'We felt that we had seen the greatest that could be known on the earth at this time, and though we might not believe every claim their followers set forth, we surely had been blessed in the privilege of meeting him.'[20]

After she left 'Akká, Margaret could not forget 'Abdu'l-Bahá, but it took time for her lesson to be learned. Letters were exchanged with the Master and she began to see His station as the Centre of the Covenant:

> There surely was nothing in the bare room in which this Centre received us, nor in any attempt to exhibit healing or miraculous powers to prove the truth of his position. He did not even mention the Great Manifestation, whom he represented, in whom his hopes and adoration are centered, but with the simplest words, he expounded the revelation of God in nature and in man, from a

wonderfully impersonal standpoint.

Did he not wish us to believe in that which to him was of the greatest importance in the world, and for which thousands have died by the most cruel tortures? Was it a matter of indifference whether we took back to America from an outsider's standpoint a testimony of this truth that the Avatar, for the twentieth century, in reality, had come to fulfil the prophecies never yet fulfilled? With the calmness of one who can afford to await the results, and with the humility of one who knows his station in the work, both in this world and in that invisible one (the Cause-world), he made no effort to convince or to affect his hearers. All this, however, did not come at once to my mind, but has been the outgrowth of the years that have intervened between that day in Acca and this . . . When thinking of the generous amount of time he had given me, I felt I must write a letter expressing thanks and my appreciation, and on the way from Alexandria to Marseilles I did so; then dismissed the subject from my mind . . . One day, a most exquisite letter written in Persian, with a translation into English, came to me and I felt as never before when reading those words which vibrated through me as would music from the chords of a grand organ, nor could I understand the power that could cross the seas and oceans, and give me a sense of such nearness and spiritual longing. From that time to the present moment, Abbas-Effendi, or 'Abdul-Baha' has been to me an ever growing mystery, his letters have been filled with a spirit so great and holy that its equal cannot be found unless it be in the epistles of the New Testament . . .

In Acca, on the shores of the Mediterranean, dwells a man who is the center of thought of all the lands, whom the noblemen, the great, the wealthy, rejoice to meet even for one day. He is a comforter to the poor and unfortunate and a healer to the sick.

His home is a prison, where He has been placed on account of His dreaded influence upon the people of that land. He has the freedom of the city and through the goodness of God, the Sultan of Turkey has now given Him permission to visit the holy resting-place of His Father, just outside the city of Acca. He spends much time in writing tablets to His followers and in preparing, for future circulation, the wonderful utterances of His Father. He never allows Himself the barest comforts that the ordinary working man of

America would think a necessity. He will not own two garments, for He gives daily to the poor, often sharing His meal and that of His family with some hungry man, woman or family. He sleeps but little and is up at all hours writing, praying or instructing a devoted one who may be leaving for some foreign country. He never speaks or thinks of Himself, the one thought and aim of His life is to do the work that He has come to perform. The best exponents of this Revelation are met in the land where they have been called to suffer martyrdom for their faith.[21]

Ella Goodall and Helen Hillyer

In early March, Ella Goodall (later Cooper) and Helen Hillyer met the departing Phoebe Hearst group in Cairo. Ella had learned of the Faith in California from Helen who had heard of it from Phoebe Hearst. Ella then taught her mother, Helen Goodall, about the Faith and the mother-daughter pair became powerful teachers of the Cause.

From Cairo, their trip became a little eventful, particularly a train ride in Egypt. Ella and Helen boarded the train in Cairo and were going to Port Said. Things started out well but then, Helen wrote,

> when we reached Ismalia we remained quietly in our compartment, bought oranges and dates out the window and of course were greatly interested in watching the crowd, a seething mass of humanity. Finally, we felt the train move, and after a few minutes I said to Ella, 'Something is wrong. We are going back toward Cairo,' and I pulled the bell cord on the side of the car. Soon excited conductors came running along the outside step from both directions yelling . . . I said I feared something was wrong, that we wanted to go to Port Said where we had a steamer to catch . . . He said . . . he would dump us out at the next station where we could get a train back to Ismalia and then catch the next accommodations to Port Said. He did literally dump us out, but I could hardly call it a station. There was simply a platform and a couple of wooden benches in what seemed to us a portion of the Sahara. Soon, however, up out of nowhere came men and children curious to know who and what we were. They spoke a little French and we soon made them understand we were waiting for a train to take us to Ismalia.

After two or three hours' wait that seemed much longer, something on wheels came along that we boarded and we were once more on our way. It was well into the evening and quite dark when we reached our goal for the night, for of course no more trains were going to Port Said till the morning. There was a miserable little hotel in the station, and as the town did not look that we would fare any better going farther, we negotiated for a meal and a night's lodging. We elicited quite a bit of curiosity having arrived at that hour and on that train, so quite a number of very queer people came snooping around even after we were shown to an apartment, which consisted of a very open-air bedroom with porches on two sides. We decided we would not undress at all, so crawled up onto the large bed that was well draped with mosquito netting and there we remained practically bolt upright all night.

We were called and left at an early hour on the first train to Port Said. When we arrived there, I was all primed for a heavy reprimand to the Thomas Cook's agent for having been so remiss as not to have informed us we should have changed cars the afternoon before at Ismalia, but when I saw the distressed look on his face change to one of relief when he found us, and when he said he had been wiring frantically to Cairo to know where we were and that he had had the steamer held for us till our arrival, of course all was forgiven.[22]

When Ella finally reached 'Akká on 5 March, she was in heaven:

The Greatest Branch ['Abdu'l-Bahá] is all and more than anyone could ask. He is a perfect ideal of Christ and I shall never forget the look on His face as he stood in the Tomb [of Bahá'u'lláh] lighting the candles and again when He bowed His head praying just outside the room . . . He looked as if He were receiving instructions from His only superior. His face was heavenly in its sweet calm and He never shed a tear though everyone else was weeping terribly. His power is unmistakable: though a prisoner He holds the government in His own hands.[23]

[The Greatest Holy Leaf] was so simple – with the simplicity of the truly great – that she put us at ease at once, and we were delighted to discover that she had a keen sense of humor and her eyes were lovely blue. Like all the ladies of the Holy Household she showered us with her love and it was not long before we had the temerity to respond to that glorious character. Hers was the responsible position in the prison home – she seemed to be the center about whom all the women revolved not those of family alone but pilgrims and resident believers as well. It was evident that all instinctively conceded to her a spiritual authority second only to the Master.

In her room the gatherings of the household took place. It was the prized privilege of the visiting pilgrims to join the family there for the early morning tea, 'Abdu'l-Bahá being the only man present . . .

The Greatest Holy Leaf, or Khanum, as she was called, which means, The Lady, being the chatelaine of the home, always carried her bunch of keys and never failed to oversee all domestic affairs of the household and under the most primitive conditions. She seemed to us to be always so perfectly balanced between the spiritual and the practical.[24]

Ella was also impressed with one of the youngest members of the household, Shoghi Effendi, who was just two years old at that time. Ella was with the ladies and 'Abdu'l-Bahá when the future Guardian of the Faith came into the room:

Having dropped off his shoes he stepped into the room, with his eyes focused on the Master's face. 'Abdu'l-Bahá returned his gaze with such a look of loving welcome it seemed to beckon the small one to approach Him. Shoghi, that beautiful little boy, with his exquisite cameo face and his soulful appealing, dark eyes, walked slowly toward the divan, the Master drawing him as by an invisible thread, until he stood quite close in front of Him . . . While we breathlessly watched to see what he would do, the little boy reached down and picking up the hem of 'Abdu'l-Bahá's robe he touched it reverently to his forehead, and kissed it, then gently replaced it, while never taking his eyes from the adored Master's face. The next moment he turned away, and scampered off to play . . .[25]

Little Shoghi Effendi may have been very reverential in the presence of his grandfather, but Rúḥíyyih Khánum later wrote that he described himself as 'the acknowledged ringleader of all other children. Bubbling with high spirits, enthusiasm and daring, full of laughter and wit, the small boy led the way in many pranks.'²⁶

One morning during the devotional chanting soon after Ella arrived

> there was a young Syrian girl in the Household who was teaching the Daughters English. She was a Christian and knew nothing of the Bahai belief, but one day as we all listened to the chanting, she suddenly burst into tears and ran from the room. They all smiled and quietly awaited her return. In a few minutes she came back, and when asked what made her cry, she shook her head and could only reply, 'It was so beautiful – it was so beautiful.'²⁷

When Ella and Helen went to the Shrine of Bahá'u'lláh with the Master, He took them into the inner room and gave them candles with which to light the candelabras in each of the four corners. Ella and Helen left 'Akká on 23 March.

Naw-Rúz 1899

Naw-Rúz, the Bahá'í new year, was celebrated on 21 March and the Bahá'ís in 'Akká all gathered at 'Abdu'l-Bahá's house, the men in one room and the women in the room of the Greatest Holy Leaf. The Master visited the room of the women and passed sweets to everyone, after which his daughter Rúhá Khánum chanted. Then 'Abdu'l-Bahá went to visit the men. Finally, He visited the gathered children and gave each a few coins. After the celebration, Lua Getsinger went to the Tomb of Bahá'u'lláh for the last time with Rúhá Khánum. They travelled in a closed carriage and, upon arriving, went into a small room and remained hidden until all the men had visited with 'Abdu'l-Bahá and had gone. Then they had their own visit. 'Abdu'l-Bahá led them into the Tomb and raised His voice in supplication for Lua. After leaving, Lua wrote:

> What this day was to me no one can ever know. My work, my work, my deeds must tell in the future whether or not He prayed for me in vain. I can only say I wanted to fall at His feet then and there, and give my heart, my soul, and my life for the dear and sacred mouth that had spoken on my behalf. I then prayed for our teacher who was the means of giving us the Truth in America, I felt that

if I should live a thousand years I could never ask God enough to repay him for what he has done for me and for those I love in my dear native land. I can never do it: God only can pay my deep debt of gratitude by answering my supplications for his welfare. As we turned away, my eyes lingered lovingly upon the Sacred Place, – and in my heart I could only feebly thank God for His great mercy and many blessings which I can never deserve, though I give my life for His sake by shedding my blood in His Cause – which I pray may be my happy lot, when His Will in me is done.[28]

As Lua prayed for her teacher, Ibrahim Kheiralla, he was well advanced in his path toward becoming a Covenant-breaker. On 26 March, the Kheirallas left Haifa for Port Said. His wife, Marian, didn't stay there long, but left for Europe while Kheiralla tarried. Marian remained faithful to the Cause while Ibrahim Kheiralla's ego carried him to the nethermost fire. When he arrived in New York, he went to his friend Anton Haddad and tried to get him to write and sign a letter to 'Abdu'l-Bahá, telling him,

I know . . . that the Master, 'Abbás Effendi, loves you and will believe your statements, so I wish [you] to write him a letter in which I [Kheiralla] will describe to him my present conditions, and beg him to write to the rich people in this country to help me in return for the invaluable service I had rendered the Cause . . . I would also like the Master to authorize me to publish my book as the fundamental basis of the Bahá'í teachings in America. I also wish 'Abbás Effendi would send me some tablets in which he praises my work, and commands the believers to listen to what I say and obey me and not to listen to other people who are only people of sedition and strife. I want you to sign this letter with me . . .[29]

Anton Haddad refused and remained faithful to 'Abdu'l-Bahá.

The day after Lua prayed for Kheiralla, she and Edward met with the Master and He told them that, when they reached Cairo, they should see Mírzá Abu'l-Faḍl and 'Abdu'l-Karím, 'who would tell us some things we wished to know'. He added that they should, however, be back in America six weeks after leaving 'Akká. The Getsingers' last day with the Holy Household was 23 March. During her final meeting with

'Abdu'l-Bahá, Lua broke down in tears and He encouraged her saying, 'Do not cry – be happy. I will go with you in spirit – the separation of the body is nothing, I will go with you.' He then allowed her to follow Him to the room where He wrote His Tablets. As she watched Him work, she noticed that He had photographs of Thornton Chase, Mr Clark and Howard Struven on His table. When the Master saw her looking at them, He said, 'You must tell them that I kissed their pictures and am glad to have them; that they are my sons and My heart longs to see them so I may kiss them.' Then He called Edward in and presented him with a bottle of pomegranate juice. To each He gave a bottle of rose oil, and then they left.[30]

Ali-Kuli Khan

One young man who arrived in late spring of 1899 began his pilgrimage from Tehran with ten others at night in a blizzard, by saying 'My friends – no more talk, no more lip service. The time has come to seek Him out. No more postponements, no more thoughts of preparation for the journey. Let whoever is willing, follow me!'[31] His ten companions were turned back at the Russian border when they were denied passports, but the instigator, Ali-Kuli Khan, whispered to the Governor, who happened to be a Bahá'í, that America had discovered the Bahá'í Faith and that he could be useful to 'Abdu'l-Bahá because he spoke English. The Governor issued the one passport.[32]

The solitary Khan continued on with little money, encountering many difficulties, including a voyage across the Caspian Sea in stormy water. He was terrified that the ship would sink and repeatedly asked the captain whether it was possible. The captain always replied, 'Oh yes, Pretty soon now. Pretty soon.'[33]

Surviving the storm, Khan arrived in Baku where he spent a week in the company of Ḥájí Mírzá Haydar-'Alí, a totally dedicated Bahá'í later known as the Angel of Carmel. Khan also slept on the floor because he had vowed not to sleep in a 'comfortable bed' until he had arrived in the presence of 'Abdu'l-Bahá. From Baku, Khan suffered an even worse sailing to Istanbul. Travelling steerage, it was a horrible experience for all except one woman named Rúhání who told them that pilgrims with permission to visit 'Abdu'l-Bahá would reach their destination safely.[34]

Then came the spring morning, just before dawn, when Khan's ship anchored about a mile offshore from Haifa. At that time, Haifa had no port so people were rowed ashore. He was met by a number of believers and taken to the coffee house of Ḥusayn Effendi who informed him that the Master was at that moment in Haifa. Khan, after his long and gruelling journey was suddenly terrified at the thought of meeting 'Abdu'l-Bahá and broke down, crying 'How can one such as I, one with so many shortcomings – how can I stand in the presence of One from whose all-seeing eyes nothing whatever is hidden?' Khan was then informed that 'Abdu'l-Bahá would see him immediately. Arriving at a house, Khan looked up and saw that 'standing tall before him, was One in turban and robe, One with a full beard, dark but with much gray intermingled, and a face just as Khan had always visualized the countenance of Bahá'u'lláh.' Khan promptly fainted.

The Master raised up the fallen Khan, put His arms around him and kissed him on both cheeks, then had him taken to another room and given some tea. After only a few minutes, He called a recovering Khan and told him that

> The Blessed Perfection, Bahá'u'lláh, has promised to raise up souls who would hasten to the service of the Covenant, and would assist me in spreading His Faith. His Cause has now reached America and many in the Western world are being attracted to His Teachings. You, with your knowledge of English, are one of those souls promised me by Bahá'u'lláh. You have come to assist me by translating His Sacred Writings as well as my letters to the friends in America and elsewhere in the West . . . You must reside with me and assist me in my work.[35]

With that introduction, 'Abdu'l-Bahá handed Khan a packet of letters to translate into English. When he opened them, Khan was stunned to find them all written in Arabic: 'But my Master, these are not in Persian! These are in Arabic.' Khan didn't know Arabic. Smiling and with deep love in His eyes, 'Abdu'l-Bahá took a double handful of rock candy from the table and put it in Khan's hands, saying 'Go, and eat this candy. Rest assured, the Blessed Perfection will enable you to translate the Arabic into English.' Khan was indeed able to translate those letters.[36]

Before leaving Khan that first meeting, the Master then pointed to a bed in the room that He Himself had used and dismissed him with

'This is your bed. Sleep in it.' Khan could not sleep in the Master's bed, however. For the next three nights, he slept beside it on the floor as he had done for the previous two years. On the fourth day, Ustád Muḥammad-'Alí asked him, 'Are you aware that you are disobeying the Master?' This shocked Khan, so his visitor said that 'you have not slept in the Master's bed, as He told you to do'. That night, though with great trepidation, Khan broke his bed fast.[37]

'Abdu'l-Bahá told Khan that he would develop the power to speak to huge audiences and Khan accepted it because the Master had said it. It later became true. 'Abdu'l-Bahá said something similar in Tablets to Dr Hermann Grossmann, who later became a Hand of the Cause, and to O. Wolcott. The Master wrote to Dr Grossmann that 'When you speak, do not think.'[38] To Mr Wolcott, he wrote: 'The souls who are free from every tie and are baptized with the Holy Spirit, while speaking, are inspired with the Divine Inspiration. This is why it is said that when you are speaking, you should not think; you should speak what the heart is inspired to.'[39]

Anton Haddad

Ali-Kuli Khan had come to Haifa to work, and so did the next visitor to 'Abdu'l-Bahá. In America, the Bahá'í community was splitting into two camps, those who followed the Covenant-breaking Kheiralla, who had taught the Faith to many of the early American believers, and those who remained faithful to 'Abdu'l-Bahá. Those who had participated in the Hearst pilgrimage had learned how inaccurate Kheiralla's teachings were and he became desperate to maintain his position and prestige. Phoebe Hearst sent Anton Haddad to ask the Master what to do. Anton clandestinely left New York in July 1899, hoping not to be noticed by Kheiralla's group. Unfortunately, Anton ran into relatives of Kheiralla in Marseilles, France, and soon the misguided founder of the American Bahá'í community was writing to the Master trying to discredit him.[40]

Anton reached Beirut, worried about not having the Master's permission to continue to 'Akká. After the Hearst pilgrimage, because of the disturbances raised by the Covenant-breakers, 'Abdu'l-Bahá had withdrawn permission from all pilgrims to go to 'Akká. Therefore, Anton was surprised and immensely relieved upon his arrival to find a telegram from 'Abdu'l-Bahá which said, 'Let Haddad come without permission.'[41]

When Anton arrived in 'Akká, 'Abdu'l-Bahá's reaction to the events in America surprised him. 'Abdu'l-Bahá said: 'I am very sorry for Kheiralla, a most precious crown was prepared for his head in the spiritual kingdom, but now he has covered himself with a great stain and much mud. However, I supplicated God, the Almighty Father, to have mercy on him and to forgive him his sins and to protect him from the vanity of the world . . .'[42] 'Abdu'l-Bahá carefully instructed Anton in the verities of the Faith over the next two weeks. Anton took thorough notes, which were corrected by the Master Himself, then hurried back to New York in November 1899. By early 1900, he had published a pamphlet called *Message from Acca*, which was distributed to the Bahá'ís across America and did wonders in guiding the young American Bahá'í community.[43]

1900

In 1900, 'Abdu'l-Bahá sometimes stayed in a rented house in Haifa about a block from the beach; however, He primarily lived in 'Akká. The house in Haifa He used as an office and a place where he could meet with pilgrims. The house had an open courtyard with rooms on three sides. The Master's room was sparsely furnished with a bed, several chairs and a large table at which He did his writing. The table also had flowers, rosewater and a plate full of rock candy. Travellers stayed in a room at the back of the house and Siyyid Taqí Manshádí, who sorted the Master's mail, had another room in which he lived. Initially, Ali-Kuli Khan stayed in this house, but later moved to 'Akká, staying at first in a caravanserai and then in the House of 'Abdu'lláh Páshá.[1]

Ali-Kuli Khan soon became one of the targets of the Archbreaker of the Covenant, 'Abdu'l-Bahá's half-brother Mírzá Muhammad-'Alí, because he knew that Khan was from a distinguished Persian family and feared that his translations of 'Abdu'l-Bahá's Writings into English would attract more Americans.

The arrival of the first American pilgrims during the previous year had greatly antagonized the Covenant-breakers and they had increased their efforts to bring 'Abdu'l-Bahá into disrepute. Ibtiháju'l-Mulk, a wealthy Persian Bahá'í from Gílan, arrived on pilgrimage in 1900. He was a Bahá'í firm in the Faith and absolutely dedicated to the Master. The Covenant-breakers quickly tried to turn Ibtiháju'l-Mulk from 'Abdu'l-Bahá. Mírzá Áqá Ján, who had been Bahá'u'lláh's amanuensis for forty years, but who was now allied with Muhammad-'Alí, wrote to Ibtiháju'l-Mulk and tried to create doubts about 'Abdu'l-Bahá. Ibtiháju'l-Mulk already knew about the Covenant-breakers and ignored the letter. The Covenant-breakers didn't stop with simple harassment of 'Abdu'l-Bahá and the Bahá'ís. One Covenant-breaker poisoned 'Abdu'l-Bahá's water jug and another tried to stab Him with a knife.[2]

1900

When Ibtiháju'l-Mulk arrived, he asked 'Abdu'l-Bahá if he could give a feast for the other pilgrims and the Bahá'ís who lived in the area. The Master gave His approval. The feast was held on a Sunday and included Mrs Keating and her daughter, from Chicago, and Marian Kheiralla, the wife of Ibrahim Kheiralla, who despite her husband's breaking of the Covenant had remained faithful to 'Abdu'l-Bahá. The Master served the guests Himself.[3]

Ali-Kuli Khan's biographer records his account of how 'Abdu'l-Bahá then led the group, including Ibtiháju'l-Mulk, to the Tomb of His Father:

> ... after it [the feast] the Master led the assemblage to Bahjí. Prior to entering the Tomb, a water jar filled from a neighboring stream on His shoulder, and they following with their jars the same, 'Abdu'l-Bahá watered the flowers growing outside. Then, at the door, He anointed each guest with attar of roses.
>
> Inside, and for the first time in Khan's hearing, the Master Himself chanted the Tablet of Visitation in the Shrine, His voice so strong and sweet, the air of the Tomb so holy, that the believers were carried away from themselves to realms undreamed of before.
>
> After the Tablet was chanted, 'Abdu'l-Bahá requested the Western believers to sing a hymn in English. And many there shed tears hearing the Western strains following the Eastern, their echoing voices fulfilling the prophecy that, with the coming of Him Who lay there in the Tomb, East and West would embrace each other like unto two lovers.[4]

Sarah Farmer and Maria Wilson

In January 1900, Maria P. Wilson, from the Boston area, and Sarah Farmer, from Green Acre, the future Bahá'í school, boarded the *S.S. Durst Bismarck* for the Mediterranean Sea and Egypt. Once on their way, Sarah discovered two friends, Josephine Locke and Elizabeth Knudson, also on the ship. Sarah soon noticed that her two friends were reading a book on deck which they would quickly conceal whenever Sarah approached them. Sarah's curiosity finally led her friends to reveal that they were reading the *Hidden Words*, by Bahá'u'lláh. After reading what was in the little book, Sarah immediately wanted to visit

'Abdu'l-Bahá. She and Maria cabled for permission to visit and it was granted. When the four women reached Egypt, they met some of the Bahá'ís living there, which allowed them to learn more about the Faith. They arrived in Haifa on 22 March and the next day took a carriage to 'Akká. They were not impressed with the ancient town as they passed through the 'stench and confusion of the narrow street'. Then they entered the courtyard of the Master's house and saw Him at the top of the steps and immediately forgot everything else. That night, Sarah wrote in her diary, 'Heart too full for speech – received by our Lord.'[5]

Sarah Farmer had many questions that she hoped 'Abdu'l-Bahá would answer. To ensure that she didn't forget any of them, she wrote down fifteen questions on paper and placed the sheet in her Bible. When 'Abdu'l-Bahá called for her at five the next morning, she dashed off for her interview, forgetting her Bible and, therefore, her questions. When she was seated before Him, the Master turned to the interpreter and said, 'Tell Miss Farmer that this is the answer to her first question . . .' 'Abdu'l-Bahá then proceeded to answer each question in order until, unable to restrain her emotions, Mrs Farmer burst into tears of happiness. Though exhilarated, she returned to her room to regain her composure.

In 1892, at a lecture on the future of humanity, Sarah had suddenly recognized that it was 'the dawn of a New Day and Peace for humanity' and saw a way that she could help:

> I saw the picture of Green Acre with its acres of beautiful fields and pines and the river with the Inn high above its bank. But instead of a small summer resort it had become a great center of learning. Throngs of people were coming to it by boat, carriage, even walking. On the shore was a large tent with people comfortably seated listening to a series of Conferences on progressive subjects, free of charge so that all could come. There were all races and creeds there, and happy children and young people ready to learn how to make their lives of value. Peace was the aim of everyone's efforts . . . And I saw also that in the years ahead the Conferences would grow into a school and the school into a University . . .[6]

'Abdu'l-Bahá told her that her dream had been real and that there would, indeed, be a university there, as well as a temple for the worship of God.

Sarah and Maria only stayed in 'Akká for four days, but Maria made a second pilgrimage a few years later when the Master told her: 'When I come to America I will visit you.'[7] When He did get to America, He did more than just visit her – He stayed in her home for ten days.[8]

Arthur and Elizabeth Dodge, and Anna Hoar

On 24 September, Lua and Edward Getsinger returned to Haifa with Anna Hoar and Arthur and Elizabeth Dodge.[9] Arthur Dodge was a successful lawyer, journalist and magazine publisher who became a Bahá'í in 1897 and who was later named a Disciple of 'Abdu'l-Bahá.

The new pilgrims were met at 3 a.m. by a group of believers including Anton Haddad.[10] Arthur always remembered the 'great spiritual light' in their faces which made it 'easy to distinguish the believers from the other natives in the street or anywhere one passed or came upon them'.[11] At that first meeting, Anna recorded her feelings:

> I shall not attempt to describe that visit, nor my first impression of Him. I could not put into words what I felt. Nor can words describe Our Beloved Master. Nor does one fully realize His Greatness, His love and gentleness, humility and grandeur, till they have passed beyond that Presence for the last time, and then it comes gradually, and the farther one recedes, the greater He appears.[12]

Each morning at 5 a.m. the pilgrims would rise and join 'Abdu'l-Bahá on a 20-minute walk to a small house at the foot of Mount Carmel directly below the Tomb of the Báb. They would sit there for an hour, sometimes with Mírzá Abu'l-Faḍl, listening to the lessons of the Master.[13]

Anna, Arthur and Elizabeth were in 'Akká for nine days. Arthur Dodge spent as much time as possible 'receiving the blessed instructions straight from the fountainhead'.[14] When he wasn't with the Master, he was with Mírzá Abu'l-Faḍl who told him much about the history of the Faith in Iran. 'Abdu'l-Bahá breakfasted with the pilgrims most mornings after which he gave them an hour-long lesson which focused on the Bahá'í understanding of Biblical passages or spiritual growth and the soul.

On the way back to New York, the Dodges stopped over in London and Arthur talked with Archdeacon Wilberforce of St John the Divine

Church, Westminster,[15] who became very interested in the Faith and later invited 'Abdu'l-Bahá to speak in his church when He arrived in London eleven years later.

Though Edward and Lua Getsinger had arrived with the other American pilgrims, they stayed much longer, for three months, until 1 January 1901. In a letter to the Bahá'ís in Chicago, Lua wrote, with the common but misguided idea of the Master's station, that

> His heart is large enough for all, and the Cup of His Love is ever running over... Oh my dear brothers and sisters, listen to His words and be comforted. The same Holy Spirit, that spoke in Jesus Christ 1900 years ago, today speaks in Him, and through him doeth all good works. Every day of His life is a pure, holy and sanctified example for all the children of earth; to walk in His footsteps is not difficult if we can but succeed in cutting our hearts from the world, and turning our faces fully to God. Therefore, let not your hearts be troubled over anything – the most important thing is to pray without ceasing, and look not to the mistakes and faults of those around you...
>
> We have found since we are here this time that our dear Master (may my life be a ransom to the dust of His feet!) explained many things to Dr. Kheiralla during our first visit, which he (Dr. K) never translated to us, as the teachings of our Lord conflicted with his own ideas... But, thank God, now everything will be made clear, for the Truth is like the light of the sun, – nothing can hide it...
>
> Our Lord has commanded my husband and myself to return to America for one year, and we leave here after one month, with Mr. Haddad and Mírzá Abdel Fadhl [Mírzá Abu'l-Faḍl], whose teachings and explanations of the Bible are authorized by our Lord, so we know that they are correct![16]

'Abdu'l-Bahá lived in a portion of the House of 'Abdu'lláh Páshá. The Master had leased one upper and one lower apartment. The lower apartment, consisting of several rooms, was the *bírúní*, a public reception area, while the upper floor was the *andárúní*, or private area, and contained two rooms, one of which was the Master's office and the other was where He entertained guests. Protestant missionaries had another apartment on the ground floor near the entrance which they used as a dispensary and a place to teach their beliefs.[17]

There were many more Eastern pilgrims than Western in those days and their pilgrimage was a bit different from those of Westerners. The few Western pilgrims had different needs and their agenda was more flexible than that for the Eastern pilgrims. The Eastern pilgrims stayed in a pilgrim house where Áqá Muḥammad Ḥasan was the custodian. They were usually awakened with a prayer chanted by one of the friends, after which they gathered for tea and breakfast. This was a time for the discussion of the activities of the Faith and continued until 'Abdu'l-Bahá passed through on His way to do His business about town. 'Abdu'l-Bahá would return for lunch, then there was a period of rest or a nap. As night fell, everyone, including resident believers, gathered and awaited 'Abdu'l-Bahá's arrival. Sometimes the Master spoke to the group and at other times, He would go upstairs and call pilgrims up individually. Duration of pilgrimage was very flexible, lasting from a couple days to several months. The pilgrims spent much of their time transcribing and copying the sacred Writings and sending 'Abdu'l-Bahá's instructions to various places. They also were commonly involved in wheat sifting, a task that occupied their hands and eyes, but left them free to converse, chant and sing. To sift wheat, a large cloth was spread on the floor and a round table placed in its centre. Bags of wheat would be emptied onto the table. The pilgrims and friends would then manually sift the wheat after which it was sent to the mill to be made into flour.[18]

Charlotte, Louise and Eleanor Dixon

On 30 October Charlotte Dixon and her two daughters, Louise and Eleanor, arrived from Washington, DC.[19] Ali-Kuli Khan was evidently impressed with the blonde Louise (of medium height) and tall brunette Eleanor because he left descriptions of them, but not of Mrs Dixon.[20]

The women were taken from the hotel to 'the house of our Lord' in Haifa. As they arrived, they saw 'standing at the open window . . . a tall Persian with a grave face, hair slightly touched with gray, and wearing the usual Persian costume . . . This was our first glimpse of this people of which we had heard so much, and the bearing of this man expressed such simple dignity that we immediately felt ourselves in the presence of one closely in touch with our Master.'

Entering the house, they were greeted by Lua Getsinger and Harriet Thornburgh, who had returned to Haifa. The women were then taken to meet the Greatest Holy Leaf whose 'features express much physical suffering, though one feels the power of her inner strength'. In her lap was three-year-old Shoghi Effendi who greeted them with 'I love you very much,' his only words of English. He then chanted a prayer.[21]

The next morning, a carriage arrived at the hotel to take the women and 'Abdu'l-Bahá's daughters, 17-year-old Rúhá and 19-year-old Munavvar, to 'Akká. In her diary, Louise wrote that she had read all the accounts of earlier pilgrims about this journey, but the reality made her heart bound

> with joy and a divine peace seemed to breathe from the brilliant sunshine and pure air. The journey took us through the streets of Haifa out to the plains beyond, around the bend of the sea which here becomes known as the Bay of Acre. On our right strode camels in dignified procession, attended by picturesque, but alas, benighted Bedouins, children of the desert. Patches of grass and green dotted amid the sand, and occasionally a lone date palm stood erect and clear out against the background, while beyond in the distance, loomed a chain of hills corrugating the horizon. To the left, our carriage wheels dipped into the sea as we sought the more solid road bed, and always before us and ahead, like a white beacon, the City of Light, a place of prisons, an abode of the Arab and Bedouin, yet blooming as the rose, for in the midst dwells the King of the earth. Driving through the streets of the fortifications, we passed the prison in which the Blessed Perfection lived and wrote for two years . . . The streets are narrow, and the stone buildings present a most ancient and oriental appearance, but after passing through the most thickly settled portion of the city, we came into the open where stands the house occupied by our dear Lord and His Family. It is a large white structure built around a court and garden, almost on the edge of the sea . . .[22]

The pilgrims were led into a room with no furniture but divans around the walls and Persian rugs on the floor. 'Abdu'l-Bahá rose from a divan and welcomed them. Louise wrote of that meeting:

> It is useless to add another to the impressions received by numerous pilgrims on first seeing our dear Lord. His figure, costume and bearing we found just as had been so minutely described to us, but

the full import of this most blessed and precious Personality can only be felt, not expressed, so that it is quite literally true to say that after the most elaborate description one has not conveyed in what it really consists.'[23]

At dinner that night, 'Abdu'l-Bahá took each of the women by the hand and escorted her to the table, 'my mother at his right hand and my sister beside her, while my place was at his left'. There were also twelve other pilgrims from Russia and Persia as well as Ali-Kuli Khan.

On 2 November, the Dixon family went to the Shrine of Bahá'u'lláh and then to the Garden of Riḍván, where the caretaker told them the story of Bahá'u'lláh and the locusts (see the story on page 73). The following day, they had both breakfast and supper with the Master and Louise noted:

Our Master eats very little Himself and often declines dishes which were served at the table. On one occasion when the sweets were served, seeing that Mr Getsinger had taken none of the cake, which was very delicious, in a most loving manner He took a portion from mother's plate and gave it to him, and then took a piece for Himself also from her plate and ate it. At another time, in the breakfast room, He gave to my sister and myself some of the white cheese of that country and said: 'It would make our minds good.'[24]

The Dixons returned to Bahjí on 4 November and, from the balcony of the Mansion, watched 'as the believers, in the beautiful costumes of their country, walked slowly and reverently, their arms folded, forming a picture' with the setting sun and animals in the fields. A few days later they left 'Akká in the company of 'Abdu'l-Bahá for Haifa.[25]

The next day they went with Rúhá Khánum to the site of the Tomb of the Báb following 'a circuitous path and our driver walked with his horses most of the way'. They then left Haifa the following day.

On their return journey, the Dixons stayed in a pension in Rome. They were still on a spiritual high and a young woman also staying at the pension was strongly attracted to them. When they met by chance in the elevator, Charlotte was able to introduce the Faith to the woman, who turned out to be Agnes Alexander, a future pioneer to Japan and Hand of the Cause of God.[26]

Laura Barney, Ellen Goin and Emma Tronvé

It was at the age of 21 that Laura Barney made the first of many pilgrimages, arriving in October with her cousin, Ellen Goin, and Emma Tronvé, a fervent Catholic Frenchwoman.[27] For Laura, this was to be a life-changing pilgrimage, leading to the book *Some Answered Questions*. When the three women arrived in Haifa, Laura sent 'Abdu'l-Bahá a message saying that she

> believed He must be the Christ Spirit of the awaited Day. I believed that this great hour was at hand for the whole world and sin itself was calling for a Redeemer. If He was truly the Saviour He had the power of awakening my sleeping soul. I sent this message because I believe the first basis of everything is, or should be, sincerity and I didn't want to appear to have deeper feelings than I truly possessed.[28]

The next morning, Ali-Kuli Khan arrived at their hotel to escort Laura and Ellen to 'Abdu'l-Bahá. When he saw whom he was to escort, the shy Khan 'nearly sank into the ground. He had never before seen such strikingly beautiful American girls . . . He could hardly get his message out' and just stared at his shoes.[29] It may have been a portent of the future because in 1904, he married the American Florence Breed. When Khan and Florence cabled the news to 'Abdu'l-Bahá, He was reported to have

> clapped His hands and sent for sweets, shared the word with the pilgrims, and celebrated with them this first fulfilment of Bahá'u'lláh's prophecy, that the day would come when East and West would embrace like unto two lovers. He blessed their marriage with a remarkable wedding Tablet, wishing them a life of achievement in both the material world and the spiritual.[30]

At six the next morning, Laura and Ellen entered the Master's home and were shown to a simple room. Laura wrote:

> When the Master appeared on the threshold I was overwhelmed, for such an atmosphere of perfect Majesty and humility surrounded His whole being. He swept into the room, and, after having given

us a most beautiful welcome, bade us be seated, then the flood of His words became to us as living water – I could not understand the language, but the spirit was so strong that we felt as though we knew the words even before they were given us through the clear translation of Aly Kuli Khan. At first we remained as though stunned, but soon to my great surprise, for it is something that I seldom do, I began to weep. They were not tears of sadness, oh no, they were tears of hope, and deep gratitude, tears that one might shed after having been released from a dark prison. For years I had tried to remove the darkness which enveloped my soul, but in vain, all had seemed useless my despair increasing tenfold after each successful struggle. I listened to the Master's words; I saw my way and saw my way clearly, my tears flowed from the source of gratitude, my chilled heart felt the warm life pulse of the love throb for the first time. The cage of darkness was shattered, and my freed soul felt the wings of the spirit upon which to soar upward to God.[31]

When Laura returned to her room, she told her friend Emma that she had a wonderful message to give her, but that she had to calm down first. Then the three women drove up to the monastery on Mount Carmel. Emma went to the chapel, knelt down and 'prayed with great fervour'. The next morning she rushed to Laura, whom she called Elsa, and told her:

'Elsa, I had such a strange dream last night; now I feel quite prepared to hear what you have to tell me.' She then related how in her dream she was kneeling in the chapel upon Mt. Carmel and her prayers were directed to the Figure of Christ on the Crucifix. She prayed for guidance and light. Gradually the figure on the Cross descended and approached her, laying His hand upon her head, and said 'Be at peace – your prayer is answered.'[32]

Laura then told her what she had learned the day before and Emma accepted the Message with 'joy and fragrance'. The next day it was Emma's turn to meet the Master. On seeing His face, she was overcome by a wave of emotion because the face she saw was the same as the face of the figure who had come down from the Cross in her dream.[33]

Laura had an immense desire to remain in the Master's household, but just before she departed, He called her to Him and said: 'To be near me hereafter, you must now go far away to do the Master's work. Have hope and confidence and you will return unto this Holy Spot. Fear not I am ever with you.' As she left, Laura had expected to be anguished, but 'instead we all felt a great peace and a great happiness'. And she realized that the first part of 'Abdu'l-Bahá's statement had already come true. Laura returned to Paris, rearranged her whole life and taught the Faith. The second part of the Master's statement then came true when, in early 1901, she was recalled to the Master's presence.[34]

Emogene Hoagg, Helen Ellis Cole and Alma Albertson

Emogene Hoagg, Helen Ellis Cole and Alma Albertson left from America and were in Haifa by 21 November.[35] Emogene was born in 1869 and had gone to a 'fashionable seminary for young ladies' where she learned Italian, German, Spanish and Persian, capabilities that later enabled her to translate *Bahá'u'lláh and the New Era*, *Wisdom of 'Abdu'l-Bahá* and *Hidden Words* into Italian, helped translate the Kitáb-i-'Ahd and the *Will and Testament of 'Abdu'l-Bahá* into German; and assisted with translating *Bahá'u'lláh and the New Era* into French. She married a wealthy New York Dutchman. She first heard about the Bahá'í Faith from Lua and Edward Getsinger while visiting Phoebe Hearst after Phoebe had returned from her pilgrimage. When Ibrahim Kheiralla began creating disunity, she went to Paris and encountered May Bolles, Helen Cole and Alma Albertson.[36]

In Haifa, the three women were collected by Isfandíyár, 'Abdu'l-Bahá's trusted servant, who took them to the Shrine of Bahá'u'lláh in a carriage pulled by three horses. They were met there by the Greatest Holy Leaf and Ḍíyá'íyyih Khánum (one of 'Abdu'l-Bahá's daughters and the mother of Shoghi Effendi, often referred to in early accounts as Zia Khanum). The three women met 'Abdu'l-Bahá later when they arrived at His house. Emogene's room in 'Akká contained nothing more than a cot, but she slept there for ten nights in 'perfect comfort'.[37] The 14 days with 'Abdu'l-Bahá were Emogene's 'spiritual baptism'.[38] The women were able to meet with 'Abdu'l-Bahá every day; He immersed them 'in the divine Message bequeathed to a dying civilization by His Father'.[39] Alma Albertson recorded that the Master said:

> Man becomes like a stone unless he continually supplicates to God. The heart of man is like a mirror which is covered with dust and to cleanse it one must continually pray to God that it may become clean. The act of supplication is the polish which erases all worldly desires. The delight of supplicating and entreating before God cuts one's heart from the world. When the taste of man is nourished by honey he never likes to taste any other sweetmeat. Therefore, prayer is a key by which the doors of the kingdom are opened. There are many subjects which are difficult for man to solve. But during prayer and supplication they are unveiled and there is nothing that man cannot find out. Mohammed said: 'Prayer is a ladder by which everyone can ascend to heaven.' If one's heart is cut from the world his prayer is the ascension to heaven.
>
> In the highest prayer men pray only for the love of God, not because they fear him or hell or hope for bounty or heaven. Thus the souls in whose hearts the fire of love is enkindled are attracted by supplication. True supplication to God must therefore be actuated by love to God only. . .[40]

Other American and Russian pilgrims were there at the same time. In one of His talks to the pilgrims, 'Abdu'l-Bahá explained progressive revelation.

> The Báb said: 'The day of Adam is, as compared with the Day of the Blessed Perfection, as a child in the womb of its mother beside a full grown and perfect man.' He did not mean that the world was then in its infancy, but that the Bounties of God then poured out upon all the people of those days were so much less than those manifested in the days of the Blessed Perfection. The day of Adam was as the rising of the sun; the Day of the Blessed Perfection as the Full noontide. The joy, fragrance and spirituality in the time of Moses compared with that in the day of Jesus was like a river compared to the sea.[41]

When the pilgrimage was over, 'Abdu'l-Bahá suggested that Emogene go to Port Said and study with Mírzá Abu'l-Faḍl. Emogene did so, writing:

I knew no one at Port Saʻíd and met none but Baháʼís during my stay there; but I was not lonely for I was treated as a sister by the kind friends. For four weeks Mírzá Abu'l-Faḍl received me at the home of Nur'u'lláh Effendi twice a day, morning and evening, and gave me such explicit instruction on the Bible that for the first time this Book became an open page. It was not without difficulty that I got the explanation. Sometimes Nur'u'lláh Effendi would give me the meaning in Italian, and at other times Aḥmad Yazdí Effendi would translate into French. Then I would put their words into English. After about two weeks Anton Effendi Haddad was sent to Port Saʻíd, and he translated directly into English. Almost every evening five or six of the Baháʼí brothers would meet with us to hear Mírzá Abu'l-Faḍl's explanations. Those were wonderful days, – to think that I, an American woman, was able to meet with these Baháʼí brothers of a different nationality and in a foreign country, and to feel so perfectly at home, just as though I had been with my own family! Probably to them it was yet a more novel experience to be able to meet with an unveiled sister. All this has been brought about by the power of Baháʼu'lláh. I was still at Port Saʻíd at Christmas time and was honored at dinner by the presence of Mírzá Abu'l-Faḍl, Aḥmad Yazdí Effendi and Anton Effendi Haddad. Dear Mírzá Abu'l-Faḍl did not wish to go into the large dining-room at the hotel, so we had a private room and he entertained us by relating Baháʼí incidents in his life.[42]

In 1919, along with Marion Jack, Emogene made a historic seven-month teaching trip through Alaska and the Yukon. She remained a travel teacher for the rest of her life.

Reverend Henry Jessup turns against the Faith

Also in November, the man who had written the address wherein the name of Baháʼu'lláh was first spoken in America arrived in Haifa. At that earlier time, on the occasion of the World's Parliament of Religions in Chicago on 23 September 1893, the address the Reverend Henry Jessup wrote was given by Reverend George Ford, who told his audience:

1900

In the Palace of Bahjí, or Delight, just outside the Fortress of 'Akká, on the Syrian coast, there died a few months since, a famous Persian sage, the Bábí Saint, named Bahá'u'lláh – the 'Glory of God' – the head of that vast reform party of Persian Muslims, who accept the New Testament as the Word of God and Christ as the Deliverer of men, who regard all nations as one, and all men as brothers. Three years ago he was visited by a Cambridge scholar [Edward Granville Browne] and gave utterance to sentiments so noble, so Christlike, that we repeat them as our closing words:

'That all nations should become one in faith and all men as brothers; that the bond of affection and unity between the sons of men should be strengthened; that diversity of religions should cease and differences of race be annulled. What harm is there in this? Yet so it shall be. These fruitless strifes, these ruinous wars shall pass away, and 'the Most Great Peace' shall come. Do not you in Europe need this also? Let not a man glory in this, that he loves his country let him rather glory in this, that he loves his kind.'[43]

By November 1900, Jessup had dramatically changed his view of the Bahá'í Faith, at least in part because his missionary work in Syria was producing very few converts to Christianity while the Bahá'ís were very successful. Zia Bagdadi wrote that in Hamadan, Iran, in the late 1890s, there were no Christians or Bahá'ís. Then, at about the same time, a group of well-funded Christian missionaries and three Bahá'ís arrived and began teaching. The Christians spent 'enormous sums of money', while the Bahá'ís, Mírzá Abu'l-Faḍl, Ḥájí Mírzá Haydar-'Alí and Mírzá Ebuir Azdak [sic], were poor. Within a year, 700 people became Bahá'ís, but not one converted to Christianity.[44]

Where Jessup had once praised the teachings of Bahá'u'lláh, now he passionately condemned them. Jessup arrived in Haifa with his wife and Captain Wells, a chaplain from the Philippines. They stayed at the Pross Hotel on Mount Carmel where an American lady who had become 'enamoured of this system of mysticism' was staying. Captain Wells 'had come there for the express purpose of keeping her out of that abyss of religious platitudes'. Jessup wrote, 'We spent four and a half hours in conversation with her. She could give no reason for following Abbas Effendi, excepting a kind of hypnotic fascination.'[45]

Jessup and Wells called on 'Abdu'l-Bahá the next day. Jessup wrote that He was 'an elderly and venerable man, very similar to scores of venerable Moslem and Druse sheikhs I have met in this land'. Of the Faith promoted by 'Abdu'l-Bahá, Jessup said that it 'may result in good if it spreads among the Sunni Moslems of Turkey and Egypt as it has among the Shiahs of Persia . . . But I cannot understand how a true Christian can possibly exchange the liberty with which Christ makes us free and the clear, consistent plan of salvation through a Redeemer, for the misty and mystical platitudes of Babism.'[46] After leaving 'Abdu'l-Bahá's presence, Jessup wrote that He had the 'painful feeling that he was accepting divine honours from simple-minded women from America and receiving their gifts of gold, without a protest or rebuke'.[47]

Jessup did not differentiate between 'Abdu'l-Bahá and His Covenant-breaking half-brother Mírzá Muḥammad-'Alí, thinking them both to be followers of Bahá'u'lláh. In his book, Jessup wrote that 'In March, 1901, Rev. Mr. Bray of Wisconsin dined with Mohammed Ali [Mírzá Muḥammad-'Alí] and Bedea Effendi [Badí'u'lláh], brothers of Abbas. They showed him the tomb of their father, Beha Allah, who they insisted was an incarnation of the Holy Ghost. "What," said Mr Bray, "is this the tomb of a dead Holy Ghost?" Mohammed Effendi was perplexed and made no reply.'[48]

Because of his narrow-mindedness and spiritual blindness, Jessup wrote that

> Beha-ullah in Acre claimed to be an incarnation of God and on his death a few years ago his son, Abbas Effendi, succeeded him and is running the 'incarnation' for all that it is worth, and that is worth a good deal, as pilgrims constantly come from the Babite sect in Persia and bring their offerings of money with great liberality . . .
>
> The Babite movement in Persia started out as an attempt at a reform of Islam and ended by the leader claiming to be divine and invulnerable in battle, but when he died, another was found ready to succeed to his pretensions.
>
> They teach a strange mixture of truth and error, of extreme liberality and unscrupulous persecution of those obnoxious to them.[49]

Unlike Jessup, some who came to argue were not so set in their ways. Sarah G. Herron arrived on pilgrimage in December 1900 and during her time there, 'Abdu'l-Bahá told the story of the visit of a group of materialist scholars who had asked Him about the Immaculate Conception.

> The scholars said it is impossible for a child to be born without a father, and said nothing could change their opinion regarding it. They left the subject and began speaking of geology – scientific facts well known. They were led to speak of their idea of evolution of man from the atom and molecule all through the different stations until at last man was evolved from all these previous conditions. Then Abbas Effendi said: 'Well, did the first man who was evolved have a father and mother, as you said a child must have that comes into the world?' They said: 'Why no, of course not.' Then the Master said: 'Well, if God could make the first man who came upon the earth without a father or mother, could He not make Jesus Christ also without a human father?' They were confounded and said nothing more, but after that they were converted and went away believers.[50]

1901

In January of 1901, Mason Remey, Helen Ellis Cole, Ethel Rosenberg, Harriet Thornburgh and Lua and Edward Getsinger were on pilgrimage, staying until March, except for the Getsingers who left for a while and returned in March.[1] May Bolles had hoped to go with them, but 'Abdu'l-Bahá told her not to.[2] Harriet taught English to a dozen members of the household and also cared for Ali-Kuli Khan when he became ill.[3] This was the first of seven pilgrimages Mason was to make to 'Abdu'l-Bahá.

Edith and Marie-Louise McKay

Edith McKay and her mother, Marie-Louise McKay, came on pilgrimage during this time and stayed with the Getsingers. When Edith and Marie-Louise first met 'Abdu'l-Bahá, they found themselves on their knees weeping with joy. Edith wrote:

> Those were two wonderful weeks. We would go each morning very early to the Master's house and He would teach us, answering our numerous questions, explaining the scriptures and many things we had ignored. There were always two or three interpreters for different languages. After that, the Master would dictate His Tablets, often two or three at the same time, answering hundreds of letters which He received; then all of a sudden He would rise and go towards the door where a crowd was waiting for Him. He would then go to town, visiting the poor and the sick and healing them.[4]

A year after their pilgrimage, Edith and her mother moved to Switzerland. There Edith met Dr Joseph de Bons, a Swiss doctor. Edith and Joseph were married and he immediately accepted Bahá'u'lláh when His message was presented to him.[5]

Ali-Kuli Khan left Haifa to go to America at the request of 'Abdu'l-Bahá as a translator for Mírzá 'Abu'l-Faḍl as he taught the Faith and helped the American believers remain steadfast in the face of Kheiralla's activities. Ali-Kuli Khan wasn't happy about this and complained that he could 'hardly speak to two people'. 'Abdu'l-Bahá responded, 'You will speak to hundreds. You will speak to thousands. You will speak to millions.' Satisfied that what the Master had predicted would come to pass, he was not surprised when, on arriving in America, he was asked to speak on the radio.[6]

Edith Jackson and Sigurd Russell

On 1 March, Laura Barney returned to 'Akká with Edith Jackson and Sigurd Russell. Edith Jackson was a Bostonian who had married a wealthy Frenchman who had since died. Sigurd Russell was the 15-year-old son of friends whom Edith had more-or-less adopted. When they started their journey to 'Akká, Sigurd did not believe in God and Madame Jackson was full of doubts. By the time their pilgrimage was over, Sigurd had become one of the 'firmest and most devoted followers of the Master' and Madame Jackson left 'full of faith'.[7]

In previous years, great feasts had been held with visitors from both East and West. In 1901, however, the activities of the Covenant-breakers forced their cessation. But one day, when Edith Jackson was present, a number of Eastern pilgrims, 'practising extreme caution and prudence, had been able to arrive unnoticed from various directions and gathered in the pilgrim house'. 'Abdu'l-Bahá chose that time to gather everyone together at a feast. It was a marvellous event with people of Muslim, Christian, Jewish, Zoroastrian, Hindu and Buddhist backgrounds, each wearing their native clothing, together in the same room, joyous to be together and united in the Faith.[8]

Starting the Shrine of the Báb

'Abdu'l-Bahá had started building the Shrine of the Báb in early 1900 on the spot specifically pointed out by Bahá'u'lláh Himself. The biggest problems with the construction were the constant efforts of the Covenant-breakers to stymy the work. At the end of 1900, Mírzá Muḥammad-'Alí sent representatives to Damascus to report that

'Abdu'l-Bahá was building a fort on Mount Carmel from which He would launch a revolt. In response to these lies, 'Abdu'l-Bahá was visited by the Válí of Beirut in November 1900. The British Vice-Consul in Haifa, James H. Monahan, reported that

> 'Abbas Effendi, the chief of the Babists, who seems to be now permanently living in Haifa instead of Acre, began last summer to build a large house on Mount Carmel for an unknown purpose. About the beginning of October the work of building was stopped when half-finished, and it seems probable that the Turkish government stopped it. However, it is said that it will now soon be resumed. The visit of the Vali may perhaps not have been unconnected with this matter.[9]

The Deputy Governor of Haifa was also against the building of the Shrine, though the Governor approved. The Governor was friendly with the Bahá'ís and appointed a three-man commission to investigate the problem. When they reported that there was no cause for concern, the Deputy Governor rejected their report. 'Abdu'l-Bahá visited the Deputy Governor in his office, but the man was adamant. The Master then accompanied the man to his house in hopes of finally persuading him to relent, but, by the time they arrived, he had not. 'Abdu'l-Bahá decided that His attempt had failed and the Deputy Governor climbed up the steps to his house. Just as he began to climb the third flight, he suddenly collapsed and died. This opened the way for construction to continue.[10]

In order to build a road to the building site, 'Abdu'l-Bahá needed a certain piece of land, but the owner, at the instigation of the Covenant-breakers, refused to sell. Finally, after two months of negotiation, he agreed. 'Then', the Master remembered, 'he reneged. Again he agreed. Again he reneged. A third time he agreed and a third time he reneged.' The owner then demanded that the Bahá'ís return some trees that had been removed during one of the times of agreement. 'Abdu'l-Bahá agreed. The man then wanted a fence built between their properties and 'Abdu'l-Bahá said he would build a wall. Next the man wanted a mediator and Sádiq Páshá was selected and approved. A meeting was arranged with the owner and the mediator, but the owner failed to show up. When they went to the owner's house, he refused to come out. 'Abdu'l-Bahá said:

I was extremely sad. That night I did not sleep, did not eat supper and did not even have tea; I did not meet with anyone, sat in the darkness and said a prayer of the Báb. Close to dawn I fell asleep. Before noon, Ustád Muhammad 'Alí came and said that the interpreter from the German consul and the consul's nephew were waiting for me. I went to see them. The nephew said that a tract of land belonged to a German woman and we could have as much of it as we wanted. I had been sad and now I was happy.

I went to the land registry and found the documents related to the transaction all ready in the Consul's own handwriting and signed by him with no condition attached. I said that I would have to purchase it. He said that they had come forth to serve, to resolve problems, not for greed and profit . . . with utmost joy and happiness the access road to the Shrine was opened.[11]

It was difficult for 'Abdu'l-Bahá to oversee the project while living in 'Akká, but He did not have the funds to buy or build a house in Haifa. Seeing the problem while visiting Him on pilgrimage, Edith Jackson offered money for the construction of a house and Laura Barney helped to purchase land on the eastern side of the German Colony.[12] Construction started soon thereafter and the house was usable in 1906. The following year, 'Abdu'l-Bahá began moving His family into the new house. For a number of years, it was known as the Jackson House. Today, we know it as the House of the Master.

Mírzá Habíbu'lláh Afnán

Mírzá Habíbu'lláh Afnán, who had attained the presence of 'Abdu'l-Bahá in 1897 and 1898, returned in 1901. On his previous visit in September 1898, he had seen the Master's power to do many things at once when the Mufti of 'Akká, the Qadi of 'Akká and the Motosarraf of 'Akká were all visiting Him. He wrote:

> The Master was busy revealing verses. His pen moved extremely rapidly across the page. Meanwhile, He was conversing with the Iranian believers in Persian, with the Mufti and the Qadi in Arabic and with the Motosarraf and several of the Pashas in Turkish. All the while His pen never stopped moving. The divine spirit had

enveloped the atmosphere and anyone who ventured a question was favored with an answer until that blessed Tablet was completed and 'Abdu'l-Bahá set the pen down.[13]

On this pilgrimage, Habíbu'lláh and his family stayed with 'Abdu'l-Bahá for forty days. The day after their arrival, 'Abdu'l-Bahá called them and said that He had intended to ask them to stay in the Holy Land to help Him with the construction of the Shrine of the Báb, but instead of that work, He wanted them to return to Shiraz and become the caretakers of the House of the Báb. 'When you arrive in Shiraz,' he told them, 'I will give you the complete instructions. This task entrusted to you is the most important of all services and worthy of the greatest reward before the Divine Court. Truly, future kings and monarchs will long to have been present on this day and been numbered among the servants and attendants of that Sanctified Threshold.'[14] He then gave them instructions about how to receive pilgrims and visitors to the House of the Báb and how to manage it.

Habíbu'lláh was in 'Abdu'l-Bahá's presence one day when He received an envelope containing nothing but a blank sheet of paper. The Master smiled and said, 'The servants want to test us. Woe betide them on the day when God decides to test His servants!' 'Abdu'l-Bahá then proceeded to write an answer on the blank sheet. The 'test' had been sent by Áqá Siyyid Muḥammad-Ṣádiq.[15] Ṣádiq's wife, Fá'izih, had become a Bahá'í some years before and this had enraged him. For years they fought over the Faith. Many Bahá'í teachers, including Mírzá Ḥaydar-'Alí, became involved in trying to teach Ṣádiq, but all encountered the same hostility. One day Mírzá Ḥaydar-'Alí quoted a verse from the Qur'án that supported his argument, but Ṣádiq vehemently replied that such a verse could not have come from the Holy Book. The next day, Ṣádiq himself had discovered that very quotation in the Qur'án and was suddenly ashamed of his actions. To resolve his dilemma, he wrote a series of questions for 'Abdu'l-Bahá. In the envelope to the Master, however, he placed a blank sheet of paper; the actual letter he put in his safe.[16]

When 'Abdu'l-Bahá's reply to Ṣádiq arrived, it began, 'O thou who posed a test for 'Abdu'l-Bahá! Is it seemly for a man like thee to test a servant submissive and lowly before God? Nay by God, it is given to the Centre of the Covenant to test the peoples of the world.'[17] It also answered every question Ṣádiq had asked. He was very ashamed and prostrated himself at his wife's feet, asking her forgiveness. In the letter, the Master said He had answered the questions only because of the services of Ṣádiq's wife for the Faith. His reply also invited him and his wife on pilgrimage. After their pilgrimage, Ṣádiq and Fá'izih Khánum became stalwarts of the Faith and defenders against Covenant-breakers.[18] (There is another version of this story in *Sweet and Enchanting Stories*, compiled by Aziz Rohani, in which Ṣádiq gives the letter with the questions to the Local Spiritual Assembly to hold until the answer was received. This version says that it was Ṣádiq who requested the pilgrimage after receiving his answer. Adib Taherzadeh, in the story above, used Mírzá Ḥaydar-'Alí's written account of the incident. Since Ḥaydar-'Alí was there, his version is considered to be the more accurate one.)

Laura Barney and Mason Remey

Laura Barney was anxious when she arrived for her second pilgrimage. She had formed an ideal image of the Master from her first visit and now worried that a 'great disillusion might be awaiting me'. But when she came into His presence, she 'instantly realized that this ideal was an absolute reality and far beyond my anticipations'.[19] One day she was with the Master when two Eastern pilgrims came into His presence and she said that it was the first time she had truly understood the meaning of reverence: 'Their reverence for Him was perfect for they realized and knew who He was!'[20]

Mason Remey arrived for his second pilgrimage and spent eleven days with the Master in March. He commented on how 'Abdu'l-Bahá could see the inner beings of the pilgrims and was 'The one who knows and understands all conditions of soul, for his understanding penetrates deeper than the mind. I was deeply impressed by his understanding of my inner-self.' He noted that the Master could

> penetrate the heart and silently give that divine strength and assurance which every soul craves . . . The advice and admonitions of The Master are both special and general in their nature. To individual souls he gives special and personal advice, through the carrying out of which each soul receives strength and enlightenment . . . Not everyone who visits The Master and sees him with the outward eye, sees him with the inner spiritual eye. Outwardly he is like any

other man, but inwardly he is entirely different. He stands unique! The indwelling spirit within him we only see as we look beyond his human personality.[21]

Yúnís Khán and William Hoar

Youness Afroukhteh, better known as Yúnís Khán, arrived in April 1901 to help 'Abdu'l-Bahá with his ever-increasing work and to help translate to and from English. Following his first pilgrimage in 1897,[22] he had been busily working in a bank in Persia when he was handed a telegram that read 'Youness Khán is to come. 'Abbás.' Within two weeks, he was on his way, expecting to be away for a few months, not knowing that it would be nine years before he returned.[23] While on his way, he met an American, William Hoar.

William Hoar's journey to Haifa was adventurous. He left New York on 19 April, travelling by way of London, Paris, and Egypt, where he met the Yazdí brothers, Muḥammad and Aḥmad, in Alexandria and Port Said respectively. Aḥmad Yazdí gave him a fez to wear while in Palestine, together with many messages and letters to take to 'Abdu'l-Bahá. Because of the dangerous situation in Haifa and 'Akká due to the actions of the Covenant-breakers, William was sent from Port Said to Beirut and told to find Mustapha Bagdadi, one of the early believers and a contemporary of Bahá'u'lláh.[24] Upon his arrival in Beirut, William hired a dragoman (an interpreter and/or guide) who promised to take him to Mr Bagdadi the next day. Being a total stranger and not knowing any of the local languages, William was anxious.

> The next morning, as I approached the bazar of Bagdadi, it occurred to me that I did not know the language, that I could not speak either Persian, Turkish or Arabic, and I was somewhat at a loss to know how I should make myself known, not caring to tell my interpreter who or what I was, or what was my object in visiting Bagdadi. However, I trusted to fate, and as I approached the shop, I observed two young men sitting behind a counter, and not knowing what else to say, I approached them with the Bahai salutation, 'Allah-o-Abha', which I afterwards found to be an open sesame to the hearts and possessions of my brother Bahais in the East. Instantly upon hearing this salutation, the faces of the two young men brightened, and they

looked the welcome which it seemed to me they could not express. Not knowing what else to do or say, I said, 'I am from America and can only speak English.' One of the young men responded immediately, 'I speak English', and instantly the situation was relieved.

We entered into conversation, and I learned that the young man who informed me he could speak English, was Eunis Kahn [sic], who was then on his way from Teheran, Persia, to Akka, Syria, where he was to take the place as English interpreter to Abdul Baha, previously occupied by Ali Kuli Khan, whom I had met in Port Said on his way to America.

I was then taken by the other young man, who proved to be the son of Mustapha Bagdadi, to his father and introduced to him as a brother Bahai from America.[25]

Mustapha Bagdadi entertained the American and gave him a tour of the city:

I then returned to my hotel to meet my dragoman who was to come for me after luncheon to take me for a ride through the Mount Lebanon District, which lasted all the afternoon. It was a most charming drive, in the spring of the year; the country was green, attractive and beautiful, and the air laden with the perfume of fruits and flowers.[26]

William wrote that Mr Bagdadi was the 'very personification of goodness and kindliness'. He had two sons, one of whom, Zia, was at that time studying medicine in America and who was to become very important in that community.

That night William and Yúnis K͟hán boarded the steamer for Haifa, arriving there at 3 a.m. They were met at the dock in Haifa by a 'band of brothers', that included Siyyid Taqí Mans͟hádí. William was overwhelmed by the warmth of his welcome: 'It seemed as if the greatest pleasure that these dear brothers had in life while I was with them was in ministering to my wants and comfort.' After breakfast, William met 16-year-old Amín Fareed, who became his constant companion and interpreter. William said, 'I felt utterly lost when he was not at my side.'[27] A year later, 'Abdu'l-Bahá would send Fareed to America as Mirzá 'Abu'l-Faḍl's servant and cook. When called by the Master to return to 'Akká in 1904, Fareed refused and stayed in America. After accompanying the Master through North America and Europe, Fareed went against 'Abdu'l-Bahá in 1914 and became a Covenant-breaker.[28]

After spending a day awaiting 'Abdu'l-Bahá's call, it came and Yúnis Khán and William joined Siyyid Taqí Manshádí and Nuru'lláh Effendi for the trip to 'Akká. Interestingly, their carriage had been made in America. Soon William was being led into a long, high-ceilinged room where he would stay during his visit. After a short while, the double doors were suddenly

> thrown open, and a group of Persians entered. Foremost among them was a venerable, white robed figure with a long flowing white beard, and a most benign and beautiful countenance, and him I at once took to be Abdul Baha. However, I was mistaken, for he was not Abdul Baha, but an uncle of Abdul Baha, the brother of the Manifestation.
>
> Suddenly the group parted, and a figure strode forward, who I immediately knew by his very presence to be none other than Abdul Baha. He is not a tall man, but is, nevertheless, a man of commanding presence, with a noble head splendidly set on regal shoulders, a man who would command attention and respect in any assemblage.
>
> To me, his was a personality of ineffable sweetness and charm, a reposeful dignity impossible to describe. In his face was the light of a divine love, and his smile a glimpse of the heavenly radiance. I shall never forget that smile; it came but rarely, but when it did come, lighting up a countenance habitually sad, it was beautiful to behold.
>
> He approached me, took both my hands in his, gave me an affectionate salutation and welcome, seated me on the divan and took a place beside me. I turned and looked into his face . . .[29]

Lunch was soon announced. Being the primary meal of the day, it consisted of vegetable soup, cucumbers, roast lamb, sweetmeats and bread. William wrote:

> Abdul Baha always has a guest at the noon-day meal, and I, of course, was the guest of the day, and to meet me were invited two Persian believers, one of them a man of majestic presence, who had been with the Manifestation almost from his boyhood, who had

suffered with Him in exile, and who was the faithful friend of Abdul Baha – Haji Niaz [Ḥájí Níyáz, from Egypt] Kermani. Kermani is an old man, six feet tall, with a long white beard – a splendid type of the Oriental man, sweet, gentle, but, withal, commanding and strong – such a man as an artist seeking a model for an Isaiah would choose. I spent very many happy hours with Kermani . . .

Sometimes we talked about the friends in America, and the progress of the Cause all over the world, and at other times the conversation of Abdul Baha was on the instructions of the Kingdom.[30]

William began asking questions and carefully recording the answers. Each day, the power of 'Abdu'l-Bahá affected William until he became 'a complete and true teacher of the Faith'.[31]

As for Yúnis Khán, he wrote that he 'tasted the sweetness of reunion and experienced once again all the emotions and feelings which had so filled my being the first time I attained His presence; His kind and loving words rejuvenated my drooping soul.'[32] This was the first time Yúnis Khán was to translate for the Master: 'My first hour in the presence of the Beloved of hearts was spent in a fragmentary and disjointed attempt to translate His words, as I sat utterly intoxicated by His presence.'[33]

When that first meeting had ended, he 'was summoned to His presence alone. In a hushed voice the Master confided: "You have to be here with us. Trust no one but me. Whatever is in your heart, confide it to me only. Trust no one, this land is in turmoil and the troublemakers are waiting in the wings. Be vigilant."'[34]

On the afternoon of his first day, William was taken to the Riḍván Garden. There he found the

Bahai pilgrims and the exiles of Akka were gathered – a splendid group of men, cleanly dressed, intelligent, and apparently prosperous. One can never tell, by looking at the Bahais in the East, whether they are rich or poor. There is no pretence or show about them, nevertheless, there is that in their appearance which one sees only in the well groomed man. One could not tell the merchant from the barber, or the scholar from the shoemaker – brothers all.

I was taken by the arm and introduced to each one of them individually, and as I was introduced, I was told what the occupation and calling was of the one to whom I was presented. A nice, cleanly dressed young man was introduced to me as the barber; another as the shoemaker; another as a merchant, and so on through the entire group. There seemed to be no distinctions among them. It was a community of perfect equality, and they were loving and gentle and perfectly free in their intercourse with each other . . .'[35]

The next day, William went to the Shrine of Bahá'u'lláh with 'Abdu'l-Bahá and had the bounty of being alone in the room containing the remains of the Manifestation of God.

Returning from these powerful experiences, William went to his room and discovered a Turkish soldier looking over the family photographs he had brought and spread about his room. Using signs, the soldier asked if the photos were his and, using signs as well, William indicated that they were. Then 'Abdu'l-Bahá walked into the room and introduced Lává Páshá, a Turkish general who was the second in command of 'Akká. Lává Páshá had come specifically to meet 'Abdu'l-Bahá's visitor. Meeting him destroyed William's preconceived notions about the Turks and he thoroughly enjoyed the general's company. The next day, the general returned and the American and Turk sat with 'Abdu'l-Bahá asking each other questions about their respective countries.

The novelty of having an American there brought 'Akká's commanding officer, 'General Kerif Pasha, a grizzled Turkish soldier', to visit the following day in the company of the Master. He was there as a courtesy to William since he was a friend of 'Abdu'l-Bahá. Before leaving 'Akká, William noted that 'The Governor was his [the Master's] friend; the military men, from the humblest lieutenant to the General in command, seemed to revere him, and he seemed to me to be more a personage of distinction and honor than a prisoner and exile . . .' One of the Master's friends was a Judge of the District, 'a splendid looking man, tall, full bearded, with magnificent, dome-like head and a countenance of great intelligence and sweetness . . .'[36]

On Thursday, 'Abdu'l-Bahá and William were invited for dinner with Lává Páshá. Told to be ready at 7 p.m., William dressed carefully in a black suit topped by his fez. William was to go with 'Abdu'l-Bahá, but the Master was not present. After he had waited for over an hour, an escort arrived to take William to the dinner. When he arrived, 'Abdu'l-Bahá still wasn't there, but nobody seemed to be anxious. William's military hosts seemed to know that whatever delayed the Master was important and it was not until He was present that dinner was served. Finally, at 9 p.m., He arrived. William was seated between Lává Páshá and a District Judge. William deemed the dinner 'indescribable', and then set forth to describe it:

> It was served in courses, as we serve them, knives, forks and spoons being provided for me, the rest eating in true Oriental fashion with their fingers. As one dish was served, Liva Pasha turned to me and said, 'This dish was prepared by an artist.' I replied, 'I can very well believe it', for anything more delicious I had never eaten. It was a chicken, prepared I know not how, but, as I have said, delicious. Some sweetmeats were passed to me, and as the plate was put before me, I was told that these were called 'Judge's mouths'. I ate one, and turning to the Judge said, 'These are indeed sweet, and I can only say that I hope justice is always as sweet in the mouth of our friend as these condiments.[37]

After an amazing meal, William talked with Lává Páshá:

> During our conversation at the table I sat at the right of Liva [Lává] Pasha and engaged him in conversation most of the time, with frequent references to Abdul Baha, when, suddenly, he turned to me and striking the table with his hand, with great vehemence he said, 'We believe Abbas Effendi to be the greatest man living in the world today.' I replied that many others held him in like esteem; that there were some in far away lands . . . This seemed to please him, for I found out afterwards that Liva Pasha was the devoted, loving friend of Abdul Baha . . .
>
> The dinner over, we repaired to an anteroom where we sat and smoked and talked, the soldiers telling the stories of their adventures and experiences, and all seemed happy. Abdul Baha sat a lone and solitary figure, apparently not interested in the conversation, nobody taking offense or seeming to notice it; but the instant that Abdul Baha indicated a desire to speak, every voice was hushed and every head was bowed while He discoursed. He told them that He, too, was a soldier, but that his warfare was not carnal; that He did not fight with the sword and with guns but that His weapon

was the Sword of the Spirit, and His armor the Breastplate of Righteousness.³⁸

One day, William saw that something unusual was happening, but didn't know what. Finally, Amín Fareed told him that the commemoration of the Ascension of Bahá'u'lláh was about to take place. The Master hadn't told him about it because He thought it would be too long and tiring for a Westerner. When William asked 'Abdu'l-Bahá if he might participate, the Master agreed, but even so, made arrangements to 'provide a place to which I might retire to sleep. But', William wrote,

> I disappointed them, showing as much endurance as any without apparent effort. While we were sitting in the Garden along towards midnight, Kermani, who is an exceedingly humorous character, was chaffing me about my ability to sit the night out. I assured him that I could. Once, after a lull in our conversation, I chanced to look at Kermani, and I noticed that his noble head was bowing and falling, and that finally it sunk upon his breast in sleep. I watched him for a moment or so and then touched him upon the knee, Upon his awakening, I said to him, through Ameen, 'Could ye not watch with me one hour?' I shall never forget the benign look that he bent upon me as he said, 'O my brother, I have been watching these seventy years.' My heart was touched, and for a moment I could say nothing.³⁹

William's long description of the commemoration is very interesting:

> During this day no Bahai eats from morning until evening. An early breakfast is taken and the fast is not broken until after sundown. In the afternoon of this day we went to the little rest house erected by Abdul Baha located near the Holy Tomb. Shortly after our arrival we saw coming down the road a cavalcade of soldiers and others, and in their midst rode Abdul Baha. As Abdul Baha reined in his little white ass at the gate of the house, a young Turkish officer, dismounting quickly from his horse, went to the side of Abdul Baha and falling to his knee, assisted him to alight, after which he kissed his hand and remounted his horse. This devotion and attention to Abdul Baha was general. Everyone seemed to love him. A Turkish

gendarme is sent with him wherever he goes for his protection, not as a guard. He was at that time allowed absolute freedom, and so careful were the authorities of his welfare, that wherever he went this guard accompanied Him.

No Bahai sleeps during the night following this day. At sundown a feast is prepared, consisting of bread, fruit, tea and a freshly killed sheep. This meal is served by Abdul Baha's own hands. His guests are seated about the table, and He Himself goes about serving first one and then another, not neglecting even the humble Turkish soldier who was his guard and who loved Him. After his followers had eaten, Abdul Baha himself sat down and received food from their hands. After this tea is served, and Abdul Baha retires to the little upper room in the rest house before mentioned, and spends the time in meditation and prayer, frequently sending for one follower and then another for an interview.

Toward midnight he sent for me, and the experiences and emotions of the few moments spent with him in the little upper room at midnight, I can never describe or forget. After my interview I returned to the others, and sharply at midnight a procession was formed and with slow and reverential step marched to the Holy Tomb. Each one was provided with two candles which he carried in either hand. The uncle of Abdul Baha, of whom I have already spoken, the brother of Bahaollah, and myself, were requested to head the procession. At the word from Abdul Baha we started, and as we went up the little slope and came to the foot of the hill on which the tomb is located and then arrived at the top of that hill, I looked back and the scene in the soft moonlight and at that hour of that band of devoted men each possessed, I believe, of the spirit of a martyr, was strange indeed and produced in me a profound impression, such as I can never forget.

Arriving at the tomb, some of the brothers, melting some of the wax from the candles, stood them on the railing surrounding the Garden, while others thrust their candles in the earth, after which they gathered around the little garden seated on the ground in Oriental fashion, to await the coming of the dawn. The thoughtfulness of Abdul Baha showed itself in my case, for knowing that I was an Occidental and unused to sitting as our Oriental brothers do I was provided with a chair placed on a platform raised just above the ground and next to the Tomb. Then began the reading and chanting of the tablets, first by one and then another, and then by Abdul Baha Himself, until the dawn. The celebration of this day of the Ascension lasts from dawn to dawn, and ends with this ceremony at the tomb.

After the chanting of a tablet by one of the brothers, Abdul Baha sent word to me that he would like to have me sing one of our Christian hymns . . . You can refuse Abdul Baha nothing, and, whether I could sing or not, I would certainly have made the effort in deference to his request. I sang for him that familiar old Episcopal hymn: –

'Wearied of life, and burdened with my sin,
I look at heaven and long to enter in . . .'

Thus the night wore away, until finally the dawn was announced, and with a benediction and blessing from Abdul Baha, we were dismissed.[40]

On William's last day in 'Akká, 'Abdu'l-Bahá gave Yúnis Khán written instructions for him, but told Yúnis Khán that he was to avoid giving names or in handing over the actual Tablet. Accompanying William and Yúnis Khán was Amín Fareed, who as we have seen had developed a close relationship with William, but whom Yúnis Khán described as a 'young imposter' with 'a long experience in treachery and deception'. When Yúnis Khán explained what 'Abdu'l-Bahá wished him to do, William asked for the written instructions and it became obvious that Amín had managed to raise suspicions against him. He was forced to send 'Abdu'l-Bahá a telegram and ask Him for permission to pass over the written instructions.[41] The instruction involved meeting with the Persian Ambassador in Washington, DC, and attempting to alleviate the persecution of the Bahá'ís in Iran.[42]

Because of his later steadfastness in the face of Kheiralla's rebellion, William Hoar was declared by Shoghi Effendi to be a Disciple of 'Abdu'l-Bahá.

Confined to 'Akká

Mírzá Muḥammad-'Alí tried every way possible to create problems for 'Abdu'l-Bahá. In addition to approaching the politically powerful, he also spread lies and rumours in the Christian and Muslim religious communities. 'Abdu'l-Bahá claimed to be God, he repeated to anyone who would listen. One day, an American missionary, 'very patriarchal with a long white beard,' arrived from Beirut and marched into 'Abdu'l-Bahá's reception room. Without preamble, he demanded from the Master whether He claimed to be God. When 'Abdu'l-Bahá tried to greet his belligerent visitor, the visitor interrupted Him, repeating, 'I hear you claim to be God.' Though 'Abdu'l-Bahá calmly said He had not made any such claim, the missionary's mind was closed and he refused to listen, continuing in his accusatory mode. Yúnis Khán said 'the scene made him think of Christ, hungry in the wilderness, and taunted by Satan, who told Him: "Command that these stones be made bread."'[43]

Muḥammad-'Alí's schemings were revealed by his brother Badí'u'lláh in 1907, when he briefly returned to the protection of the Covenant. In a letter he wrote to 'Abdu'l-Bahá, he said immediately that after the passing of Bahá'u'lláh,

> Mirza Mohammed Ali said to me: 'The Blessed Beauty (Bahá'u'lláh) – Exalted is His Station! – said: "We have written something and it is in Our depository." . . . I saw that, through Mirza Majduddin [Majdu'd-Dín], Ali Riza, his sister, and the mother of Mirza Shua'u'llah, he (Mohammed Ali) carried the blessed trusts (the writings of Bahá'u'lláh) by way of the window and the gallery of the Behji to his own place. He took away all the traces of the Supreme Pen and the special Tablets revealed for the beloved of God . . .
>
> Among other things he said to me that the preservation of the blessed writings was referred to him by a blessed command, that he possessed a Tablet from the Supreme Pen to that effect. He did not even allow this servant to read the writings . . . For a long time, by means of allusions and hints . . . he gave me to understand that he possessed a Tablet from the Supreme Pen concerning His Holiness Abdul-Bahá, which, he said, if he should reveal, the name of Abdul-Bahá would be effaced . . . Some time elapsed . . . and I asked him for it, but every time he offered me an excuse and sought a pretext to avoid it. Finally, prior to the imprisonment in the most great prison of Akka, one day he took out of a drawer a blessed Tablet from the Supreme Pen, wherein were mentioned the deeds, the actions . . . of Mirza Yahyah (Subh-i- Ezel), mentioning him often as 'My brother'

... I read it and remarked: 'This has no connection with these days'. . .
He said: I have permission from the Blessed Beauty (Bahá'u'lláh) to
use my pen in the blessed writings (interpolate) for the protection
of the Cause. Now, since some souls have exaggerated (the station of
Abdul-Bahá) and the Master claims Divinity, I will erase the word
'My brother' and insert in its place 'My Greatest Branch,' which I
will show to people in order to check his influence.[44]

Now, in 1901, Mírzá Muḥammad-'Alí's shenanigans resulted in both
he and the Master, as well as all the Bahá'ís, being confined to within
the walls of 'Akká, something the Covenant-breaker had not expected.
It happened on 20 August:

'Abdu'l-Bahá . . . was informed, in the course of an interview with
the governor of 'Akká, of Sulṭán 'Abdu'l-Ḥamíd's instructions order-
ing that the restrictions which had been gradually relaxed should be
reimposed, and that He and His brothers should be strictly confined
within the walls of that city. The Sulṭán's edict was at first rigidly
enforced, the freedom of the exiled community was severely cur-
tailed, while 'Abdu'l-Bahá had to submit, alone and unaided, to the
prolonged interrogation of judges and officials, who required His
presence for several consecutive days at government headquarters
for the purpose of their investigations.[45]

The Governor imposed restrictions on all Bahá'ís, regardless of whether
they were faithful to 'Abdu'l-Bahá or Covenant-breakers. Though He
accepted His incarceration, 'Abdu'l-Bahá persuaded the Governor
to have all the believers as well as all the Covenant-breakers, except
for Mírzá Muḥammad-'Alí and Badí'u'lláh, freed from the strict confinement within the city walls that was imposed upon Him.[46] For
'Abdu'l-Bahá, the confinement meant that He could not visit the Tomb
of His Father.

British Vice-Consul Monahan wrote on 30 September:

The Persian Babist leaders Abbas Effendi and his two brothers
are shut up within the walls of Acre by an Imperial Iradé [order
or decree] which arrived in the middle of the quarter. It is supposed that the Ottoman Government took alarm at Abbas Effendi's

increasing wealth and influence especially his influence over Americans and other foreigners. His disciples are however at large in and around Haifa and Acre . . .[47]

Though he had been the cause of his own imprisonment, as well as that of 'Abdu'l-Bahá, Mírzá Muḥammad-'Alí tried his utmost to place the blame elsewhere. Badí'u'lláh, in his letter of repentance, wrote:

> Although they have been the cause of this great matter, yet every day they arranged a new fiction and spread it here and abroad. Once they said a Christian gentleman, among the friends of His Holiness Abdul-Bahá, who resides in Egypt, had spoken publicly of the Cause, in a church, without caution and wisdom, and this had caused the imprisonment. At another time they said that his Honor Mirza Abul Fazl . . . had composed a book and published it, and, this having fallen into the hands of the doctors of Azhar (University) had caused this misfortune. In short, they have done all they could, secretly and publicly.[48]

Badí'u'lláh also explained how the Covenant-breakers brought others into their circle:

> The first thing they do is to appear most obedient to the Divine Laws and night and day engage themselves in the writings of the verses to such a degree that the newcomer imagines that they are absolutely evanescent and absorbed entirely in servitude, having no thought or purpose save the Blessed Cause and the Blessed Verses. After a while they give vent to certain mentions and insinuations in order to hinder the listener from turning to the firm command of the Covenant of God. That is to say, they begin to interpret and misconstrue some of the verses, and some they interpolate and transpose with perfect delicacy, giving one to understand they are wronged. They convey all that which tends to instil enmity and hate in the new-comer's heart against His Holiness, 'Him whom God hath willed' – Abdul-Bahá. Later, they encourage him by various means to say evil things against Abdul-Bahá, and they, themselves, outwardly voice the Verses of Bahá'u'lláh.[49]

VISITING 'ABDU'L-BAHÁ

To most, this imprisonment was terrible, but to Yúnis Khán it was also a blessing because earlier, in Haifa, the Master would commonly visit the poor at night and without a lantern-bearer. Murders were common and some of the believers would secretly follow 'Abdu'l-Bahá until He was safely home. One night, Yúnis Khán was following 'Abdu'l-Bahá through the dark streets when an assailant fired a pistol at the Master:

> We had not quite reached the midpoint when suddenly I saw three shots fired at Him from the alley to our right. At first I remained unconcerned, for I had become accustomed to the sound of gunshots at night. However, on the second shot I saw the flash of fire coming from the barrel of a gun being fired in the direction of 'Abdu'l-Bahá. I ran toward the alley. The third shot was fired before I reached the intersection but I saw someone fleeing. A second person who was halfway up the alley also ran away. Both ran toward the beach. At this moment I was but a few steps from 'Abdu'l-Bahá. The Master's gait did not change. He strolled along with the same dignity and stateliness that were the distinguishing characteristics of that radiant and heavenly Being. Unperturbed, He continued His steady strides without paying the least attention to what had just transpired.[50]

Three months after his first report, Vice Consul Monahan again wrote:

> The Babist leaders . . . have not yet been allowed outside the walls of Acre. It is said that the Persian Government demands that they should be kept thus confined. The construction of the Babist house on Mount Carmel . . . which has been several times stopped by the Turkish Authorities and resumed, was again resumed and is being carried on actively. Two young American gentlemen, disciples of Babism, arrived in November and stayed two or three weeks in Acre. They presumably came to console Abbas Effendi and transact business with him. I have heard that a considerable amount of money was received during the quarter from America for the Babists.[51]

The 'two young American gentlemen' mentioned in Vice Consul Monahan's report were probably William and Wendell Dodge (see below, page 77).

The rumours created by the Covenant-breakers affected the understanding of many.

Thomas Breakwell, Herbert Hopper and Isabella Brittingham

Thomas Breakwell was an Englishman who lived in Louisiana and worked at a cotton mill. Spending the summer of 1901 in Europe, he had encountered May Bolles. The day after meeting May and learning of the Faith, he realized that 'Christ has come again!' and became a Bahá'í. Within a very short time Breakwell joined Herbert Hopper, who had permission to visit 'Abdu'l-Bahá in 'Akká, and the two departed France for the Holy Land.

Breakwell, Hopper and Isabella Brittingham, travelling separately, arrived in early September, just days after 'Abdu'l-Bahá's strict confinement in 'Akká had been imposed.[52] In describing her trip to 'Akká, Isabella noted that, because of the renewed confinement of the Master, in addition to a passport and a visa, they also needed a letter of recommendation from the Turkish Ambassador to the Governor of 'Akká.[53] As her ship approached Haifa from Beirut, Isabella said:

> From the lips of the Orientals about me, on the steamer, I heard the name, 'Abbas Effendi', 'Abbas Effendi', 'Abbas Effendi'. Presently Haji Mirza Hassan Khorassani who was sitting not far from me commenced to talk and he also said 'Abbas Effendi' and presently he came to say 'Baha Ullah'. Presently Mirza Rouhy came by me and dropped down in a seat in a quiet way and said: 'These Orientals are talking of our Lord, and they are all saying what a wonderful person he is and one man especially said that our Lord had taken his son and was educating him and looking after him, and spoke in such a beautiful manner of Him.' And so it is, unbelievers and believers alike recognize a greatness in the presence of our Lord.[54]

Herbert was called first to 'Akká and Isabella spent the afternoon in Haifa in the presence of Munírih Khánum. Later, Thomas Breakwell arrived at the hotel and Isabella wrote that 'Although we had never met each other, yet in one moment, through the precious Spirit of this Glorious Revelation, we were as brother and sister talking together – with tears of happiness upon our faces . . .' Early the next day, Isabella and

Thomas were called to 'Akká and made that much-described journey through the waves. Isabella wrote that they talked little and read some of the Writings. When they arrived at the Master's house, Isabella wrote:

> A row of beautiful Oriental brothers in the Faith awaited, there, our coming, and greeted us in the NAME of that One Who has made the world one home, – and then, still following our guide, we ascended an outer staircase and were ushered into a large ante-room, most simply furnished, in Oriental style, and were requested to be seated, and then were left alone. The hour was that of noon, – golden and calm. We sat there with thought in suspension. A great stillness fell upon me. Love seemed vibrating everywhere. In a few moments a messenger entered, and in low tones invited us to 'partake of a material and a Spiritual feast.' We followed him silently, passing through an upper court which had for its roof the blue sky, and entered a long room, advancing a little and then involuntarily pausing . . . At that upper end, which was slightly elevated, was spread a table for the noon meal, with a simple snowy cloth and pure white china . . . Around the room were standing, in perfect silence, with folded arms and bowed heads, a number of the Oriental brothers whom I had previously met, – awaiting the entrance of our Lord. We had not long to wait. At the far end, beyond the table, a door swung calmly open, and a Figure, all beautiful and majestic, entered, clad in white flowing robes, and advanced toward us. It was the MASTER. So different was He – so absolutely All-Spirit – so much more glorious than the photograph taken of Him by a believer, many years ago . . . that I did not, for one instant, recognize Him. The next instant I knew my Lord – and then I lost all earthly consciousness in that Presence. Those about me said that I called: 'O, it is my Master!' – and that I ran to Him, – but I did not know that I had done so. I only knew that I found myself There, before Him, kissing His beautiful Hands, which were extended toward me. Then they said He left me and went to greet Mr. Breakwell, who was standing dazed and motionless. I do not remember the Master leaving me, but dimly remember seeing Him greet my fellow pilgrim. Then they said He returned to me and taking me by the hand led me to my seat at the table, but I remember nothing of this. That Great Vibration had broken up the old conditions, and I was lost to the consciousness

of this world then, and for hours thereafter, although I, doubtless, mechanically lived and moved. I had entered that Great Light, and Its Power already had begun the work of disintegration.

Great days followed; too great, too sacred, to speak much of. For with what language of the flesh can we portray them? Only those who have been vouchsafed the blessedness of attaining that Visit, and have continuously prayed during the pilgrimage thither to be emptied and cleansed that they may be filled by Him, know what that Visit means to the longing heart.[55]

May Bolles described the timing of Breakwell's schedule and his meeting with 'Abdu'l-Bahá a bit differently:

When he and Herbert Hopper arrived in the Prison of 'Akká, they were ushered into a spacious room, at one end of which stood a group of men in oriental garb. Herbert Hopper's face became irradiated with the joy of instant recognition, but Breakwell discerned no one in particular among these men. Feeling suddenly ill and weak, he seated himself near a table, with a sense of crushing defeat. Wild and desperate thoughts rushed through his mind, his first great test, for without such tests the soul will never be unveiled.

Sitting thus he bitterly lamented: Why had he come here? Why had he abandoned his projected journey and come to this remote prison, seeking – he knew not what? Sorrow and despair filled his heart, when suddenly a door opened, and in that opening he beheld what seemed to him the rising Sun. So brilliant was this orb, so intense the light that he sprang to his feet and saw approaching him out of this dazzling splendor the form of 'Abdu'l-Bahá.

He seldom mentioned this experience which transformed and transfigured his life.[56]

One day the three pilgrims went to the Riḍván Garden. While there, the gardener, Abu'l-Qásim, told stories of the time Bahá'u'lláh was in the garden. One he told was about the locusts:

At one time when the Blessed Perfection, Baha'u'llah, was in His little room at the Rizwan, a swarm of locusts filled the Garden. This troubled Abul Kasim and he sought the Presence of the Blessed

Perfection and told Him of their being there. The Blessed Perfection replied: 'Go and entertain them. They are our guests.' Abul Kasim obeyed, gathering all the fruits and vegetables he could find, and placed these in the Garden. The locusts rapidly devoured these and then flew up and settled upon all the trees, shrubs and flowers, and upon every part of the Garden.

Again the gardener sought the Blessed Presence, and expressed his fear that the locusts would destroy everything, and especially the mulberry trees. The Blessed Perfection replied: 'This is well. Let them devour them.' The gardener supplicated: 'This will not be good, for there will be no shade trees for Thee under which to sit.' The Blessed Perfection replied: 'Because you do not wish them to remain, very well.' And He then went down into the middle of the garden, took the Hem of His Garment in His Hand, and waving it, uttered, thrice, these words: 'Abul Kasim does not want you! God protect you!' Immediately, upon His uttering these words, the locusts arose in a body, and flew away.[57]

Isabella stayed in 'Akká for five days. Then, on her last night in Haifa, she and eight others went to the Tomb of the Báb and, 'sitting in an almost unbroken silence, looked across the blue waves to Acre, the City of Love and Peace for the whole world, watching it until the sunset gold deepened into rose and then turned into ashes, and the Holy City was hidden from our eyes by a mist; then by the light from a lantern . . . we descended the mountain.'[58] Isabella was later named a Disciple of 'Abdu'l-Bahá by Shoghi Effendi.

Yúnis Khán remembered that Breakwell would 'usually be seen reciting the verses of the Bible in glorification of the Kingdom of God' and that while in the presence of 'Abdu'l-Bahá was 'enthralled by the matchless beauty of the Beloved, and as he completed his pilgrimage and received permission to depart, he evinced moving signs of deep adoration and veneration'.[59]

Breakwell did not have time to mix with the other believers in 'Akká. When he left, Yúnis Khán accompanied him to Haifa. As the two young men waited for the ship, Breakwell 'gazed longingly out of the window towards 'Akká, fervently reciting prayers'.[60] Breakwell soon began an amazing correspondence with Yúnis Khán after his departure, writing every two weeks. In his second letter, Breakwell wrote 'But I ask God for calamity; I desire undiminishing pain. I long for suffering without respite. I yearn for enduring agony and torment so that I may not for a moment neglect the mention of the Beloved.' He worried about his parents, but 'Abdu'l-Bahá assured him they would accept the Faith, which they did. Soon Breakwell was in the hospital where he wrote, 'I am ill and bedridden in the hospital for consumptives. The fire of love has well nigh consumed me. I am happy. Pray that God may not deprive me of this pain.' In his next letter, he wrote, 'I am intoxicated with the wine of suffering and pain and am prepared to receive the supreme blessing.' There was no next letter. Breakwell had passed away – and the Master knew without a letter telling Him so.[61]

'Abdu'l-Bahá wrote a Tablet of Visitation for him, telling Yúnis Khán, 'I wrote it with such emotion that I wept as I wrote. You must translate it well so that he who reads it will not be able to hold back his tears':[62]

> O Breakwell, my beloved! Where is thy beautiful countenance and where is thy eloquent tongue? Where is thy radiant brow and where is thy brilliant face?
>
> O Breakwell, my beloved! Where is thy enkindlement with the fire of the love of God and where is thy attraction to the fragrances of God? Where is thy utterance for the glorification of God and where is thy rising in the service of God?
>
> O my dear, O Breakwell! Where are thy bright eyes and where are thy smiling lips? Where are thy gentle cheeks and where is thy graceful stature?
>
> O my dear, O Breakwell! Verily thou hast abandoned this transitory world and soared upward to the Kingdom, hast attained to the grace of the Invisible Realm and sacrificed thyself to the Threshold of the Lord of Might!
>
> O my adored one, O Breakwell! Verily thou hast left behind this physical lamp, this human glass, these earthly elements and this worldly enjoyment!
>
> O my adored one, O Breakwell! Then thou hast ignited a light in the glass of the Supreme Concourse, hast entered the Paradise of Abhá, art protected under the Shade of the Blessed Tree and hast attained to the Meeting (of the True One) in the Abode of Paradise!
>
> O my dearly beloved, O Breakwell! Thou hast been a divine

bird and, forsaking thy earthly nest, thou hast soared toward the holy rose-garden of the Divine Kingdom and obtained a luminous station there!

O my dearly beloved, O Breakwell! Verily thou art like unto the birds, chanting the verses of thy Lord, the Forgiving, for thou wert a thankful servant; therefore thou hast entered (into the realm beyond) with joy and happiness!

O my beloved, O Breakwell! Verily thy Lord hath chosen thee for His love, guided thee to the Court of His Holiness, caused thee to enter into the Rizwan of His Association and granted thee to behold His Beauty!

O my beloved, O Breakwell! Verily thou hast attained to the eternal life, never-ending bounty, beatific bliss and immeasurable providence!

O my beloved, O Breakwell! Thou hast become a star in the most exalted horizon, a lamp among the angels of heaven, a living spirit in the Supreme World and art established upon the throne of immortality!

O my adored one, O my Breakwell! I supplicate God to increase thy nearness and communication, to make thee enjoy thy prosperity and union (with Him), to add to thy light and beauty and to bestow upon thee glory and majesty.

O my adored one, O my Breakwell! I mention thy name continually, I never forget thee, I pray for thee day and night and I see thee clearly and manifestly, O my adored one, O Breakwell!

Verily I beseech God to make thee confirmed under all circumstances. Do not become despondent, neither be thou sad. Ere long thy Lord shall make thee a sign of guidance among mankind.[63]

A year later, Yúnis Khán was sorting the mail with the Master when 'Abdu'l-Bahá suddenly plucked out a letter, saying 'What pleasant fragrance emanates from this envelope, open it quickly and see where it comes from. Hurry up.' Inside was a postcard with gold-coloured handwriting and a single violet. The words, which said, 'He is not dead, he lives in the Abhá Kingdom,' were written by Breakwell's mother or father. 'Abdu'l-Bahá 'leapt from His seat, seized the postcard, placed it on His blessed forehead and wept'.[64]

Herbert Hopper, Breakwell's companion, died in 1908 at the age of only 34, possibly by tuberculosis caught from nursing Breakwell.[65] Hopper had told 'Abdu'l-Bahá that he desired to be a martyr for the Faith. After his passing, the Master confirmed that he had done so.

William and Wendell Dodge

On 16 November, William and Wendell Dodge, the 18- and 21-year-old sons of Arthur and Elizabeth Dodge, were the next Western pilgrims to arrive, staying in the Master's household until 4 December, a total of 19 days. William recorded that 'Abdu'l-Bahá entered their room at 'Akká at 4:15 p.m. on their first day and said, 'Welcome, my boys,' and then chanted a prayer for them. They ate every noon and evening meal with the Master. William noted that there were usually 19 at the table, including 'Abdu'l-Bahá and them. A frequent dinner guest was General Badrí Beg of the Turkish army.[66]

One day at dinner, a thick soup was served. At one point, William put his spoon down in the soup to adjust his collar. When he brought his hand down, he inadvertently hit the handle of the spoon with his elbow, and soup splashed out onto the beard of the Eastern pilgrim next to him. William was terribly embarrassed, but 'Abdu'l-Bahá laughingly said, 'Do not worry; that is a blessing.' Wendell then asked, 'Who gets the blessing, Bill, you or the friend with the whiskers?' 'Abdu'l-Bahá laughed again.[67]

Wendell and William's interpreter was Amín Fareed and he was not happy about what he obviously considered to be their flippant attitude. The youth were extremely happy to be with 'Abdu'l-Bahá and joyously expressed that happiness. Fareed told them that when entering the presence of the Master, they must be reverential, walking in with heads bowed, hands clasped and without smiling. They felt rebuked and, at the next meal, did as Fareed suggested. But 'Abdu'l-Bahá ignored them completely and they felt even further rebuked. Back in their room, the two boys talked about the problem and finally decided that they were just bad actors, resolving to be their natural buoyant selves. So, the next time they entered the dining room, they smiled cheerfully at the Master Who returned their smile, took them into His arms and said, 'That's the way I want you boys to act; be natural, be happy.'[68]

On 18 November, the boys went with Siyyid Muḥammad Taqí Manshádí in and around 'Akká. In spite of the friendliness of some of the Turkish soldiers, they were cautioned not to walk openly with the resident Bahá'ís because of the suspicions that might arouse. The young men, therefore, walked through 'Akká by themselves, not rejoining their guide until they were well beyond the city walls.[69]

One day, 'Abdu'l-Bahá went to the boys' room and presented them with ten ringstones on which the Greatest Name had been engraved. He blessed and kissed each one then chanted a prayer.[70]

On 28 November, William had a private interview with 'Abdu'l-Bahá. He wrote that

> I was impatient at heart because I do not know God, and because I am not able to teach or work in the Cause of God. Without [me] saying a word, Our Lord said, 'You must not be in a hurry. Your wish will be fulfilled. You will be strengthened and confirmed by God.' Our Lord said a seed cannot grow immediately and bear fruits, but it must grow in accordance with Nature's Law.[71]

There was considerable confusion about the station of 'Abdu'l-Bahá, with many early Bahá'ís believing Him to be the Spirit of Christ. Because of this, on 1 December, the Master dictated a special Tablet for William and Wendell:

> In this greatest period there are only two Manifestations, the Blessed Báb (may my soul be a ransom to him) and the Manifestation of the Blessed Perfection (Glory be to Him).
>
> We are all servants of the threshold of Baha and the one who serves most in His Holy threshold is the most beloved. My greatest wish and desire is submissiveness and servitude at His Holy Threshold. My name, Abdul Baha, means the servant of God; my heart is the servant of Baha, and my spirit is the servant of Baha and rejoices only in this name . . .
>
> Therefore, in order that there may be no discord, all of the believers in the truth must not mention me except as Abdul Baha, the servant of God. The essential thing is love. I must love you, and you must love me. Such is the meaning of the truth, while untruth means rancour, discord and hatred. All else save love is merely outwardly uttered words.[72]

William and Wendell's last day was 4 December and 'Abdu'l-Bahá allowed them to go the Shrine of Bahá'u'lláh and see the photograph of Bahá'u'lláh. At 2:45 p.m., William and Wendell Dodge boarded the carriage and returned to Haifa.

Soon thereafter, an American journalist, William E. Curtis, visited 'Abdu'l-Bahá and came away with different and mixed feelings. Curtis obviously did not know of the devious activities of the Covenant-breakers, so was influenced by rumours. He wrote that 'Abdu'l-Bahá was

> a clever, learned and respectable man, having a magnetic presence, attractive manners and a great deal of tact . . .
>
> Abbas Effendi is a fascinating mystic, a man of most impressive presence and conversation, and his voice is musical and mesmerizing. He seems to have a mercenary tendency, however, for he never lets an American leave him without an appeal for funds for the propagation of the faith.
>
> He has been quite successful in that, as in other directions. Every year numbers of Americans come to see him and have brought him gifts of money, the most of which has been used in the construction of a shrine and temple upon Mount Carmel . . . As the movement is supposed to be secret the Turkish authorities became alarmed at the number of American visitors and their liberal contributions, so Abbas Effendi was prohibited from leaving Acre and has not been able to complete the shrine.[73]

The Covenant-breakers never let a chance go by to denigrate the Master.

1902–1903

With the reimposition of restrictions on 'Abdu'l-Bahá and the constant nefarious activities of the Covenant-breakers, it became extremely difficult for pilgrims to visit 'Akká after Wendell and William Dodge. Mírzá Muḥammad-'Alí and his henchmen were looking for any excuse to make trouble for the Master and therefore were on watch for any Bahá'í pilgrims trying to enter the city. Because of the Covenant-breakers' slanders and concocted allegations, the local authorities scrutinized the Master's activities very closely. In addition to this surveillance, three houses that 'Abdu'l-Bahá had rented in Haifa for pilgrims were closed up and He had no room in His home for visitors. Some pilgrims from the East were able to attain the presence of 'Abdu'l-Bahá by using extreme caution, but it was a full year after the Dodge boys before the next Western pilgrims, Madame de Canavarro and Myron Phelps, were granted permission to come to 'Akká by the Master.[1] But before they arrived, however, a major event in the history of the Bahá'í Faith occurred in Ashkabat.

The Maṣhriqu'l-Adhkár in Ashkabat

On 28 November 1902 the cornerstone of the first Maṣhriqu'l-Adhkár, House of Worship, in the Bahá'í world was laid in Ashkabat, now the capital of Turkmenistan. Mr M. M. Holbach sent a report to *Star of the West* that described the event:

> The Mashrak-el-Azkar, or Bahai temple, at Eskabad, is indeed a sign of the times. That Russia should have permitted its erection is little short of a miracle. That the first church in the world erected not for the worship of sect or community, but for the members of all churches and all sects to meet in union, should be in a country

we have always associated with religious intolerance, gives food for thought.

Thirty-three years ago the first Bahai teacher went to Eskabad. The now populous city had not then come into existence. Eskabad was merely a camp of 60,000 soldiers in the wilderness.

Aza Mohammed Riza, the present guardian of the temple, was the teacher who carried the Bahai gospel of peace and brotherhood to military Eskabad. He was a mason by trade, and in company with a fellow workman, also from Persia, who shared the new faith, he worked with his hands at building the new town, but at the same time he built even better than he knew, for from this small beginning has sprung the thriving Bahai community, which is roughly estimated at 1,000 persons, who, stimulated by a donation of 2,000 rubles from Abdul-Baha himself, have given so liberally of their worldly goods that Eskabad can claim forever the proud distinction of having erected the first Temple of Peace in the world.

At first the Russian government refused permission for the erection of the temple, and a special petition was sent by the Bahais direct to the Czar, who had the matter inquired into, and, finding that so far from there being anything political in the background, the followers of BAHA'O'LLAH are enjoined never to take up arms or join in any revolutionary movement against the state, gave the required permission. The Russian government sealed its approval when the Governor of Eskabad – Koropatkan, who afterward distinguished himself as general in the Russian-Japanese war – came in state to lay the foundation stone and deposited a silver box containing papers descriptive of the circumstances relating to the building. At this same ceremony the highest representatives of the different religious bodies in Eskabad – Christians, Mohammedans, Jews and Armenians – were present by invitation.[2]

Besides being the first Bahá'í House of Worship in the world, it was also the inspiration that caused the American Bahá'ís to aspire to emulate them and build a Mashriqu'l-Adhkár of their own.

Madame de Canavarro and Myron Phelps

In December 1902, two Americans arrived in 'Akká: Madame de Canavarro and Myron Phelps. They arrived from Beirut in the company of Dr Arastú Khán who had travelled from Iran. The two Americans were deeply involved with Buddhism at the time, but were attracted to the Bahá'í teachings. Mme de Canavarro had spent prolifically to promote Buddhism and was very knowledgeable in its philosophy. When she first met 'Abdu'l-Bahá, she humbly kissed the Master's hand.

De Canavarro and Phelps were full of questions and wanted answers, not talks. A problem, however, quickly arose because they had different questions and understandings and wanted different answers. This forced 'Abdu'l-Bahá to give two answers to most questions and created friction between His guests. As Yúnis Khán, the interpreter at these meetings, wrote: 'since the enquirer [Mme de Canavarro] and the recorder [Mr Phelps] had different views, they disagreed as to the meaning of the replies and the frequent repetition of the concepts made the task that much more arduous for 'Abdu'l-Bahá.'[3]

The first problem arose when reincarnation was discussed. Phelps insisted on including his own ideas along with the answers of the Master so that the book he wished to publish would be of more interest to reincarnation-inclined Europeans. Within a couple of days, there was a 'fracas'. Mme de Canavarro was not able to understand 'Abdu'l-Bahá's explanation of one of the principal concepts of the Bahá'í Faith. The lady suddenly verbally attacked the translator, Yúnis Khán: 'in furious objection . . . she addressed me angrily in harsh and unintelligible words. She was so irate that she was unable to speak clearly.'

Poor Yúnis Khán was caught in the middle between an angrily incoherent visitor and a puzzled 'Abdu'l-Bahá who kept asking what the woman was saying. The woman, though, gave the young man no time to answer either Him or her. Finally, things calmed down enough for the woman to clearly state her problem:

> Why is it that you Easterners must always be the pioneers and standard-bearers in the field of religion, although you obviously do not possess any particular qualifications or accomplishments to justify that status? In turn, we Westerners must become dependent on you to share such knowledge with us secondhand. First, you

obviously have no erudition to qualify you to understand such spiritual concepts. We are the ones who introduce the subject matter and share with you the guidance to understand the issue. Then we must wait for your response. If it weren't for us Westerners, how could you hope to understand such issues? The problem is, once you comprehend the subject matter, you get the answer first and then I have to receive the answer from you. Worse still, you receive the mysteries of the Kingdom and the divine realities directly from the Master without any intermediary (meaning that you drink from the fountainhead) whereas we have to obtain our knowledge from you (meaning that we drink stagnant water). Why should I focus my eyes and ears on your mouth and wait for the answer to my query?[4]

Even in the face of such arrogant spiritual blindness, 'Abdu'l-Bahá maintained His tranquillity and patiently explained that

the effects and influences of the mysteries of the Kingdom are spiritual, not material. Ear and tongue are material faculties. If the soul is not susceptible to receiving the divine favours, of what use are ears and tongues? These spiritual concepts are directed to your heart. I speak to you with the power of spirit and you receive these heavenly concepts with your whole being, with pure intentions and a radiant heart. The essential requirement is true, sincere and heartfelt communication. Praised be to God, that spiritual connection is established. Whatever you have heard so far are the blessings of the Holy Spirit. My connection with you is direct. The tongue of the translator is only a material and physical faculty.[5]

With this, the furore died away and Mme de Canavarro listened more with her heart and less with her ears. During the rest of their stay, she absorbed 'Abdu'l-Bahá's spiritual message, but Mr Phelps was more concerned with his own ideas. Yúnis Khán translated half of his book into Persian and the Master made many corrections, but Phelps still wrote what he wished and the book, *The Master in 'Akká*, though very interesting, is littered with errors and misinterpretations.[6] Even so, Phelps was affected by 'Abdu'l-Bahá and had a deeper understanding of His Station than many:

We of the so-called 'Christian' lands think, perhaps, that if Christ were to appear again upon the earth the good news would burden the telegraph, that His words and daily life would be marshalled forth under double headlines for our convenient perusal at breakfast or on the rapid-transit trains, giving us the interesting information without interrupting our important occupations. Ah no! We but deceive ourselves. The Man of Nazareth might pursue His holy life on the banks of the Jordan and the shores of Gennesaret [Galilee] for a generation of men, but the faintest rumor of Him would not reach our ministers or our stockbrokers, our churches, or our exchanges.

Imagine that we are in an ancient house of the still more ancient city of 'Akká, which was for a month my home. The room in which we are faces the opposite wall of a narrow paved street, which an active man might clear at a single bound. Above is the bright sun of Palestine; to the right a glimpse of the old sea-wall and the blue Mediterranean. As we sit we hear a singular sound rising from the pavement, thirty feet below – faint at first, and increasing. It is like the murmur of human voices. We open the window and look down. We see a crowd of human beings with patched and tattered garments...

It is a noteworthy gathering. Many of these men are blind; many more are pale, emaciated or aged. Some are on crutches; some so feeble that they can barely walk. Most of the women are closely veiled... There are perhaps a hundred in this gathering...

A door opens and a man comes out. He is of middle stature, strongly built. He wears flowing light-colored robes. On his head is a light buff fez with a white cloth wound about it. He is perhaps sixty years of age. His long grey hair rests on his shoulders. His forehead is broad, full, and high, his nose slightly aquiline, his moustaches and beard, the latter full though not heavy, nearly white. His eyes are grey and blue, large, and both soft and penetrating. His bearing is simple, but there is grace, dignity, and even majesty about his movements. He passes through the crowd, and as he goes utters words of salutation... He stations himself at a narrow angle of the street and motions to the people to come towards him... As they come they hold their hands extended. In each open palm he places some small coins. He knows them all. He caresses them with his hand on the face, on the shoulders, on the head. Some he stops and questions...

This scene you may see almost any day of the year in the streets of 'Akká . . . you may see the poor of 'Akká gathered at one of the shops where clothes are sold, receiving cloaks from the Master . . .

On feast days he visits the poor at their homes. He chats with them, inquires into their health and comfort, mentions by name those who are absent, and leaves gifts for all.

Nor is it the beggars only that he remembers. Those respectable poor who cannot beg, but must suffer in silence – those whose daily labor will not support their families – to these he sends bread secretly . . .

This man who gives so freely must be rich, you think? No, far otherwise. Once his family was the wealthiest in all Persia. But this friend of the lowly, like the Galilean, has been oppressed by the great. For fifty years he and his family have been exiles and prisoners. Their property has been confiscated . . . Now that he has not much he must spend little for himself that he may give more to the poor. His garments are usually of cotton, and the cheapest that can be bought . . .

For more than thirty-four years this man has been a prisoner at 'Akká. But his jailors have become his friends. The governor of the city, the commander of the Army Corps, respect and honor him as though he were their brother. No man's opinion or recommendation has greater weight with them. He is the beloved of all the city, high and low. And how could it be otherwise? For to this man it is the law, as it was to Jesus of Nazareth, to do good to those who injure him. Have we yet heard of any one in lands which boast the name of Christ who lived that life? . . .

This Master is as simple as his soul is great. He claims nothing for himself – neither comfort, nor honor, nor repose. Three or four hours of sleep suffice him; all the remainder of his time and all his strength are given to the succor of those who suffer, in spirit or in body. 'I am,' he says, 'the servant of God.'

Such is 'Abbás Effendi, the Master of 'Akká.[7]

Dr Arastú Khán, who had arrived with Madame de Canavarro and Mr Phelps, had gone on pilgrimage shortly after the death of his brother, Aflátún. Their grandfather had been one of the first Bahá'ís from a Jewish background and had been the court physician to Muhammad

Shah. Mysteriously, during the first days of his pilgrimage, 'Abdu'l-Bahá always addressed Arasṭú Khán by his brother's name, which thoroughly confused him. Then one night when he and Yúnis Khán 'were following the Master through the narrow crooked streets of the prison city, the Master again addressed him as Aflāṭún and said, "Do you know why I call you Aflāṭún? It is because I desire his truth and spirituality to appear in you."' This comment caused Arasṭú Khán to rapidly develop those qualities as he worked at translating letters from Western Bahá'ís. He stayed in 'Akká for a year.[8]

Hippolyte Dreyfus and Edith Sanderson

During the last days of the visit of Mme de Canavarro and Mr Phelps, Hippolyte Dreyfus, from France, and Edith Sanderson, an American living in Paris, arrived in 'Akká. Hippolyte had made his first pilgrimage in 1901 at the age of 31 and had become 'totally enkindled and attracted, longed to be of service to the Faith and even yearned to sacrifice his life and gain a martyr's death'.[9] This time, he stayed for three weeks and enjoyed many 'philosophical and intellectual discussions'. 'Abdu'l-Bahá requested Yúnis Khán to spend his time with Hippolyte. One day, Hippolyte told his companion, 'Today I inadvertently played the role of Adam and was terribly embarrassed.' Yúnis Khán didn't understand this statement and asked for a clarification.

> Don't ask! I am afraid I may be driven out of paradise. You see, I always lock the bathroom door when I bathe. This time I neglected to make sure that the door was locked. When the Master knocked on the bathroom door and called my name, without thinking I asked Him to come in. He opened the door while I was naked. I was terribly embarrassed: I realized I had done what Adam did![10]

Contacts and enemies

A young woman called Mademoiselle Letitia came to 'Abdu'l-Bahá's home and taught French to the children. One day a French believer arrived and 'Abdu'l-Bahá asked Mademoiselle Letitia, who was not a Bahá'í, to translate for Him. Túbá Khánum told the story:

During the visit of a French believer 'Abdu'l-Baha called upon Mademoiselle to interpret for Him, as the pilgrim was very eager for instruction and there was no one else who could speak his language.

Mademoiselle, being a Catholic, and knowing nothing of the Baha'i teaching, became very much embarrassed over her task, which quite amused 'Abdu'l-Baha.

Some days later she evidently confessed to the nuns in the convent, who keep strict watch over her, and for several days she looked very stern and forbidding.

Finally 'Abdu'l-Baha called her to him and said: 'Letitia, tell the good nuns that they need have no fear. I asked you to interpret for me because there was no one else to speak French, not because I desired to teach you. We have so many Baha'is who come here begging with all their hearts and all their love for instruction, that only to them do we give our precious teachings. You would have to beg and beg and beg before I would give it to you, and even then I might not do so; for it is not so cheap as to be bestowed where it is not wanted.

'Stay in the home if you like, or go if you are not happy here. We are glad to have you if you care to stay; but free your heart of all fear that we will try to make a Baha'i of you.'

Mademoiselle is very sweet and they all love her. Her parents live at Haifa and 'Abdu'l-Baha has been wonderfully kind to them; they are very poor. She is always happy here, but of course she does not know why.[11]

As for his enemies, 'Abdu'l-Bahá never let them feel anything but love. In the early 1900s, a fanatical Protestant missionary from Scotland named Miss Ramsey was trying to convert souls to Christianity. Every day from morning until evening, she would go from door to door, reading the Bible to the people in each house. She did much charitable work at her own expense for forty years.

> She was not friendly to the Bahai Cause but the Master showed her every kindness because she was very faithful to her Christ . . . For quite a time she used to go to Abdu'l-Baha's house and read the Bible to the members of his household. They listened to her most attentively, and finally she concluded that they were converted. One

day she was reading when one of the family asked her the meaning of the verse just read, but she could not give it. They explained to her that this was a prophecy concerning the appearance of Baha-o-llah.. She became very wroth and left the house.[12]

Yúnis Khán described her as 'consumed with the fire of religious prejudice and hatred', which made her a ready target for the Covenant-breakers who quickly 'fanned her flames of rancour until she became a true enemy of the Faith'. Since the Protestant Mission had a dispensary and rented an apartment in the building in which 'Abdu'l-Bahá lived (the first room visited today by pilgrims in the House of 'Abdu'lláh Páshá), she was forced to pass Him several times a day. Whenever she encountered 'Abdu'l-Bahá, 'she would writhe in agony, grimace and lower her head while quickening her pace to a run'. One day as she passed by, looking upset, the Master called her over and asked, 'Miss Ramsey, do you know how much I love you?'

'How much?' she asked.

'Look in your heart and see how much you hate me, and to that extent I love you,' He responded. 'Stunned by the answer, she began to stammer', writes Yúnis Khán, 'then turned and hurried away.'

'Abdu'l-Bahá gave her a farewell banquet when she finally returned to Scotland.[13]

1904

George and Rosa Winterburn

On 5 February, George and Rosa Winterburn arrived in Haifa. Because of the difficulties at the time, their arrival was unmarked; they appeared to be just more tourists, but theirs had been a difficult and bewildering journey from America to Haifa because of the intrigue and onslaught of the Covenant-breakers. When the Winterburns arrived in Paris on their way to Haifa, they received a telegram instructing them to wait until further notice. After several months 'in a state of anxiety and prayer' the permission to continue arrived and they travelled on to Port Said. But, again, they were met with word from 'Abdu'l-Bahá to wait. 'Bewildered and disconcerted,' the Winterburns remained in Port Said until, a full year after their departure from America, they were finally allowed to complete their journey.[1]

Shortly after arriving in Haifa, the couple entered a small store whose owner, they knew, was a Bahá'í. The shopkeeper took them to the home of 'Mírzá Yazdí'. Rosa wrote that once there, Mírzá Yazdí 'served us tea and by some rapid means let the believers know that we were there'. Soon a few believers arrived, including Mishkín-Qalam, the famous calligrapher, who said that though he had been sick, news of their arrival 'had so cheered his heart and strengthened him that he was able to come and bring greetings to us and to express his love for us'. The Winterburns were amazed at the love and hospitality they had received from Bahá'ís in Port Said, Alexandria and Haifa.[2]

After an hour of companionship, the couple left for 'Akká. As they were getting into the carriage, one of the friends said, 'You are going now to your greatest test.'[3] This question bothered them for a long time. The Winterburns described their trip to 'Akká:

The drive is along the shore of the bay and takes about two hours.

Starting from Haifa we are facing Acca all of the way. At first, it is just a white city on the water, but, as one gets nearer, the minaret and domes become distinct, and the buildings and walls begin to take shape.

Soon we were there, under the walls, through the gate, up the narrow streets, built for defence; then through the second line of fortifications by means of a second gate, twisting around right-angled corners, with streets just wide enough for the wagon and its three horses, with pedestrians close up to the walls to get out of the way, and so on to the house of Abdul-Baha. There loving greetings were awaiting us and many willing hands to carry luggage and parcels for us. We were conducted up the long flight of stone steps to the second story, and shown into the room where Abdul-Baha usually receives His visitors.[4]

The Winterburns spent some time with Yúnis Khán until 'Abdu'l-Bahá entered. Before meeting the Master, Rosa feared what her reaction would be. She had heard about how overwhelmingly emotional that first contact could be, so she had prayed that she would look into His face with smiles only. She wrote:

The entrance into the Holy Presence came as simply and naturally as into that of some dear friend. We wondered somewhat, my husband and I, for we had thought it impossible to meet Him whom our hearts so reverenced and loved without being overcome with emotion. Hours passed, we met Him face to face, felt the touch of His hands, basked in the light of His smile, and still we had not been overcome by any mighty wave of irresistible feeling; and still we wondered. Days passed. The life in Acca had received us, had taken us into its loving arms, and still we were wondering when and how was to come that mighty sweep of power. It did not come. The dominance of the Lord spoke to us only through His love, everywhere triumphant. The influence of Abdul-Baha expressed itself in the peace around us that was always unbroken. His wisdom was manifest in the reverence of the gray-haired men who bowed before its decisions in unquestioning acceptance. The efficiency of His teachings was illustrated in the eagerness of those who had been Zoroastrians, Mohammedans, or Christians to all live together there in perfect love and unity, under His sheltering care; and in their determination to carry with them to the ends of the world the same peace and harmony that wrapped them in its folds in that dreary, but glorious, little prison city, Acca.[5]

The arrival of the Winterburns was kept a secret even from the few Bahá'ís still resident in 'Akká. Rosa stayed with the women of the Holy Household while George was given a small room of his own. Yúnis Khán noted that George, 'who had endured so much pain and agony to achieve his heart's desire obviously had great appreciation for the blessing granted to him. He hardly ever left his room and spent much time in prayer and meditation.'[6]

One day, George asked Yúnis Khán if he could meet a Persian Bahá'í. Coincidentally, a Bahá'í from Bombay, who had previously been a Zoroastrian and was there with his son, had specifically asked to meet the two Americans, because the sacred book of the Zoroastrians prophesied that 'a new world should be discovered, and that in the "last days" people from this new world should meet with the people of Zoroaster, that they should meet in the worship of the same God, in the same place'. To him, their meeting was the fulfilment of that prophecy.[7] When the old Zoroastrian and the Winterburns came together, 'there was an indescribable outburst of feelings, cries of joy filled the room. Mr. Winterburn ran to meet the old man and embraced him, while his wife took the child in her arms, as tears of happiness flowed and the meaning of the phrase, "East shall embrace the West", was truly demonstrated.' Yúnis Khán said his translation skills were not needed, though one spoke only Persian and the others just English. He said that he 'just stood there and shared in this outburst of intense emotion, until at last each wiped away the other's tears from his own face and they sat down'.[8]

Initially, the Winterburns were only supposed to stay in 'Akká for three days, but their entrance had been so clandestine that 'Abdu'l-Bahá allowed them to stay longer. By the fifth day, however, they had been noticed, so 'Abdu'l-Bahá had to tell them it was time to go, saying that the officials had begun to comment on their stay and to wonder at the length of it.[9]

The Winterburns spent six days with 'Abdu'l-Bahá in 'Akká, being in His presence at lunch and dinner every day and sometimes for short visits in the morning or afternoon. Rosa said that she had not had those 'great experiences of emotion that some visitors to His Presence have been seized with; but a great peace fell upon my soul, a tranquillity and a surety took possession of me, such as comes from nowhere else. That is the pervading atmosphere of the Holy House, a calm security that no cataclysm can shake . . .'[10] When George was with 'Abdu'l-Bahá, 'he sat in a state of utter awe and wonderment' at the bounty he had been given after his 'year-long odyssey'.[11]

After six days, the time came to leave. The Winterburns wrote:

> We lived a lifetime in those six days. The outside world disappeared. The past had never been. There was no future. It was as if the moment in that Presence were all of life, and that it was eternal. 'Prayer, peace, glory, and praise' enveloped us from the moment that Abdul-Baha took our hands in His in a welcoming grasp until He said, 'Go back and serve!' and we left His physical presence perhaps forever in this world.[12]

As they left 'Akká, the Winterburns pondered two questions: Why hadn't they felt 'some overwhelming conviction of the sanctity of the Presence in which we had spent six such bliss-filled days?' and what was that greatest test they were supposed to have undergone? The first question answered itself when they looked back on their experience:

> We realized at last that when we first entered His presence so quietly, it was as if we had been taken gently up by the first swell of a great tidal wave, raised so tenderly that we had been scarcely conscious of the uplift; we had been carried on and on, higher and higher, until, as the tidal wave may sweep over coast, rocks, and even cities, we had been carried high over all worldly consciousness, and it had become to us as if the world were not. As this realization came to us, we prayed that we might never again be upon that lower spiritual level where we had been when that wave lifted us and bore us so high into the realms of absolute, common-sense, unquestioning conviction.[13]

But what about that greatest test? As 'Akká faded behind them, they realized that the test had been passed without their knowing it. They wrote:

... incorporation of the living spirit of God in a human body could never be a stumbling block now to our steps. We had met a man, it is true, a man with all the needs and elements of humanity; but it had been to realize how perfect an instrument of the Lord the human body may become. How else could God have spoken to us so forcibly as through those human lips that let fall divine wisdom? As through those human eyes, whose glances bore into one's soul a conception of the love and tenderness of God? As by that human tongue that never uttered a harsh or unkind word? As through that stately form, unbowed by all the grievances of the world or by the sufferings of long years of prison life and deprivation? Surely, if man is the greatest work of God, man must also be the most perfect messenger of God to man.[14]

Frank Frank and his guide

Mr Frank Frank also arrived in 'Akká during those perilous times. He was a new Bahá'í who desired to meet 'Abdu'l-Bahá. Like the Winterburns, when he arrived in Port Said, he received a message telling him to wait. The Bahá'ís in Port Said pleaded with 'Abdu'l-Bahá to grant permission to Mr Frank and it was finally given, with the stipulation that he use 'great caution and vigilance'. When Frank arrived in Haifa, a man approached him with the salutation 'Alláh'u'Abhá', professing to be a Bahá'í and devoted to 'Abdu'l-Bahá, and saying that the Master had helped him set up a printing business. The man also asked about the American Bahá'ís, including their names and backgrounds. Further, he requested to accompany Frank to 'Akká and act as his translator.[15]

When Frank arrived in 'Akká, the resident believers recognized the supposed translator and quickly sent word to 'Abdu'l-Bahá that Frank had arrived with a 'deceitful spy'. Yúnis K͟hán wrote that ' 'Abdu'l-Bahá was quite annoyed. He instructed me to "go and attend to the traveller downstairs and send the troublemaker to me".' Yúnis K͟hán carried out the Master's instructions, then asked Frank 'Where did you get to know this rascal?' Frank told his story, to which Yúnis K͟hán replied, 'Everything that he has said is true, except that he has just left out one detail: he happens to be a deceitful man, a collaborator of the Covenant-breakers and an associate of the enemies of the Faith.' Frank was aghast at what he had done, but was soon called into the presence of

'Abdu'l-Bahá, where he poured out his devotion and servitude.[16]

Leaving Frank, Yúnis Khán encountered Mírzá Núru'd-Dín and asked, 'How was Mr Guide thrown out?' Mírzá Núru'd-Dín said, 'Whatever it was, it was heaven-sent, because he repented and promised never to approach any of the friends of God again.' Later, 'Abdu'l-Bahá explained that he had rebuked the man, saying,

> What sort of deception and hypocrisy is this that you commit against your own religion? You are a Christian and receive an income from the Protestant Society, and yet you betray your own Faith by bringing American travellers to me so that I may invite them into the Bahá'í Faith? To them you say negative things about your Faith. But by guiding them to me you betray your own conscience. Do you want me to write a few words which would cause your dismissal?[17]

This threw the 'guide' into a panic and he promised to never again approach American Bahá'í pilgrims. Yúnis Khán reported that the man 'ran all the way back to Haifa'.[18]

Mr Frank was amazed at the hospitality he received and could hardly believe that he was given the bounty of actually having dinner at the table of 'Abdu'l-Bahá. He said that he had never imagined that he would be treated as such, saying he had expected that 'I would have to prostrate myself from afar, like visiting the Pope, approach on my knees and be dismissed after a short visit. And now I see that we eat at the same table! Since I never consider myself worthy of such a station, please ask if I may be excused.' 'Abdu'l-Bahá, of course, simply poured out more loving kindness and 'heart-warming attention and regard'.[19]

Like many pilgrims, Mr Frank had brought a gift to the Master, a small Egyptian silk carpet. But unlike most people, Frank set a condition on its acceptance: 'that whoever may in the future be the recipient of this gift from the hand of the Master must be a Bahá'í. I would not be happy if a non-Bahá'í were to step on it.' The Master agreed, saying 'Rest assured, I will find a good place for it so that no non-Bahá'í may tread on it.' 'Abdu'l-Bahá gave that rug a station far beyond its donor's wish: it covered the bench on which the photographs of Bahá'u'lláh and the Báb were placed.[20]

Mr Frank only stayed in 'Akká for two days, but his 'simplicity and inner purity' kept him in the minds of the resident believers for a long time. One remarked to 'Abdu'l-Bahá: 'I see that the American friends have overtaken us Persian believers and have surpassed us in every service.' The Master responded with, 'From America, I await the appearance of a few people. Soon they will appear. And then you will behold unprecedented victories for the Cause.'[21]

Azíz'u'lláh Azízí

Azíz'u'lláh Azízí, travelling with Hand of the Cause Ibn-i-Aṣdaq, Siyyid Hasan Hashimi-Zadeh and Ustad Mahmud Khabiri, arrived in 'Akká in early 1904. It had been an eventful journey. While in Anzali, a town on the Iranian coast of the Caspian Sea near Rasht, they had been quarantined in a wooden building when a fire broke out. They only survived because of the efforts of Khabiri. Then, when they reached the Russian town of Badkubih,[22] they were put into quarantine. When finally released, they travelled to the Black Sea, planning to sail to Beirut. The captain of their ship refused to allow them to board for some undisclosed reason. Then, 'an Italian ship had pity on us and greed for money prompted the captain to accept to take us to Beirut. But he failed to keep his promise and left us stranded in Istanbul', where they were again quarantined. This time, their baggage was 'disinfected' with steam. The steam ruined all their leather items, including their shoes.[23]

Finally arriving in Haifa, they went to a coffee shop called Sahlan wa Siyyid, where they found someone waiting for them. The pilgrims prayed all the way from Haifa to 'Akká, where they had to register, and obtained Turkish visas. Azízí described 'Akká as

> a city with a very foul environment. It was exceedingly filthy. Its alleys were dark and narrow. There were scarcely any trees or greenery of any kind . . . This run-down and ruinous city was under martial law. It had only one gate, which was constantly patrolled by guards. Leaving the city itself was difficult. It was hardly possible for anyone to make it out to the surrounding fields and escape the pitiful environs of the city with its looming and threatening towers. At dusk, the bugles would sound and all the hustle and bustle would grind to a halt. Everyone had to return to their houses, which were no better than holes, and remain there. Close to the house of 'Abdu'l-Bahá, a

military garrison was stationed which kept close watch at the least movement of the friends . . .

Most of the Bahá'í pilgrims would become ill. After traversing the long distance between Tehran and 'Akká, with primitive means of travel and lodging overnight in low-grade inns and weathering adverse climates, they had to face the unhealthy conditions of 'Akká and became even more distressed when witnessing the hardships of 'Abdu'l-Bahá.[24]

Azízí and his companions found rooms in a caravanserai, then were called into the presence of 'Abdu'l-Bahá. Azízí described that first meeting with the goal of their desire:

> Even though I wanted so much to behold that peerless Beauty, I did not dare raise my head and thus did not know quite what to do . . . We kissed the ground out of respect. His holiness 'Abdu'l-Bahá was holding a lamp in His blessed hand and was paying special heed to each one's face. Right away I realized that 'Abdu'l-Bahá was showing his own face, fulfilling what I had always longed for before . . . Then He said, 'You are very spiritual.' He said many things, but due to my inner anxiety at the time, they did not remain in my mind. But what I do remember is that He said, 'The chief of the guards informed us that a group of our friends have entered 'Akká, whereupon we replied, "Yes, indeed – some from Iran, some from India and some from other places have come to visit us."'[25]

Later, all of the pilgrims had a private interview with the Master. For his, Azízí wrote:

> I was so nervous, I had difficulty even keeping my balance. Immediately 'Abdu'l-Bahá said, 'Bismellah (In the name of God), enter.' I obeyed and took my place on a chair, but experienced such trembling as could not be described. The trembling became such that even the chair was vibrating and making noise. 'Abdu'l-Bahá was very kind, even though I had lost my composure. He ordered tea to be brought and served me with His own hands and bade me drink. As I drank, I felt better and began to calm down as my anxiety ebbed away. He asked me about the events of my journey and my

travelling companions. I had a few things to say, as there were more than a few mishaps, and I had some complaints about one of the friends, but as I was about to make mention of that, He said, 'Yes, I know, but so long as there are youth so strong and steadfast in the Cause, as you – who are as an immovable mountain – actions of people like that are not worthy of mention.'

By this single statement, many points became obvious to me. I was now confident that both apparent and hidden aspects of people were crystal clear to 'Abdu'l-Bahá. No need was there for self-disclosure from one like me. Suddenly I became conscious once again that I was in the presence of 'Abdu'l-Bahá, the 'Mystery of God'. Then 'Abdu'l-Bahá in a loud voice addressed one of the friends known as Aqa Muhammad-Rida Qannad. He said, 'I have written a prayer for the martyrs of Yazd. I will chant it to you, listen as well.' He began to chant by heart. The timbre of His voice had such impact upon me emotionally, that I am incapable of explaining its effect, especially the power and magnificence He manifested in that hour. Aqa Mirza Adib Taliqani, the Hand of the Cause [Ḥájí Mírzá Ḥasan-i-Adíb], had a very close relationship with me. With extreme kindness, he had related to 'Abdu'l-Bahá the events and the sequence of the debate which had taken place in my house that historic night, especially of my father's temper, anger and dissatisfaction over my joining the Bahá'í religion. At times 'Abdu'l-Bahá would make mention of that episode and would remark as to its significance.[26]

When 'Abdu'l-Bahá and the pilgrims went to Bahjí, He stated that 'the children of Israel would return to this land, attain independence and exercise sovereignty. The children of Israel would become renowned throughout the world.' The prediction greatly surprised Azízí and he wrote:

> Such statements of 'Abdu'l-Bahá and His blessing upon these mean and ill-tempered people, after all the poverty and powerlessness, along with all the pride I had witnessed, was simply beyond belief. Jerusalem was in the hands of the Arabs, who were strong and prejudiced and they [the Jews] were just a handful of impotent, meek, timid and homeless lot of old Jewish men. O God! What a blessing this was, what a profound statement. Just how were the Jews to

achieve their sovereignty and independence? As it stood now, the Arabs did not even let the Jews visit their own Holy Places. How then would the Arabs ever permit them to have their own government and self-rule?[27]

Azízí was also surprised that when 'Abdu'l-Bahá invited the pilgrims for lunch, He served them Himself. The Master

> would hold a vessel in His hand and would pour out water for everyone to wash their hands for lunch. At the table, He would take care to personally show hospitality to the guests, or see to it that each was served. He would also entertain those present with anecdotes so humorous that everyone would burst with laughter and were hardly able to contain themselves. The Master would often say, 'Food should be taken with happiness.'[28]

'Abdu'l-Bahá had been building the Shrine of the Báb at this time and the Covenant-breakers sent false rumours to Istanbul that the Master was constructing a fortress on Mt Carmel. These rumours resulted in a 'task force' being sent to investigate the matter. The arrival of the task force resulted in 'Abdu'l-Bahá telling Azízí that it was time for him to leave 'Akká.

Investigation and interrogation of 'Abdu'l-Bahá

A group of Turkish investigators appear to have arrived to interrogate 'Abdu'l-Bahá sometime later in 1904, though the time is quite uncertain (see also the next chapter). Yúnis Khán had gone to France for a time and returned to find that 'quiet and deadly calm dominated the city . . . The resident friends seldom showed up for a visit . . . and no permission was granted to anyone to enter 'Akká'. He wrote that 'Miss Barney hardly ever left the House of 'Abdu'l-Bahá except on certain occasions to visit the Shrine of Bahá'u'lláh, which was undertaken with great care and caution'. Howard and Mary MacNutt, who arrived in January 1905, had to use extreme caution in order to reach 'Abdu'l-Bahá's house in 'Akká, so this investigation probably occurred sometime in the latter part of 1904.

While the Winterburns, Mr Frank and Azíz'u'lláh Azízí were basking in the presence of the Master, the Covenant-breakers were busy. The Governor of 'Akká, who had freed the Covenant-breakers when 'Abdu'l-Bahá, all the Bahá'ís and the Covenant-breakers were confined to 'Akká in 1901, was very attached to the Master and was upset at the injustice that kept 'Abdu'l-Bahá confined within the city walls. He told 'Abdu'l-Bahá that He should not consider Himself to be a prisoner, but should come and go as He pleased. This was not with the permission of the authorities in Istanbul and the Master declined. Then one day, the Governor requested to visit the Shrine of Bahá'u'lláh, but he wanted it to be in the presence of 'Abdu'l-Bahá. The Master agreed and was at Bahjí for the Governor's rites of pilgrimage.

But still 'Abdu'l-Bahá kept Himself confined to 'Akká. The Governor decided to try again, but this time he brought along important members of the government. The sight of 'Abdu'l-Bahá leading a procession that included the Governor of 'Akká, Faríq Páshá, Lává Páshá and General Badrí Beg, 'who humbly walked behind Him, bowed themselves before the Shrine of Bahá'u'lláh and emulated 'Abdu'l-Bahá in kissing the Threshold as they entered the Shrine,' was a huge shock to the Covenant-breakers, driving them to come up with a new plan. And the plan they came up with was to bring charges against the very Governor who had freed most of them from their incarceration in 1901.[29]

Mírzá Muhammad-'Alí drew up an indictment against 'Abdu'l-Bahá and various officials that was pure fiction and sent it to the Sultan and other authorities. The document attacked any official who viewed 'Abdu'l-Bahá favourably. In *God Passes By*, Shoghi Effendi writes of the Covenant-breakers' efforts:

> Through verbal messages, formal communications and by personal interviews the Covenant-breakers impressed upon these notables the necessity of immediate action, shrewdly adapting their arguments to the particular interests and prejudices of those whose aid they solicited. To some they represented 'Abdu'l-Bahá as a callous usurper Who had trampled upon their rights, robbed them of their heritage, reduced them to poverty, made their friends in Persia their enemies, accumulated for Himself a vast fortune, and acquired no less than two-thirds of the land in Haifa. To others they declared that 'Abdu'l-Bahá contemplated making of 'Akká and Haifa a new Mecca and Medina. To still others they affirmed that Bahá'u'lláh was no more than a retired

dervish, who professed and promoted the Faith of Islám, Whom 'Abbás Effendi, His son, had, for the purpose of self-glorification, exalted to the rank of God-head, whilst claiming Himself to be the Son of God and the return of Jesus Christ. They further accused Him of harboring designs inimical to the interests of the state, of meditating a rebellion against the Sultan, of having already hoisted the banner of Yá Bahá'u'l-Abhá, the ensign of revolt, in distant villages in Palestine and Syria, of having raised surreptitiously an army of thirty thousand men, of being engaged in the construction of a fortress and a vast ammunition depot on Mt. Carmel, of having secured the moral and material support of a host of English and American friends, amongst whom were officers of foreign powers, who were arriving, in large numbers and in disguise, to pay Him their homage, and of having already, in conjunction with them, drawn up His plans for the subjugation of the neighboring provinces, for the expulsion of the ruling authorities, and for the ultimate seizure of the power wielded by the Sultan himself. Through misrepresentation and bribery they succeeded in inducing certain people to affix their signatures as witnesses to the documents which they had drawn up, and which they despatched, through their agents, to the Sublime Porte.[30]

When the document reached Istanbul, it had its desired effect and investigators arrived. The Governor was dismissed and a new, antagonistic one, put in his place.[31] The Master's house was put under constant surveillance and 'Abdu'l-Bahá sent away all pilgrims and most of the resident Bahá'ís.[32]

The investigators called 'Abdu'l-Bahá in for interrogation several times and demanded answers to the charges. The Master demolished them all. Finally, the investigators mentioned a group of witnesses who had been 'cajoled, bribed or forced' to give evidence contradictory to 'Abdu'l-Bahá's statements. At this, 'Abdu'l-Bahá declared the charges to be false and walked out, unhindered.[33] 'So imperturbable was 'Abdu'l-Bahá's equanimity', Shoghi Effendi wrote, 'that while rumors were being bruited about that He might be cast into the sea, exiled to Fizán in Tripolitania, or hanged on the gallows, He, to the amazement of His friends and amusement of His enemies, was to be seen planting trees and vines in the garden of His house.'[34]

Finally, one night when everyone was 'besieged by fear and agitation,

'Abdu'l-Bahá left the house and walked slowly to the port. He arrived at the city gate and looked out to sea. Then he glanced at the investigator's warship and walked home. A short time later, the ship sailed into the darkness and the investigation ended.[35]

Edith Jackson and Sigurd Russell

In mid-April, Sigurd Russell and Madame Edith Jackson returned to 'Akká for their second visit.[36] Sigurd asked 'Abdu'l-Bahá about the status of Pope Leo XIII, who had died the previous year. The Master's answer was:

> His condition, there, in the world of the spirit is the same as it was here. While here, his eyes were not opened to the real spiritual light neither did he comprehend the real truth of God. Thus, when he left the earth, his spiritual eyes were not opened – neither his spiritual ears. He occupied a great and exalted station in this world, inasmuch as he was chosen and elected by man to be a mediator between them and God. Therefore, it was human and not divine.
>
> Let us consider a little, the differences between his life and the life of Christ. Jesus, the Son of God, walked barefoot in the wilderness without a place to lay his holy head. His shelter was the canopy of heaven, his lamp, the stars and often his food consisted of the grasses of the field or uncooked corn . . . His glory and dignity consisted not in the opinion of man, but in doing the will of his Father in heaven: and, though he was nailed to the cross, his divine head crowned with thorns, today his name is revered, his memory held sacred, his glory fills the earth and his divine sonship is acknowledged by the whole world, because he was chosen by God and not by man.
>
> But the 'Pope' while upon this earth, lived in the Palace of the Vatican, surrounded by every comfort and luxury, dressing in the most beautiful garments and softest of raiments, sleeping upon the beds of ease, partaking of the daintiest of food, wearing a crown of gold upon his head . . . but even now, though he has been dead but a short time, the world is already busy with the new 'Pope' and he is nearly forgotten . . .
>
> Thus, think of the difference between him and Christ and you

will see that the fame of the 'Pope' was of short duration, while that of Christ is eternal.[37]

Ethel Rosenberg, Laura Barney and *Some Answered Questions*

Laura Barney and Ethel Rosenberg arrived on 21 April[38] for a year-long stay during which Laura worked with 'Abdu'l-Bahá on what became the book *Some Answered Questions*. Ethel Rosenberg was acting as Laura's secretary. It was Laura's third pilgrimage and she was to return several times more: in the spring of 1905, then again in the autumn of the same year. Also in 1905, at the request of 'Abdu'l-Bahá, Laura, along with Hippolyte Dreyfus and Madame Lachenay, both from France, travelled to Tabríz, Mákú and Ashkabat, the first Western Bahá'ís to do so.[39] After spending the winter in Cairo, she was back in 'Akká in the spring of 1906. She returned yet again in 1908, and then with her husband, Hippolyte, in 1918. Laura's final visit to 'Abdu'l-Bahá was in 1921.[40]

Ethel Rosenberg had become a Bahá'í in 1899. After her first pilgrimage in 1901, she travelled to America where Mírzá Abu'l-Faḍl taught her much about the Faith. When Lady Blomfield became a Bahá'í in 1907, the two women became pillars of the English Bahá'í community. Ethel was greatly bothered by 'Abdu'l-Bahá's troubles and asked 'why He, Who was so perfect, should have to endure such sufferings'. He answered: 'How could they (God's teachers) teach and guide others in the way if they themselves did not undergo every species of suffering to which other human beings are subjected?'[41] Ethel was allowed to remain at 'Akká until 24 December.[42]

Laura was young and wealthy, but she was very happy to live in a prison if it allowed her to increase her understanding of her Faith. Because of her purity of heart, 'Abdu'l-Bahá favoured her and He commonly used humour to encourage and enlighten her. Once He asked her, 'In the heat of this summer season you should be living in the beautiful mountains of Switzerland. What are you doing in this dilapidated city of 'Akká spending time with us prisoners?' Laura spent much time with the ladies of the Holy Family, in part helping them improve their English.[43]

Like many books, Laura's didn't start off as a book. She had questions and wanted answers. She said the 'answers were written down in

Persian while 'Abdu'l-Bahá spoke, not with a view to publication, but simply that I might have them for future study'. The collected questions and answers became a book because she believed 'that what has been so valuable to me may be of use to others, since all men, notwithstanding their differences, are united in their search for reality'.[44]

'Abdu'l-Bahá's day was exceedingly busy and the only time He had to answer her questions was at lunch. Since He usually only ate one meal a day, consisting of olives, bread and cheese, answering Laura's questions sometimes cost Him his lunch. After one session, He wearily, but happily, remarked that 'It is encouraging that after all this labour, at least she understands the concepts. This is refreshing. What would I have done if after all this effort she still failed to comprehend the issues?'[45]

When working on the questions at lunch, 'Abdu'l-Bahá sat at the head of the table with Laura on His left and Ethel next to her. Yúnis Khán sat on 'Abdu'l-Bahá's right, across from Laura, and other pilgrims would fill the table. Yúnis Khán translated Laura's questions from English to Persian, then translated the Master's answers back into English. Ethel recorded both the questions and the answers. This wasn't always easy, according to Yúnis Khán, since he had to clearly understand the question before he could pass the concept of the question to 'Abdu'l-Bahá, then he had to translate the response accurately into English. Ethel wrote down everything she heard.[46]

'Abdu'l-Bahá wasn't the only one who sometimes didn't eat much during these sessions. Once Yúnis Khán was so carried away with his translations that the Master had to sneak the subject of eating into the answers He gave. One day, 'Abdu'l-Bahá abruptly turned to Laura and asked:

'How do you translate the word "*motarjim*" into English?'
'Interpreter,' she responded.
Then He asked, 'What is "*gorosneh*" in English?'
'Hungry,' she replied.
Then with His blessed finger He pointed at me [Yúnis Khán] and exclaimed, 'Hungry interpreter, hungry interpreter.'[47]

In spite of not always getting much lunch, 'Abdu'l-Bahá never lost His sense of humour. Once, when He was explaining the 'nonexistence of evil', the Master suddenly turned to Yúnis Khán and said with a smile,

'Now she will ask why, then, did God create the scorpion?' Hardly a minute had passed when the Amatu'l-Bahá [Laura] asked the question. 'Abdu'l-Bahá said: 'What did I tell you? Now in response tell her that this is the nature of things. It is true that the scorpion is evil, however it is only evil in relation to us; in relation to its own environment it is not evil. This poison is its means of defence; with its stinger it protects itself. But since the nature of the poison is not conducive to our wellbeing we consider it evil.'[48]

Soon, the questions and answers were circulating around 'Abdu'l-Bahá's family and they realized that

> if Miss Barney had not immersed herself in the depths of this divine Ocean, those precious gems would have remained undiscovered forever; those heavenly jewels would have been left concealed in the depths of the storehouse of meanings. And now that these hidden gems had come to light, what could be better than to record them in the Persian language so that they might remain intact and inviolate for posterity in the annals of the Faith.[49]

So, an amanuensis joined the luncheon group to record everything in Persian. Such a great idea entailed much more work for 'Abdu'l-Bahá since He now had to review and correct two transcripts. And when the earlier questions and answers were put back into Persian, He had to check those as well. Laura rapidly became fluent in Persian and was able to help immeasurably.[50]

Sydney Sprague

Sydney Sprague arrived from America on his first pilgrimage in October. Before he arrived, he had written to 'Abdu'l-Bahá expressing an interest in India. Once in 'Akká, he didn't want to leave, trying to make himself useful by teaching grammar, geography and physiology in the Bahá'í school. On the second day of his visit, 'Abdu'l-Bahá came to the small house Sydney shared with two Persian Bahá'ís, inspecting everything. He found a few things which He determined were not good enough for Sydney. New curtains were made and a carpenter was brought in. Then, Sydney was called into the presence of the Master.

1904

He had only been a Bahá'í for two years and was unprepared for the Master's request:

> I was told that the Master wished to speak to me. I found him in the large room upstairs, which looks out on to the Mediterranean, sitting on the divan. He beckoned me to come and sit beside him, and after taking my hand and holding it in his, in a grip of steel, he said to me very impressively: 'I wish you to leave for India to-night.'[51]

Sydney was thunderstruck, writing that it was true that he 'had wished before to go to India, and had written to the Master while I was in Paris asking that I might be allowed to do so some day, but while in Akka I had forgotten everything except that I wanted to live there always. The Master knew my thought.' 'Abdu'l-Bahá said 'I only desire your happiness. It will be a very good thing, a very good thing, if you will go now to India, but if you wish to stay in Akka longer you may do so . . .'

As Sydney remembered: 'I realized the importance of it all. I was to be the first Western Bahai to go to the far Orient, and carry tidings that my fellow Believers in Europe and America are one in love and unity with their Oriental brethren.' The Master, as Sydney was finding out, 'never commands or compels obedience, he only sweetly suggests, and his followers have found that to follow his suggestions will surely lead them on the right way'. 'Abdu'l-Bahá had held Sydney's hand in His 'vice-like grasp' during the whole interview and Sydney said he 'felt, too, as though he were imparting to me some of his own strength and courage'.[52]

Before Sydney left, 'Abdu'l-Bahá invited all the pilgrims then present, about 40 men and women, to supper. Sydney was mesmerized by the scene:

> We sat around that common table, old and young, rich and poor, dark and fair; the various coloured robes and turbans giving striking colour to the scene. We represented five of the world's great religions, and many different races. We had come from places as far away as America on the one hand and India on the other. We had been complete strangers a few days before, but now we all felt a warmth of friendship and affection for one another.
>
> The Master was the servant and waiting upon everyone, heaping

rice on every plate, much to the discomfort of some of the Eastern pilgrims 'who could hardly bear that the Master should wait on them'.⁵³

Other visitors

Not all visitors to 'Abdu'l-Bahá were the pure of heart and seekers after the truth, but most were affected by the Master. 'Akká's deputy commander, Lává Páshá, would enter the Master's house through the back door, without an appointment, shouting for a cup of sweet coffee as he entered. Once inside, he would bow and try to kiss the Master's hand, making a point of reverently kissing his fingers when the Master pulled his hand away. Lává Páshá would soon be comfortable and laughing loudly before introducing a topic on which he wanted to have a 'heated' discussion. All during this interruption, 'Abdu'l-Bahá's pen would continue to reveal Tablets until Lává Páshá had his sweet coffee.⁵⁴

At one time, two 'high-ranking Muslim divines' stopped for a visit. Yúnis Khán indicated that though they might not have been the most devout Muslims, they were welcomed into the pilgrim house and attained the presence of the Master. Later, 'Abdu'l-Bahá said, 'These people are not here to seek the truth,' and told Yúnis Khán and Mírzá Haydar-'Alí to establish a warm friendship with them. One night, when signs of weariness were beginning to show on the Master's face and the pilgrims were dismissed for the night and stood up, one of the Muslim Shaykhs humbly asked for a Tablet addressed to a high-ranking Iranian Muslim divine.

> 'Abdu'l-Bahá replied, 'I have written to him recently; that should suffice.'
> But the Shaykh insisted, 'I wish to be granted the honour of carrying to him such a gift.'
> 'Abdu'l-Bahá then consented, 'Very well, I shall write it.' As we began to leave the room, the Master said to Áqá Mírzá Núru'd-Dín, 'I am very busy, but I do not want to put this off. I may as well write it now, or I won't have another opportunity to do so. So come and sit down and I will dictate a few words' . . .
> The melodious chant of the Master filled the air, as divine verses in the Arabic tongue, indescribably eloquent and sublime, and with

the rapidity of copious rain, flowed from His lips. God be praised, the atmosphere that dominated the hearts and minds of those present is beyond description.⁵⁵

With the requested Tablet, the two Muslims left, as did Yúnis Khán. Outside in the darkness, 'Abdu'l-Bahá's secretary heard the two men talking. One said, 'It certainly was a strange phenomenon. It affected me deeply.' The other replied, 'Yes, the words were not His; yet He who spoke them spoke the truth.' Later at dinner, the divines 'seemed intoxicated, as though they had just awakened from a trance'. When they left the next day, they were 'utterly transformed'. Such was the power of 'Abdu'l-Bahá.⁵⁶

Hájí Mírzá Haydar-'Alí at another time went to visit a Christian priest in Haifa who occasionally bothered the Bahá'ís. He went up to the priest and asked: 'What is this hanging from your neck?' The priest said that it was the cross of Christ. Mírzá Haydar-'Alí then rebuked him, saying, 'Christ suffered so very much on the cross . . . Why have you hung that from your neck? You should be wearing something that Christ liked, something that served Christ.' 'Like what?' asked the priest. 'Christ had a donkey that served him well and He liked it,' replied Mírzá Haydar-'Alí. 'It is better that you make a statue of that donkey and wear it on your neck.' This upset the priest tremendously and he stormed over and complained to 'Abdu'l-Bahá, who said he would 'talk to Hájí'. But when Mírzá Haydar-'Alí next came into the Master's presence, 'Abdu'l-Bahá said: 'O, man of right conduct, again you have gone and uttered right things?'⁵⁷

One day an American atheist, an unsightly small dog in her arms, basically forced her way into 'Abdu'l-Bahá's presence. Her first comment was, 'I have heard a lot in America about your greatness. They tell stories about you, but I really have not understood the reality of the situation and I want to know what the truth of the matter is.' The Master quietly told her, with His usual eloquence, of the unity of God. The woman simply laughed and said, 'I am astonished that you can compose so spontaneously, and with such eloquence and fluency, such sophisticated verses of poetry in proof of an imaginary thing. What does "God" mean?' It was obvious that she mistook normal Bahá'í expressions for 'poetry'. 'Abdu'l-Bahá only smiled and continued in a similar vein. The woman then said,

I am not capable of understanding such concepts; moreover, I am in no way willing to lose my freedom; and furthermore, I have no attachment to any imaginary being. But I do wonder what purpose all this knowledge, wisdom and philosophy serve? If you only knew what high-ranking scientists and scholars have written books refuting all such thought! And now your followers in America walk in your path. But if you come to my home town of Boston in America, you will see this kind of talk enjoys no support. The atheists of Boston are world-renowned.

Again, 'Abdu'l-Bahá smiled and continued speaking as He had done before. Finally, with her dog increasingly restless in her arms, she left, saying that she would return in five days. 'If your God is the true God, then ask Him to guide me . . . Let's see what this God of yours will do for me.' But then, 'You have a God to whom you look for guidance; where can I look, who have no such beliefs?'

'Abdu'l-Bahá had not shown 'the slightest hint of displeasure, and treated her with extreme gentleness and compassion' and was not surprised when she returned the very next afternoon agitated and uncomfortable. 'I spent a restless night and so missed my planned trip this morning. Before I came here I was quite confident in my beliefs, but now I am anxious and unsure. Please, either grant me guidance or confirm me in my original belief.' She then courteously listened to the Master for an hour. As she left she said, 'I now realize that there is something of substance here. There are realities, the understanding of which is beyond my capability.'

The next day she did not return, but the day after she did, 'weary and distressed'. She talked again with 'Abdu'l-Bahá and left considerably happier. She was gone for four or five days, but then returned and moved into the Master's house saying she wouldn't leave until her mind was at ease. This time, when 'Abdu'l-Bahá summoned her, she came with an attitude of reverence and without her dog. She listened to the Master in 'a state of lowliness and selflessness' that demonstrated her 'submission and obedience'. When she left for America a few days later, she did so 'contented and joyful; the heavenly fragrances of her faith and certitude spread to every part of that land'.[58]

Anna Watson was in 'Akká on 18 October when 'Abdu'l-Bahá told about a dream He had about America. In the dream, He said, there were many sincere, earnest souls there. He said that in His dream He thought He was in a large room with a number of Persians . . . These told Him that there were many earnest believers in America, but that they were far apart, and all playing on different musical instruments, so that they did not play in harmony. Abdul Baha said, 'I will see what I can do. Finding one, I told him to stay until I brought others to him, but when I came back with another, the first had gone away, piping on his instrument. And so it was; I could never get them together.' He added, 'When I awoke, I was very tired.'[59]

The unity, or disunity, of the American believers was constantly on His mind. To Howard and Mary MacNutt a couple of months later, 'Abdu'l-Bahá spoke on the importance of having unity:

> Then shall the bounties of the Blessed Perfection descend upon you. Divine Assistance will be given you, and from your meeting the Love of God will be spread to all men.
>
> Strive, strive always that ye may be united. If one single sheep strays away from the fold, do all in your power to bring it back. Kindness and love must be your means of gathering all together.[60]

1905

At the end of 1904, nine pilgrims left New York bound for 'Akká. These included Mírzá Abu'l-Faḍl, Percy and Aloysis Woodcock and their two daughters, May and Eva, Mary Lucas, Julia Grundy, and Howard and Mary MacNutt. Because of the dangerous conditions in 'Akká, when they arrived in Port Said, 'Abdu'l-Bahá telegraphed them instructions to arrive in several small groups.

Howard and Mary MacNutt, and Julia Grundy

Julia Grundy and Howard and Mary MacNutt, together with Laura Barney whom they encountered in Port Said, were the first to arrive on 2 January 1905, by a small steamer, the *Mariout*, from Alexandria. Howard was an early convert of Kheiralla in New York who had abandoned his teacher when Kheiralla had broken the Covenant.

Their arrival was not easy, as Mary MacNutt recorded, saying they

> cast anchor about a mile and a half from shore . . . Great surf boats had come off from Haifa filled with half naked Arab boatmen straining their splendid muscles at immense oars. In a few moments the Mariout from bowsprit to rudder was pandemonium. These bare-footed sons of Ishmael literally swarmed over us, yelling, screaming, gesticulating; a jargon and babel of voices as if the one with the strongest lungs was most entitled to employment. None of us after our wild experiences with wind and wave on the Mariout had the physical energy to resist so we were lugged down the long swaying rope ladder like so many bags of grain and carried away shoreward by our vociferous captors. But the sea still had its claims upon us. At first the boatmen steered down into the point of the bay intending to land us through the surf but realizing almost too late that this was hazardous we turned about

and fought back with straining oars to the dilapidated wharf at the Custom House where we were dragged by muscular arms from above and pushed by strong shoulders from below up to a rickety terra firma, drenched and soaked by waves which still leaped hungrily after us. Thus we landed at Haifa on the afternoon of January 2nd, by what we afterward termed the 'Haifa lift'.[1]

Mary then went on to describe Haifa:

... we drove along the shore front, practically the only street in old Haifa to the foot of Carmel. To ascend the mountain by the most direct road, we passed through the German Colony or modern Haifa, a village or community of devoted German Christians who settled here in 1868 to await the promised Coming of the Lord, the very year in which Bahá'u'lláh was sent to 'Akká just across the bay. Over the doorways of some of the thrifty little houses is written 'Der Herr Kommt' (The Lord Cometh). The German Colony offers a striking contrast to the old city; clean streets well laid out, neat modern villas, shade trees, lawns and flower beds, everything evidencing thrift and industry. The native houses are quite the reverse. The Oriental builds his home hostile and secluded from the eyes of the outside world, walls it up solidly from the street, leaving only a single doorway of entrance and a few narrow close-latticed windows overhead; lavishing his taste upon the court interior which he alone sees and enjoys. The type of European house is just the opposite, a thing of beauty from the outside, open and hospitable, as if welcoming a visitor ...

The road turns at right angles at the German settlement, leads directly through it and climbs the mountain as straight as it can without being a sheer gravity pitch. As we go up, the horses stumble upon loose rocks and there is plenty of mud from recent heavy rains. We pass the Tomb of the Bab, see the monastery of the Carmelite monks upon the brow of the mountain just overlooking the sea, make a couple of turns at the summit, bringing Akka into clear view and golden with sunset glory, and alight at Pross House, a small hotel standing in the middle of Carmel's head [probably in the area where today's Dan Panorama and Dan Carmel Hotels are now located]. We are the only guests, and the host Hans Schneider a lay preacher in the German Colony gives us most kindly greeting . . . His terms are very low and his suspicions incline to the belief that we are American friends of Abbas Effendi.[2]

On 3 January, Julia and the MacNutts enjoyed the view from the top of Mount Carmel in beautiful weather, 'Akká glistened across the bay and the pilgrims thought of all the Holy Figures who had walked on Carmel: Abraham, Jesus, Bahá'u'lláh. Mary continued with her detailed description:

> Only a few olives growing here and there in vineyards and gardens adorn the otherwise bare picture. From base to summit the soil is scanty, the rocks and rough ridges peeping through. As you look, the landscape seems covered with a velvety soft mosaic of carpet, but as you go about on foot the conditions are incredibly rough and hostile. Sharp edges of flint and hornblende cut your shoes like knives, briers and prickly bushes catch your clothing and a most tenacious limestone clay clogs under your feet hardening like cement wherever it adheres. There are no roads, simply donkey paths filled with rocks and stumbling places. Agriculture is practically unknown. Here and there the Arab scratches the soil with a primeval plough hitched to a pair of small wiry bullocks and scatters seed with careless hand. What there is of the soil is wonderfully fertile however. Without further care or cultivation he gathers good harvests from his rude tilling. There are no fences or boundary lines. As you look across Carmel's back the untrained eye sees nothing betokening human occupancy or habitation. After awhile growing accustomed to the picture you begin to pick out a few little huts built of rocks and mud, so secluded among natural surroundings that you come upon them before you clearly make them out. As you approach, threading your way through the rocks and briers, a lot of savage dogs rush out challenging and checking your approach . . .
>
> Sometimes these rough ramblings far back upon the mountain are attended with danger. Mr MacNutt happened on one occasion to approach an Arab hut without seeing it, and was confronted by a sinewy son of Ishmael armed with a double barrelled shot gun held toward him at full cock. The morning salutation 'Arag sa-id!' and a few copper coins relieved an otherwise embarrassing interview . . .

1905

> Sometimes in our early morning rambles we would meet Syrian girls and women coming down the mountain paths from shepherd huts far back in the interior carrying upon their heads great jars of sour goat's milk . . . on their way to Haifa. There they sit along the streets among the bazaars selling it until late in the afternoon. Then you will meet them coming homeward climbing the 'short cut' mountain paths with tireless vigor making perhaps a round trip of twelve or fifteen miles . . . balancing their jars on their heads with perfect skill, barefoot and walking swiftly among boulders and loose stones which bothered us to scramble over with nothing to carry. Some of these girls are magnificent physical specimens, veritable amazons in poise and figure.[3]

Mary described the Shrine of the Báb:

> A little more than half way up the eastern side of Mount Carmel, terraced deep into its bosom of solid rock, stands a splendid white mausoleum looking out with five great round eyes toward 'Akká upon a heavenly picture of sea and sky. Above it rises the massive beetling brows of Carmel's rough ridges and boulders gnarled and twisted into convulsive shapes like wrinkles of agony upon a giant forehead. Below, the profile of the giant face projects peacefully down the mountain slope and merges with the sea . . .
>
> The Tomb is a solid gray-white structure built of the lime-stone rock from which its site has been excavated. This rock hardens by exposure to the atmosphere and merges in color after a time into a soft mellow grayish white tone peaceful and refreshing to the eye. The terrace upon which the Tomb proper stands is built out into a projecting level, flanked upon either side by deep square subterranean cisterns hewn out of the solid rock for the purpose of storing water . . . In the centre of the terrace and leading down the steep slope between the great cisterns is a long stone stairway. From the foot of the stairway the mountain side descends sharply perhaps six hundred feet to the upper edge of the German Colony . . .
>
> The Tomb itself is about fifty feet in front width and rises about half as much in height . . . At the time of our visit (January 1905) all work upon the Tomb had been temporarily discontinued owing to an investigation by the Turkish authorities, certain enemies of

'Abdu'l Baha having circulated a report that the structure was in reality a fort...⁴

On a rainy day, Howard walked down the mountain alone to the Tomb of the Báb. When he arrived, he found it closed and no one about. He was able to scramble up and look over an unfinished doorway to see the interior. Usually, visitors to the Tomb were met by the attendant, who lived nearby. When a pilgrim would arrive, the attendant would come running with an armful of flowers, a Persian greeting and breathing the Greatest Name. Then he would find them chairs and bring tea. Howard once tried to offer him a tip for his services, but the radiant attendant 'held it a moment, said some holy words in Persian, then carefully placed it in Mr MacNutt's bosom just over his heart'.⁵

> While the MacNutts and Julia were sitting atop Mount Carmel enjoying the scene on 3 January, a well-dressed and handsome man came walking up the path. The man, clothed in all-white oriental costume with crimson tarbush came swinging up the rocky pathway at a rapid walk. At once we concluded our messenger had arrived, but without turning his head, he kept straight on, looking neither to right or left, passed over the summit and started down the path on the other side of the mountain. Something impelled Mr MacNutt to follow him which he did for half a mile. Suddenly the stranger without changing his pace, put his hand behind his back and Mr MacNutt saw that he held a letter which he dropped in the road. In a short while we were reading the letter. It was a message of instructions for us to go to Akka next day.⁶

On 4 January, the trio of pilgrims went to 'Akká. Many have described this great journey of anticipation, but Mary was the master of description. When they left Haifa they couldn't tell their carriage driver exactly where they were going, so they went ostensibly for a short jaunt along the bay. They went down 'the long street of the German Colony, turning at right angles just before we reached the sea'.

> In a few minutes we entered the old city of Haifa, threading our way along the narrow principal street lined upon either side with little bazaars, mere holes in the wall, each one presided over by a

calm-faced dignified merchant in white gown, his head topped by a lofty red tarbush. There are no sidewalks and our horses were jostled by donkeys, camels and a kaleidoscopic current of humanity, making the going very slow, but thanks to his cracking whip and Arabic yells our driver pulled us through the confusion and completed his contract by depositing us at the eastern edge of the town . . . Having dismissed our conveyance we strolled nonchalantly along the sandy beach as if a further trip in the direction of Akka was the last thing in our minds, until, importuned by an Arab who spoke a little French, we engaged him to secure us a beach-wagon for a 'promenade' along the shore as far as the River Kishon or Nahr Mukatta, a mile or so on our intended way. Reaching the river, the horses fording it, our ideas of 'promenade' expanded and after a long colloquy in kindergarten French and Arabic assisted by eloquent pantomime we bargained for transportation to Akka as if suddenly deciding to go. The conveyances which make the trip of nine miles along the surf are known as 'American wagons', high-wheeled, long canvas-covered and much like the prairie schooners of our Western plains before the railroads were built . . . Three horses abreast furnish the motive power . . . Without slackening pace and with reins hanging loose, they follow the surf out as it recedes and dexterously avoid the next wave by running up higher on the beach when it breaks, making a zig-zag course as they go, always finding hard sand for their footing . . .

As we drove along we met strings and strings of camels, usually ten or a dozen, traveling in single file, the largest in front, the procession preceded by a diminutive donkey who acts as guide and pacemaker to his giant followers. Now and then little donkeys scurried past carrying long-legged Arabs, so long of limb that they had to turn their feet up at the bottom to prevent trailing upon the ground . . . Sinewy Arab fishermen, bronze-black from toe to turban were casting their circular nets into the surf with scanty results; patriarchal old Bedouins in baggy white bloomers, gaunt and wiry in muscle and limb, passed us on foot as if the nine mile jaunt from Akka to Haifa was only a trifling morning exercise . . .

In a little while we came upon a wide boulevard lined with fine old trees and extending from Akka gate toward the Rizwan. As we drove along it we had a critical survey of the city and the inhabitants thereof. Right before us the high forbidding walls of the prison-fortress loomed up in discouraging monotony, unbroken save by a huge gateway flanked on either side by heavy bastions and military towers. Akka's population had poured itself out through this gate and distributed itself along the highway . . . men, women, children, goats, sheep, cattle, camels and donkeys in heterogeneous confusion . . . We drove on into the city through the angles and double walls of the great gate, passing keen-eyed sentries who asked our Arab driver questions, then emerged into a large court-space surrounded by barracks and coffee houses where groups of Turkish soldiers lounged and stood apart. Passing across the court, the street suddenly narrowed and we unhitched one horse . . . Every fifty yards the street ended in a blank wall, then turned at right angles in another direction, a veritable catacombs with the roof taken off. Squalid pictures of humanity were everywhere before our eyes, pestiferous odors rose to the nostrils from the filth in the passageway; it could no longer be called a street. After ten minutes slow going the conditions improved; we were passing between the high walls of buildings on either side, a few bazaars more cleanly and attractive appeared and finally we came into an open court at the far end of the city just inside the sea-wall toward the east. Our driver had received his instructions from us in the words 'Abbas Effendi' and drove straight across the court to a large doorway from whence a number of Baha'i brothers came and welcomed us with 'Allah u ABHA.' We passed into an inner court. A fountain was playing in the centre and bright faced roses welcomed us in their beauty and fragrance. We climbed a long flight of steps to the upper rooms of the house which opened upon the court of roses and were shown into a large room around which ran a low divan. We had reached the goal of our pilgrimage.[7]

Very quickly they received word that 'Abdu'l-Bahá was ready to see them. He entered quickly, saying 'Welcome! Welcome! The mercy of God is very great. Two years ago I sent for you. For a long time I have yearned to see you.'[8] Mary wrote that His 'face was light itself, the voice ringing with happiness . . . The focus of the soul of this wonderful being is in the eyes. Love lingers in their depths and tenderness quivers in flashes of sympathetic light upon the lids. If the tongue were silent the eyes would voice the Spirit's message . . .'[9]

1905

Julia and the MacNutts were in Haifa and 'Akká for a total of 18 days, ten of which they spent in the Holy Household. Howard was restricted to two visits to 'Akká for a total of five days. The second time he gained the Master's presence, he had to do so 'hidden in the rear of a covered wagon, gowned like an oriental and wearing a tarbush'. 'Abdu'l-Bahá warned him that

> Your visit here is during a time of great political difficulty. Spies are many; espionage is constant; enemies are everywhere. The Governor knows that you have arrived. It will be necessary for you to remain very quiet. Do not go outside the house and do not show yourself upon the roof during the daytime lest you may be seen by those who are watching to make trouble. Your coming to Akka is not so dangerous to yourselves as it is to the Bahai Friends who live here. They may suffer the consequences of your coming to Akka after you have gone.[10]

Julia recorded few of her own thoughts and feelings but did give many of the Master's answers to her questions. One day 'Abdu'l-Bahá sent for her and she

> found Him in a little room opening from the courtyard. He was sitting upon a raised chair, His beautiful face majestic in repose and strength turned toward the only window. He greeted me joyfully. Both the daughters were present. He said, 'I want you to carry away from Acca the joy and peace of the spiritual life.' I answered, 'It would be impossible for me to be in this atmosphere of Spirit as I have been and not receive wonderful benefit.' He continued, 'God is like the calm and limitless sea. His Bounty is overflowing and illimitable . . . Love of God, Knowledge of God is the greatest, the only real happiness, because it is Nearness to God. This is the Kingdom of God. To love God is to know Him. This is what I desire for you; – that you may walk in this path.'
>
> I answered, 'Now that you have shown me the way, I wish to walk in this heavenly path.' He said, 'You are near to God and day by day you will progress by the knowledge of God toward spiritual joy. Then you will be a source of guidance to others. In you they will now behold another person; in fact everybody will witness the change in your life. You must develop spiritual love in yourself and

in them. Physical love is very different from spiritual love. To awaken spiritual love in others is to attain peace and joy for yourself.'

I said, 'I wish to teach this Message of Light and Truth, but I feel that my efforts are small and unimportant.' He answered, 'The mountain is large but it has no intelligence. The diamond is small but it is filled with light. The elephant produces no melody; the nightingale's song is like the music of Heaven. I will pray that you may become the recipient of the Bounties of God. You will be filled with power because the Spirit will speak through you. You must not bring unhappiness to others. In the future sacrifice yourself more and more in the Cause of God. Then the Love of God will grow and grow in your heart.'. . .

I asked, 'What shall I say to those who state that they are satisfied with Christianity and do not need this present Manifestation?' He answered, 'Let them alone. What would they do if a former king had reigned and a new king was now seated upon the throne? They must acknowledge the new king or they are not true subjects of the Kingdom. Last year there was a spring-time. Can a man say, "I do not need a new spring-time this year – the old springtime is enough for me"? No! the new spring must come to fill the earth with beauty and brightness. The sun rose this morning. Shall we say to the sun, "Go away! We do not need you this morning; you were here yesterday?" If we strive to upbuild this Cause with faith and love in our hearts, it will over-power all the science, philosophy, and metaphysics of this Day. I Myself am surprised at the wonderful things that are happening. The Word of God shows such power and penetration that all will be surprised and astonished at Its advance.'[11]

One day, 'Abdu'l-Bahá came to Julia and the MacNutts unexpectedly to tell them about the Feast to be held that night. He was happy because 'At the table they will be gathered together from all parts of the world' and He hoped that this would spread throughout the world. Then He turned to Howard and asked what he thought of the idea. Howard answered, 'What could I say that would add to an already perfect wisdom!' The Master then asked Howard if he would speak at the Feast. Howard responded that 'It is a blessed privilege to listen. I am usually called upon to speak, but I love to listen.'[12] 'Abdu'l-Bahá approved of his answer, but made him speak anyway.

1905

That night at the Feast, 'Abdu'l-Bahá greeted everyone, extending His hands to the believers saying 'Welcome! Welcome!' The Master seated His guests and gave each a napkin. He embraced them and led them to their seats, after which He anointed each with attar of rose. 'Abdu'l-Bahá Himself served the dinner saying, 'This is the blessed supper of the Lord for we have gathered under the shadow of the Blessed Perfection.'[13]

When dinner was finished, Mírzá Asadu'lláh introduced Howard, saying,

> He is one of our eloquent American brothers who has great power. God has given him the power to attract souls to the Fountain of Life. His words are like a magnet. In the midst of his work he has come to visit Acca. We have not been brought into this blessed brotherhood of the East and West through miracles, but through the Word of the Manifestation of God Bahá'u'lláh. Through His Word the prophecy of Christ has been fulfilled, that they should come from the East and the West to sit down at the Table of the Lord. Jesus said that the coming of the Son of Man would be as the flash of lightning from the East to the West. All the proofs are confirmed here tonight.[14]

Before such an audience, Howard MacNutt now had to speak. He said,

> My spiritual brothers in El-Abhá! The Persian language always seemed difficult to me until I visited the Holy Household. Now I find it very easy to understand. For the Persian alphabet contains but four letters, and the Persian language has only one word. These letters are 'm', 'h,' 'b', and 't', and the word is 'Muhabbat', which means 'love'. For 'Love' is the sum total of the Persian language as I hear it spoken in Acca. That is why I am able to understand and speak Persian so quickly. The Blessed Perfection in the Kitab-el-Akdas recommended that the nations of the earth should adopt one language. This was the outer language of unity. At the same time He revealed the Divine Message of Unity in the inner language of the Spirit. This inner language is understood by His children in the East and the West. When the East and West meet in the Kingdom and commune in this inner language, the putting together of mere words is an easy matter. If men love each other, all the details of unity can be quickly settled upon.[15]

For all his brilliance and spiritual power, Howard did not understand the true station of the Master and His infallibility. By late 1912, when 'Abdu'l-Bahá was about to depart from America, this problem came to a head. When Howard failed to understand Covenant-breaking, 'Abdu'l-Bahá publicly chastised him, sinking Howard's reputation within the Faith. 'Abdu'l-Bahá, however, knew Howard's spiritual qualities and steadfastness and patiently worked with him over the next year until he was able to understand. As recompense, 'Abdu'l-Bahá gave Howard the task of collecting all of His American talks and compiling them into *The Promulgation of Universal Peace*.

Mary Lucas

When Julia and the MacNutts left Haifa, they stopped over in Beirut where they met incoming pilgrim Mary Lucas, a well-known singer. She had waited for six weeks in Egypt before receiving permission to visit 'Akká for just two days. Mary's ship anchored off Haifa on 29 January at 2:30 a.m. in rough seas and she, like all the others, had to make the half-hour journey by rowing boat to shore. Mary later wrote:

> The steamer arrived in the blackness of the night, and the Arabs who had come in the small boats to take the passengers ashore, rushed on board in a wild, excited state after their wrestle with the sea. I alone (the only woman) with a Cook's courier, and these insensate creatures went down the side of the ship, into the night, and into the sea, it seemed, as the captain commended me to GOD, for he realized how perilous the night was.
>
> Mr. .... came on deck to be with me to the last, and he was sorry to see me go down the side of the ship alone, but even at such a moment his keen sense of humor did not desert him. When the Arabs came on board screaming in their excitement . . . my friend remarked: 'Don't be alarmed, he is only telling his friends how much he loves his mother.'[16]

In spite of the rough water, Mary felt unafraid and arrived at her hotel at four in the morning.

The next day, Mary took a carriage to 'Akká, noting with interest her passage through its narrow alleys: '. . . the narrow dirty streets of Acca . . .

were so narrow that it was impossible to pass the heavy ladened camels which we met coming in the opposite direction. They were obliged to back out of the way of the carriage . . .' When she reached the house of the Master, a man in a red fez greeted her and escorted her inside and then up the long stairway. At the top, she was met by Laura Barney who led her to her room and then to lunch.

When Mary and Laura entered the dining room, 'Abdu'l-Bahá was waiting and took Mary by the hand. 'It was not in the ordinary way in which one is greeted when meeting a stranger for the first time, but as though my host were continuing a friendship which had always existed. He took me by the hand . . . and led me to my seat at the table, and not one word was spoken.' At the table He asked about her journey, then, when they had finished eating, sent her to rest. At about 4 p.m. 'Abdu'l-Bahá went to Mary's room and sat on the divan for a short while, 'saying very little'.

The following morning, Monday 30 January, Mary attended the usual morning meeting of the Household for prayers, and remembered 'how inexpressibly I was impressed by the absolute poise of the Master; His absolute naturalness; absolute freedom. There was an utter absence of any desire or effort to impress one with his greatness, which is majestic in its simplicity.'[17]

As a musician who had 'studied in America and Europe', Mary asked the Master a question about the spiritual effect of music on its listeners, and was 'amazed' at his comprehensive reply:

> . . . physical things have a connection with spiritual realities . . . melodies, though they are material, are connected with the spiritual, therefore, they produce a great effect. A certain kind of melody makes the spirit happy, another kind makes it sad, another excites it to action.
>
> All these feelings can be caused by voice and music, for through the nerves it moves and stirs the spirit . . .[18]

Mary spent the evening with Bahíyyih Khánum, the Greatest Holy Leaf, and Munírih Khánum, the Master's wife. When they asked her to sing for them, she sang the hymn 'Nearer, My God, to Thee,' then chanted a Tablet in Arabic she had been taught while in Egypt. This was supposed to be Mary's last night in 'Akká, but the next morning 'Abdu'l-Bahá made no mention of her leaving. Instead, when she entered the tea room, He called her over to sit beside him and they sat together in silence. Mary thought, 'How one is at rest in this Presence! I had no desire save to remain with Him always!' She was allowed to stay and go to Bahá'u'lláh's resting place. 'Abdu'l-Bahá asked her to sing in the Shrine and she did so, thinking 'It seemed as though I was not singing, but the voice of itself was soaring, and had left my body.'[19]

Wednesday came and still no instruction to leave. At noon, Mary watched 'Abdu'l-Bahá walking in the garden:

> He walks and holds his head like a king. Outside the garden gate were many Oriental pilgrims who had come long distances to see Him – sages, philosophers and scholars, I was told. Some had long white locks; all wore the red fez. With their flowing robes they made a picture as they stood and watched the Master, outside the enclosure. He walked about the garden and seemed [to be] examining its condition and attending to such things as were necessary, as it was spring and time for planting. As these Orientals stood and watched him there, what an impressive sight it was! As he went back and forth in the garden, their bodies followed every movement, and they were careful to keep their faces always turned toward him. They stood in the most reverent attitude with their hands folded.[20]

On Thursday at dinner, 'Abdu'l-Bahá asked Mary if she was happy because she had been allowed to stay over her appointed time. Mary replied, 'You know!' and He answered, 'Yes.' On Friday, the Master again asked her if she was happy that He allowed her to stay on and again,

> I told him, he knew, He smiled and said, 'Yes.' He then added that all He did was prompted by great wisdom. He said: 'Some see the wisdom, and some do not, and some of my wisdom is impossible for any to understand, but all that I say and do has great significance' . . . So I understood that my staying so long over the time appointed for me to leave had an important meaning.[21]

On 4 February, the Master called for Mary and asked her to sing for him. She sang two hymns, then at his request chanted the Arabic Tablet she had learned earlier. He said she sang with much feeling. He also expressed His desire that she travel home by way of Paris. Later in the day, He called her in and she had a long interview, telling Him everything in her heart. He then made her 'a cup of tea with his own hands' and again said He wished she would go home via Paris.²²

Mary's last day was 5 February and He called her and anointed her head with rose oil. She later wrote: 'Words are very weak things to express what this visit with the Master meant to me. One cannot come into this Presence without being changed in every atom of the entity. The Master said that words are incapable of expressing the things of the spirit.' Mary left after lunch the following day.²³

In the spring, Alice Barney joined her daughter Laura and stayed for a month. During that time, Alice painted the portrait of the Governor's son.²⁴

Josephine Cowles de Lagnel

Josephine Cowles de Lagnel (previously Josephine Cowles) was on pilgrimage for seven weeks in April and May. She was mesmerised:

> To me while there, each day, hour, and moment, were fraught with such deep and impressive experiences . . .
>
> After a sojourn with those beloved people of nearly seven weeks . . . it seemed like leaving Paradise, and I thought my heart would break . . . To leave an atmosphere of love, which like the fragrance of rare exotics, permeated every thought, and where every service rendered was divine, was almost beyond the power of human will . . . But then the dear Master, like a pitying Father, said –'Do not weep, I will be with you' – my heart was comforted, and again, when He told me that I was to remain until after the night of the Departure [Ascension of Bahá'u'lláh] and to receive that blessing, – I was almost happy.
>
> On that evening all the believers repaired to the Holy Tomb . . . there to spend the night. After supper we were driven there, where we met all the members of the Holy Household and the believers . . .
>
> The rooms were brilliantly illuminated with lamps and candelabra and thickly carpeted with rich Oriental rugs . . .
>
> The Tomb proper was covered with a costly and most beautiful

Persian shawl, and thickly strewn with flowers. The night was wondrously beautiful. The full moon was shining with such magnificence that it was almost as light as day. Through the open window we could see the blue Mediterranean in the distance, and the air was heavy with the fragrance of jasmine and roses. The only audible sound was the wail of a solitary night bird . . . Within the chapel the aisles were filled with kneeling women, and one of the Holy Leaves chanted the prayers. The sky, the air, the sea – and even the flowers with which the room was profusely decorated – were in perfect concord. The solemn chanting amid those prostrate forms was a scene long to be remembered; and there we remained until midnight. Then we retired to the rooms on the left of the chapel, and the men in like manner filled the places so recently occupied by us. In that gathering were venerable men who had suffered years of imprisonment, whose shining faces beamed with holy light; young men were there, too, whose every look spoke of the deep veneration and love with which they had dedicated their lives to the Holy Cause; even the little grand-children were there, whose gentle and subdued manner spoke of holy reverence. One of the venerable believers chanted the Holy Utterances and Prayers, – and for three hours they remained in solemn devotion.[25]

A few years later, 'Abdu'l-Bahá said of her that 'she came here with Mrs Jackson and remained for some time. Though she was poor, she was always happy. I had her stay with us in the Household. Here she worked very hard to cook certain dishes. She said she wished to learn how to cook Persian dishes for the Bahá'ís in America. Her great, continuous sorrow had been the dying of her only son, but once she became a believer she found true happiness.'[26]

The Ottoman Commission of Enquiry

Most Bahá'í literature refers to two Commissions of Enquiry, the first in 1904 and the second in 1907. What happened in 1904 is uncertain; something did happen, as shown in the previous chapter, when 'Abdu'l-Bahá was interrogated over a number of days. Shoghi Effendi in *God Passes By*, Adib Taherzadeh in *The Covenant of Bahá'u'lláh*, and H. M. Balyuzi in *'Abdu'l-Bahá*, all write about the two Commissions.

But Necati Alkan's more recent examination of Turkish records indicates that there was only one official Commission, in 1905, though its members may have visited 'Abdu'l-Bahá at various different times.[27]

Reports by the British Consul in Beirut and the Vice-Consulate in Haifa from June, August and September 1905, published by Moojan Momen in *The Bábí and Bahá'í Religions, 1844–1944*, note the activities and the names of the members of the Commission. Except for the year and season, they are identical with the information in *God Passes By*. The earliest mention of the Commission by the British was on 30 June 1905, whereas Shoghi Effendi records its arrival as the winter of 1907. There were great difficulties for the Master in the winter of 1907, but it was not this Commission. The final piece of this puzzle is the attempted assassination of Sultán 'Abdu'l-Ḥamíd. As noted below, that occurred on 21 July 1905.

Shortly before the Commission's arrival, 'Abdu'l-Bahá had a dream 'in which He saw a ship cast anchor off 'Akká, from which flew a few birds, resembling sticks of dynamite, and which, circling about His head, as He stood in the midst of a multitude of the frightened inhabitants of the city, returned without exploding to the ship'.[28]

The four-man Commission, headed by Arif Bey, arrived in late June because of reports sent by Adam Za'im, an Albanian. The first thing the Commission did was to question Za'im about his accusations.[29]

'Abdu'l-Bahá told the Bahá'ís to leave 'Akká for their safety. Many did not want to go and Mírzá Asadu'lláh wrote that 'Abdu'l-Bahá

> admonished them, saying, 'O ye beloved of God. These people (officials) have come especially for Me, and their purpose is not yet known. It is My Will that you should depart from here and serve God wherever you go. This is the appointed time for work; it is the season of victory. If I am crucified or exiled, or thrown into the ocean, ye should remain, nevertheless, firm as mountains; nay, your service should become greater and your endurance more. Lay your trust upon God; rest assured in the confirmation of Bahá'u'lláh; spread the Fragrances of God; help the people and lead them to the Light of God.[30]

At one point, 'Abdu'l-Bahá told Mírzá Asadu'lláh and some others that they should go to Egypt. Mírzá Asadu'lláh protested that he had no passport, but the Master told him that he would be protected. When Mírzá Asadu'lláh arrived at the pier to board the ship, the Governor and other officials were there to make sure no Bahá'í left. But suddenly, the Governor's attention was distracted by the arrival of mail, allowing Mírzá Asadu'lláh and his companions to board the ship unnoticed. 'Abdu'l-Bahá said that God told the Governor to turn his head.[31]

On 30 June, the British Vice-Consulate, Pietro Abela, reported that:

> At the close of the last quarter a commission arrived at Haifa from Constantinople ... An hour after their arrival here, they left for Acre. Until now their commission is still kept secret. They however are making enquiries about Abbas Effendi of Acre, the Chief Babist, who is accused of trying to make the Moslems of Acre Babists. It is supposed that their enquiries about Abbas Effendi will result in extorting from him a large sum of money. The Caimacam [Qá'im-Maqám] of Haifa tells me that they have to enquire also about the conduct of the Farik of Acre as many complaints have been made against him. This Commission has also called many notables and enquired about general things.[32]

With the arrival of this Commission of Enquiry sent by Sultán 'Abdu'l-Ḥamíd, the Covenant-breakers were jubilant. The Commission immediately took over the telegraph and postal services, dismissed 'Akká's Governor for being too friendly toward 'Abdu'l-Bahá, put guards on the house of the Master, and associated with the Covenant-breakers.

A year or so earlier, the authorities had called 'Abdu'l-Bahá in for interrogation several times and demanded answers to its charges. This time, while the Commission interviewed many, 'Abdu'l-Bahá absolutely refused to have anything at all to do with them. In spite of the 'wildest rumors ... being spread about Him, the serenity He had invariably maintained, ever since His incarceration had been reimposed, remained unclouded, and His confidence unshaken.'[33]

'Abdu'l-Bahá described these days to George Latimer and Mason Remey years later, in 1914:

> At the time of the arrival of the Investigation Committee, all the means of communication were closed. Spies were stationed all around, calumnies and falsehoods were hurled broadcast and the enemies,

both in Acca and in other places, were united against us, drawing up a number of false reports and sending them to the authorities in Constantinople, to instigate them and arouse their suspicion so that they may make more close our confinement. It is evident from these remarks, how difficult it was to attend to anything. One of their accusations was that I was trying to lay the foundations of a new sovereignty. Another was that I have built a fortress on the slope of Mt. Carmel which will have a commanding situation of the vicinity. Again another thing was that I have made a new flag to lead my increasing army into the active field. That I have shown this flag to the inhabitants of Acca and through Mirza Zekrollah I have sent this flag through the surrounding cities and through Sheik Mahmood I have forwarded it to the Arabian tribes and bedouins in the interior demanding their allegiance and obedience. With the assistance of the Nakazeen [Covenant-breakers] all these reports were concocted and sent to the Sublime Porte. Mirza Mohammad Ali took a large piece of white cloth and had written on it in poor hand-writing the word of Ya-Baha-El-Abha, telling them that this was the flag that I have made and delivered it into the hands of the enemies that it might be forwarded to Constantinople. The president of this Committee, who was promised the governorship of Beirut at the time, declared that the first thing that he will do, will be to cut me into two pieces and hang me on the gate of Acca as a warning to others. In short my aim was this, that during those stirring days I sent away seventy of the believers to Egypt and Russia and various parts . . . At that time I provided sufficient and adequate travelling expenses for everyone. I borrowed the money from an American who lived in Paris. In short I offered myself for a target to every calamity and affliction. Then a steamer arrived in the Bay of Acca to take me away secretly . . . When this matter was arranged I called in Seyed Ali Akbar, Aga Seyed Yaha, Mirza Assadullah, Aga Riza, Mírzá Mahmood and Mirza Hayder Ali and told them that everything was prepared for my departure; that a steamer is in the Port to take me away; that I should be let down from the wall of the fortress by a rope, ride rapidly in a carriage, climb into a boat and board the ship. Now you consult about this matter and see whether I should go or not. This Committee deliberated and finally decided that I should go. They came to me and said: 'This is very good. This is an excellent plan. Please go away and leave this present condition.

We have unanimously decided upon this matter.' Then I told them I will not go. Baha'o'llah did not leave, the Bab did not leave and I shall not leave. It is not good for the Cause of God. The well-being of the Cause of God demands My Presence here.[34]

The steamer was offered by the Spanish Consul in Haifa, Escobino, who was a devoted follower of 'Abdu'l-Bahá and the representative of an Italian shipping company.[35]

Into the middle of this situation came a 'recently declared Western believer, innocent, unsuspecting and sporting an Ottoman fez'. And somehow, in spite of all the Commission's spies, he managed to attain the presence of 'Abdu'l-Bahá. This unexpected pilgrim had little deepening or wisdom and wanted to visit all the Holy Places and meet the Master – all before nightfall.[36]

The Master spent an hour with the over-enthusiastic man, then summoned an unexpected guide: a troublesome young man, ostensibly a Bahá'í, but one who associated with Covenant-breakers and had been labelled 'a thug'. When the guide arrived, 'Abdu'l-Bahá told him:

> Take him in the carriage to all the Holy Places . . . You must tell him the name of each place and describe it properly, so that he may perform the rites of pilgrimage. But as you know, the inspectors are lying in wait, so be very careful that no one learns about this . . . Beware, beware, lest anyone find out. Bring him back here before sunset for another visit before he leaves.[37]

The troublemaker accomplished his task without problem and the American departed that night for Europe, 'happy and grateful'. The troublemaker had known that he would be the one in trouble if they had been caught, not the Bahá'ís.[38]

On 15 July, the Commission telegraphed that it had finished its investigations in 'Akká, but four days later sent another telegraph stating that it had discovered things that needed investigating in Haifa.[39] Finally, one night when everyone was 'besieged by fear and agitation', 'Abdu'l-Bahá left the house and walked slowly to the port. He arrived at the city gate and looked out to sea, then he glanced at the Commission's warship and walked home. A short time later, the ship sailed into the gathering darkness with the Commission.[40]

The populace of Haifa watched as the Commission's ship weighed anchor and headed for 'Akká. But as the night fell, the ship's lights suddenly were seen to veer away from 'Akká and out into the open Mediterranean.[41] Within a few days, it was learned that on 21 July, a bomb had been thrown at Sultán 'Abdu'l-Ḥamíd at the Yildiz Mosque in Istanbul. The Sultan escaped uninjured, but 26 others were killed and 58 wounded. The Commission's report was lost in the ensuing chaos.[42] 'Abdu'l-Bahá said the assassination attempt was when the 'cannon of God boomed forth'[43] and also referred to the bomb blast as the 'cannon blast of divine confirmation'.[44]

Shoghi Effendi wrote that all four members of the investigation Committee came to bad ends:

> The four members of the ill-fated Commission of Inquiry, despatched from Constantinople to seal the fate of 'Abdu'l-Bahá, suffered, each in his turn, a humiliation hardly less drastic than that which they had planned for Him. 'Arif Bey, the head of the Commission, seeking stealthily at midnight to flee from the wrath of the Young Turks, was shot dead by a sentry. Adham Bey succeeded in escaping to Egypt, but was robbed of his possessions by his servant on the way, and was in the end compelled to seek financial assistance from the Bahá'ís of Cairo, a request which was not refused. Later he sought help from 'Abdu'l-Bahá, Who immediately directed the believers to present him with a sum on His behalf, an instruction which they were unable to carry out owing to his sudden disappearance. Of the other two members, one was exiled to a remote place, and the other died soon after in abject poverty. The notorious Yaḥyá Bey, the Chief of the Police in 'Akká, a willing and powerful tool in the hand of Mírzá Muḥammad-'Alí, the arch-breaker of Bahá'u'lláh's Covenant, witnessed the frustration of all the hopes he had cherished, lost his position, and had eventually to beg for pecuniary assistance from 'Abdu'l-Bahá. In Constantinople, in the year which witnessed the downfall of 'Abdu'l-Ḥamíd, no less than thirty-one dignitaries of the state, including ministers and other high officers of the government, among whom numbered redoubtable enemies of the Faith, were, in a single day, arrested and condemned to the gallows, a spectacular retribution for the part they had played in upholding a tyrannical regime and in endeavoring to extirpate the Faith and its institutions.[45]

Soon afterwards the pilgrims scattered about in various cities were given permission to return to 'Akká. The threat of banishment to the desert of Libya remained for a while, but then evaporated. The Covenant-breakers' efforts had all failed. Four years previously, Yúnis <u>Kh</u>án had asked 'Abdu'l-Bahá if the Covenant-breakers would continue to thrive in this world. 'What are you saying?' replied the Master. 'They will be finished in four years . . .' 'The attack made on the Ottoman Sultan,' He said in 1905 after the event, 'and consequently his being forced to ignore the report made by the inspectors of the Commission of Enquiry, were both part of the blast of divine confirmation.'[46]

The Commission of Enquiry was mentioned in the report of Drummond Hay, the British Consul at Beirut, on 5 August 1905:

> In the annexed report from Haifa by Mr. P. Abela he mentions that a Commission with an unknown object had arrived from Constantinople composed of Aref Bey, President of the Commercial Court at the Capital, the Farik Shukri Pasha, a Luwa and two Colonels.
>
> I have since learned that they left Acre to return to Constantinople probably by the mail of this week. Their inspection resulted in the suspension of the Mutessarif Ibrahim Sarim Pasha and the dismissal of Colonel Beddri Bey [Badrí Beg] and of the Commandant of the fortress of Acre who is placed under arrest.[47]

Drummond Hay sent another report on 20 September 1905 that read:

> I have the honour to report that the secretary of the Persian Embassy at Constantinople lately visited Acre in connection with the interests of the Persian Babists residing at that place. When the Imperial Ottoman Commission visited Acre last spring as reported to Your Excellency in my despatch No. 50 of August 5th which resulted in the dismissal of the Mutessarif of Acre and other officials they appear to have made enquiries about the Babists and a report became current after their departure that Abbas Effendi and all belonging to his sect would be exiled to Tripoli in Barbary.
>
> I am now informed by the Acting British Vice Consul at Haifa that the Government has come to an understanding with Abbas Effendi and that neither he nor his followers will be molested for the present.[48]

As to Mírzá Muḥammad-'Alí, who instigated all of this, 'Abdu'l-Bahá wrote:

> The Centre of Sedition hath imagined that once the blood of this wronged one is spilled out, once I have been cast away on the wide desert sands or drowned in the Mediterranean Sea – nameless, gone without trace, with none to tell of me – then would he at last have a field where he could urge his steed ahead, and with his mallet of lies and doubts, hit hard at the polo ball of his ambitions, and carry off the prize.
>
> Far from it! For even if the sweet musk-scent of faithfulness should pass, and leave no trace behind, who would be drawn by the stench of perfidy? . . . What an empty supposition is his! What a foolish presumption! 'Their works are like the vapour in a desert which the thirsty dreameth to be water, until when he cometh unto it, he findeth nothing.'[49]

In about 1905, Mason Remey made a design for a curtain to hang at the doorway of Bahá'u'lláh's resting place. The design had a ground work 'in shades of gold silk with white borders across the top and down the sides with a heavy fringe, while in the center panel was a sunburst of nineteen points with the *Greatest Name* in the center, and the ground was embroidered with ninety-five stars'. Madame d'Ange d'Astre, who had been on pilgrimage two years previously, was living in Washington at that time and was an expert with the needle. She 'undertook the execution of this and it came out very well'.[50]

1906

Jane Whyte

Jane Whyte, the wife of Reverend Alexander Whyte, Moderator of the General Assembly of the Free Church of Scotland in Edinburgh, visited 'Abdu'l-Bahá in March. A friend had invited her and her friend, Maryam Thornburgh-Cropper, to go to Egypt for the winter. Maryam had an invitation to visit 'Abdu'l-Bahá in 'Akká, so she and Mrs Whyte travelled to Palestine as well. It was not a safe time to be there and, after only two days, the visitors were forced to depart abruptly. Mrs Whyte did not directly describe the Master, but the effect of meeting Him was obvious:

> The pilgrim to 'Akká is asked many questions on his return. Is this a prophet? A manifestation of divinity? In seeking an answer we must remember how easily, how constantly the East has ever used these names. And we must ask ourselves – what do we recognise as Divine? Is it enough of divinity to see love made perfect through suffering a life-long patience, a faith which no exile or imprisonment can dim, a love which no treachery can alter, a hope which rises a pure clear flame after being drenched by the world's indifference through a lifetime? If that is not Divinity enough for this world, what is? There is no magic here; a material world today is too fond of seeking after magic, no magic but the old magic of Faith, Hope and Love. Or you ask, is this a progressive Movement, a step forward in the history of the world? Surely there can be no question as to the answer, for what do we find here? In the heart of a Turkish country, and at the center of Muhammadan power – that most conservative, cast-iron of systems conserved in a faith which is passionate, fierce, fanatical to the death – there to find preached freedom, education at all costs, absolute equality of men and women, the frank recognition

of the value of Christian truth, the teaching that God has revealed Himself in all faiths, the love of God, and the brotherhood of all nations. What greater sign can you ask than the power to flood this old world with love and aspiration, with patience and courage?[1]

'Abdu'l-Bahá's life, she wrote, 'was in continual danger by any sudden pressure from Constantinople and at that time it was not considered wise the visitors from the West should be too much in evidence.' These two pilgrims had to leave so suddenly that they did not have a last meeting with 'Abdu'l-Bahá, so Mrs Whyte left Him a letter expressing her faith and inviting him to Scotland should He ever travel to the West. The Master responded to both, writing what was to become a well-known Tablet and staying with the Whytes when He visited Edinburgh in 1913. The Tablet, which addressed Mrs Whyte as 'Oh thou who are attracted by the love of God!', contained the 'seven Candles of Unity': political union, harmony of ideas, union of freedom, union of religion, union of nationalities, union of classes and union of one language.

William Jennings Bryan

William Jennings Bryan visited 'Abdu'l-Bahá in 1906. Bryan was an American politician and a devout Christian. He ran, unsuccessfully, for the presidency in 1896, 1900 and 1908. In 1913, he was appointed Secretary of State by President Woodrow Wilson and served for two years. Bryan strongly supported women's suffrage and the prohibition of alcoholic beverages. He was also involved in the infamous Skopes trial in 1925, where he vehemently opposed the teaching of evolution. In 1906, intrigued while travelling in Turkey by reports he heard about 'Abdu'l-Bahá, he went to 'Akká. In June, after his return to America, he wrote a lengthy article about the Turkish government of 'Abdu'l-Hamíd II, which he called 'the worst on earth'. Near the end of the article, he reported his meeting with the Master, including a number of misunderstandings:

> Abbas Effendi, now a political prisoner at Akka, in Palestine, is the head of the reform movement. He was born in Persia, and is carrying on the work to which his father and grandfather devoted their

lives. He discards force as a means of promulgating truth, and while he does not command monogamy, has set the example by having but one wife. While Abbas Effendi's father preached moral persuasion, his followers were charged with revolutionary designs and the family was exiled. After remaining a time in Constantinople under the surveillance of the sultan, the reform leaders were removed to Akka, a seaport not far from Haifa. Here, surrounded by a few followers, the son holds such communication as he can with the rest of the church in Persia, his doctrines having as yet but little root among the Turks and Arabs. It is believed in Akka that he receives financial aid from a number of wealthy Americans who have become interested in his work.

We called upon Abbas Effendi as we were leaving Palestine and found him an earnest old man with a care-worn but kindly face. His hair and beard are gray, and he speaks with animation when his favorite topic is under discussion. His doctrines are something like those of Tolstoi, but he does not carry his doctrine of non-resistance so far as does the Russian philosopher. How much he may be able to do in the way of eliminating the objectionable features of Mohammedism, no one can say, but is a hopeful sign that there is among the followers of Mohamet an organized effort to raise the plane of discussion from brute force to an appeal to intelligence . . .

At Beyrout . . . a copy of the Koran and a copy of the life of Abbas Effendi were taken from me by the censor. I had no objection to his holding them during my stay in the country, but when he informed me that they would have to be sent to Constantinople, I demurred and with the aid of our representative, Consul General Berghois, not only secured the books, but secured the promise that the right of American citizens to carry books would not in the future be interfered with at the court.[2]

Bryan was evidently impressed enough with 'Abdu'l-Bahá to try to make a second visit before returning to America, but was stopped in Haifa by the activities of the Covenant-breakers. In 1912, 'Abdu'l-Bahá attempted to return Bryan's visit by going to his home in Nebraska. The politician, however, was away campaigning for Woodrow Wilson, but the Master was able to visit with his wife and daughter.[3]

Florence and Ali-Kuli Khan

On 7 June, Ali-Kuli and Florence Khan arrived in Haifa with their year-old son, Rahim. Anchoring offshore, their ship was quickly surrounded by small boats vying to carry passengers to the shore. The Khans chose the Cook's boat, 'an enormous deep dory, high at the ends, the largest and safest, manned by eleven rowers', to carry them ashore. One of the rowers was a Bahá'í and to him they entrusted Rahim. On shore, a Turkish official noted the arrival of Khan. Once settled into a 'neat German hotel', they walked up the hill to the Shrine of the Báb. Later that evening, several of the resident believers came to greet them. The next morning, they went to the Master's new house (the present House of the Master on Haparsim Street) where they were greeted by the Greatest Holy Leaf. Florence spent most of her time with the women of the household while Khan was with the men, but when it came time for lunch, Florence was told to join the men. She asked the ladies if they were coming as well, but was told, 'We cannot do these things yet, in these countries.'[4]

On 9 June, they travelled to 'Akká. Since Khan had spent a year as 'Abdu'l-Bahá's secretary, the Master's greeting was effusive: 'Oh Khan, this is increase and blessing. You went to America one and came back three.' He then greeted Florence and said 'Praise be to God that as a result of the Revelation of al-Abhá, the East and West have embraced like unto two beloved ones. You are the first American bride to be united to a Bahá'í from Persia. God praise this great favour.' When Rahim began to get restless, the Master called the child, who toddled over and was content in 'Abdu'l-Bahá's lap.

The Khans were given a large corner room with four windows, two of which looked at the garden and two of which opened to the sea. The next morning, there was a tap at their door. They opened it to find 'Abdu'l-Bahá with a large handkerchief of white roses. 'Give the flowers to Florence Khánum and bring me back the handkerchief,' He said. This answered a long-time prayer of Florence that she would receive a rose from the hand of the Master.[5]

Though 'Abdu'l-Bahá seemed free and unaffected by the world, one just had to look out the window to see the military guard pacing back and forth in front of His house to have a constant reminder that He was, in the material world, still a prisoner.[6]

The Khans stayed in 'Akká for 33 days and Florence was invited by 'Abdu'l-Bahá to sit at the head of the table at every lunch except one, unlike many women who usually ate with the ladies of the household. She also joined the men for the evening meal, though she did not attend the men's evening meetings.

Florence was always amazed to find herself sitting next to 'Abdu'l-Bahá, being seated 'as an honoured guest at the table of Him Who is the King of all the Kings of this world'. At each meal, Bashír, the steward, would bring the food and offer it to the Master. Each time, 'Abdu'l-Bahá gestured that he should serve Florence first. Sometimes He Himself would serve the pilgrims, but usually He had Bashír serve everyone else before Him. After the meal, the Master would educate the pilgrims. One day He spoke about the 'repose of the heart . . . This is a state of true faith, which gives one such confidence, such assurance of God's bounty that the trials and tribulations of all the earth cannot affect him.'[7] On another occasion, Florence asked about the training of children. 'Abdu'l-Bahá said:

> Parents must discover that calling or profession for which their children show the most aptitude and inclination, and then they must train them in the same, by engaging their attention in that direction – for sooner or later, a child will make known his natural abilities and gifts. To train his natural abilities in a manner conflicting with them is not right. It has often been seen that parents have forced their child to study in some field desired by them, for which the child himself had no natural aptitude. Then the child squandered years of his life in that field, making no progress whatever, showing that his abilities lay elsewhere.[8]

Though He was a prisoner, 'Abdu'l-Bahá did not look on it as a limitation, but as a blessing:

> Certain officials in this city have asked me to write out a petition for them to offer higher authorities to obtain my release from this captivity. I told them, 'God forbid that I should write such a thing! This is far from what I would care to do.' This imprisonment is a rest for me. There is no hardship in it . . . When we were in Haifa, we had to endure many troubles. That is, much of our time was

taken up with responsibilities that could not be avoided, such as the encounters with people from outside. But now I rest, and my outside occupations are not even one half what they were. How can I call this a prison?⁹

Florence sometimes put on a *chador* and, completely veiled, would go out into 'Akká. One day she was hurrying across the courtyard to join the other ladies who were waiting for her at the carriage when she heard a voice call 'Khánum!' Through her veil she could see no one. In order to see better, she raised the veil and saw 'Abdu'l-Bahá standing at the top of the stairs. She thought He was calling someone else, but when she started to call for Khan to translate, He waved her on. A short time later, Khan found the Master, still at the top of the stairs, laughing heartily. Later, Florence realized that 'to a man from the East, an American woman, ungainly in her chádur, can be as comical as a Westerner in drag.'¹⁰

Once, however, Florence went out by herself when completely veiled and found herself unrecognized when she wanted to be recognized. On a Friday, when the Master gave coins to the poor, Florence went out veiled looking for Bashír and

> came upon groups of men and women waiting at the great portal. She saw a father with a sick boy, saw the well leading or holding up the ailing, people of all the local nationalities and races, patiently waiting. She walked through the portal to the outer courtyard and came upon an astonishing number of people sitting along the walls. Dozens and dozens of people. There she was, alone among strange beings, terrified that her veil would blow off and disclose her foreign face. She crossed the wide courtyard, all those eyes upon her, reached the outer gate under the tower, and at last saw Bashír with a few men believers to help. He was busy handing out a silver piece to each of the poor. The crowd surged noisily around him and he could not hear Florence's muffled cry, 'Oh Bashír, there you are!' As she pushed toward him the believers who were with him took her for an importunate beggar and someone said, 'Oh Bashír, give her her money and let her pass by.' She almost lifted her veil to protest, but remembered in time, and called out a muffled, 'I am Florence Khánum!' The believers, taking a second look, burst out laughing

and led her safely out of the mob. She stood aside and, terrified, hypnotized, watched the crowd going by. She had been to many parts of the world . . . but had never seen faces like these . . . An earlier witness to these very scenes . . . saw that 'Abdu'l-Bahá's hands were injured by the crowd He served, the backs were scratched and torn.[11]

The Declaration of the Báb, the same day as 'Abdu'l-Bahá's birthday, was celebrated while the Khans were in 'Akká. For some reason, Florence had expected Him to take His birthday off work, but He was up before dawn helping with the preparations for the celebration of the opening of the doors of divine revelation. At the celebration, 'Abdu'l-Bahá greeted about two hundred men guests, then helped serve the platters of food. While others were eating, 'Abdu'l-Bahá said:

> A year ago, on this day, there were great difficulties and great turmoil in 'Akká. However, those times were better than these, for those hardships produced good results for the Cause. Last year this Feast Day could not be celebrated here on account of the troubles, but still, it was better than now, for the very obstacles which stopped the celebration helped to spread the Cause of God.[12]

Though He had been born on this day, 'Abdu'l-Bahá made it abundantly clear that the only celebration should be for the Declaration of the Báb:

> In America the believers have celebrated this day as my birthday – but this day marks the beginnings of the upraised cry, the beginning of the spirit, the beginning of the splendor, of the advent of Bahá'u'lláh. For these must it be celebrated, and for the dawn of unity, which happened on this day, and also because it was celebrated by Bahá'u'lláh, and because He revealed many Tablets in its honor. With exceeding joy must the believers commemorate this day, and to mark it for any other reason whatever is against the Law of God. No Feast Days can be set aside or introduced except those relating to the Blessed Beauty and His Highness the Exalted Báb.
>
> Do you understand what I am saying? For if anything contrary to this be done, the Faith would become similar to those sects which

have so many holidays and feasts that out of three hundred and sixty-five days in the year, some one hundred and eighty are feast days.[13]

Florence was fascinated by many of the people who sat at 'Abdu'l-Bahá's table. Many had been imprisoned for their beliefs and were great teachers of the Faith. But one day, she asked Khan about two strange men:

'Who were those two strangers among the guests at table today?'
'Which ones do you mean?'
'Well, one of them made me think of a hissing serpent – standing on his tail and hissing. And the other made me think of one of those slugs we have at home in America that leave a slimy, glistening trail behind them wherever they go.'
'But this is amazing!' Khan told her. 'How clearly you read them!'
'Who can they be?' she persisted.
'They are two of the Master's half-brothers. As you know, all those half-brothers became the Master's jealous enemies.'
'Then what are they doing at His table?'
'They are in a phase of being forgiven. They have both expressed repentance, and begged to return to Him. He has given them another chance, and been most merciful to them. But they have remained exactly as you see them. They are the same as ever, and none of us knows what will come of it.'[14]

A few years later, the two half-brothers, Badí'u'lláh and Shu'á'u'lláh, had again become the enemies of the Master.

Florence was walking by herself one day near 'Abdu'l-Bahá's house when she saw a woman looking down on her from an open window. The woman was obviously Western. Florence saw in her eyes 'a terrible, concentrated hate'. She was startled by this and even more surprised when she later learned that the woman was a Christian missionary. This may have been the fanatical Mrs Ramsey whom 'Abdu'l-Bahá had confronted three years earlier.[15]

After 33 days, it was time for the Khans to return to America. Before they left, 'Abdu'l-Bahá gave Florence a black agate with the Greatest Name engraved upon it. On the last night, Khan called Florence out onto a dark stone parapet. In a lighted room beyond, they could see the Master pacing back and forth with His white turban pushed slightly back on His head. He was dictating tablets to Munír Zayn. The words flowed from 'Abdu'l-Bahá spontaneously and without hesitation. As Florence watched, she wished that He would pause in the lighted doorway so she could see Him better. He promptly granted her unspoken wish. As He stood there, 'suddenly a dazzling radiance began to burn about Him, growing rapidly so luminous that I was frightened and shrank back'. When she looked again, He was pacing and dictating. Florence again wished He would pause in the doorway and again He did so. And again a brilliant radiance emanated from Him. The Khans retreated to their room.[16]

A huge crowd was there to see them off from 'Akká the next morning, including Mírzá Ḥaydar-'Alí.

Back in Haifa, they spent their last hours with the Master's daughters. Florence and Rúhá Khánum stood together at the window, looking out at the port.

> 'That is the steamer that will carry you away from us tomorrow evening,' she said affectionately.
>
> 'Yes,' answered Florence with sadness.
>
> 'We envy you,' Rúhá Khánum said. 'You American women are free to travel, to see the world. You do not have to veil and live such secluded lives as we women of the East must live.'
>
> 'Would you like to travel and see the world?' asked Florence.
>
> 'Of course,' she answered simply. 'But we must continue to wear the veil until the Muslim women of Persia discard it, such is the command.'[17]

Near evening, the Khans had gone to the Tomb of the Báb for one last visit. On their way back down, Shoghi Effendi suddenly appeared out of the shadows, riding on a donkey. He had gotten permission from his tutor to ride down and say goodbye.[18]

Ali-Kuli Khan had an illustrious career. He was the Persian chargé d'affaires at the Persian Legation in Washington, DC, when 'Abdu'l-Bahá was in America, participated at the Versailles Peace Conference with the Persian delegation after the First World War, was head of the Persian Embassy in Istanbul, the Grand Master of the Court of the Crown Prince of Persia, and the Plenipotentiary to the Five Republics of the Caucasus for Persia.[19] In America, he served on Local Spiritual Assemblies in New York, Washington, DC and Los Angeles and was a member of the National Spiritual Assembly.[20]

Azíz'u'lláh Azízí returns

Azíz'u'lláh Azízí returned to 'Akká a little over two years after his previous pilgrimage.[21] He settled in the Khán-i-'Avámíd Caravanserai, where many of the resident Bahá'ís lived. After a few days, Azízí noticed that 'Abdu'l-Bahá appeared to be sad and very thoughtful, noting that he 'would talk less, and between addresses would pause for an unusually long time'. Azízí wrote:

> It was clear that He was immersed in an ocean of thought. Moreover, signs of grief were so apparent in His pure face, that the friends became heartbroken. For His joy brought upliftment and sparked warmth in the hearts of those near to Him, while his sadness would render His companions disconsolate. No one among the friends, pilgrims or locals, knew the cause.[22]

'Abdu'l-Bahá's grief bothered Mishkín-Qalam, the famous calligrapher. One day, 'with agitation and profound sadness', he told the other Bahá'ís, 'I have made up my mind that, either I will be expelled from His presence this very day and be debarred forever from gazing upon His loving face, or I will take Him out of this tremendous grief and sadness.'

Mishkín-Qalam was not a handsome man. He had delicate features, a not very attractive face, and was nearly beardless, 'having only a few threads on his chin'. He was, however, well-spoken and very humorous, making funny faces while speaking. 'The most stoic of listeners had no choice but to break out in laughter.'[23]

So, one day when 'Abdu'l-Bahá met with the Bahá'ís and pilgrims, Mishkín-Qalam

> very soberly – and without advance permission – stepped forward and with a very earnest expression on his face, started to talk. But what he was saying would make no sense. His words were nonsense – some Persian, some Arabic. His Holiness 'Abdu'l-Bahá was

listening intently to see what he was trying to say, and was unaware that something was going on. Mishkín-Qalam was talking very seriously and in between sentences would tell a joke and make funny faces. Suddenly, losing his composure, 'Abdu'l-Bahá started to laugh out loud. As a result of this display of laughter and happiness, everyone present was affected as well. Still, Mishkín-Qalam was carrying out his plot a little further to the point where everybody lost control and broke out in riotous laughter.[24]

When quiet was finally restored, 'Abdu'l-Bahá praised Mishkín-Qalam because His depressed mood had been removed, though the cause still remained a mystery.

Azízí described the accommodations at the Khán-i-'Avámíd caravansarai. The rooms were on the second floor which had a long, wrap-around balcony. All the rooms had doors that opened onto this balcony. Each room also had another door that opened onto small porches. The Bahá'ís commonly smoked cigarettes or hookahs in the rooms, until 'Abdu'l-Bahá visited one day:

> One day we were sitting in the meeting room. Some were smoking water pipes and would talk about various things. There were a few knocks on the door. The door was opened right away and 'Abdu'l-Bahá entered the room to visit the friends. The room was full of smoke. The Master then walked quietly to the other door, opened it all the way, and stepped out onto the balcony. There He stayed for more than a few minutes. He was gazing at the distant horizon. The door behind Him was still open. Then it dawned on everyone that the door was ajar to clear out the stale air in the room. When 'Abdu'l-Bahá had first entered the room, everyone stood up and removed the water pipes to a corner of the room. And still, everyone was standing, waiting for Him to re-enter the room. After 'Abdu'l-Bahá returned to that place, He made no mention of the foul air there. His greetings to the friends were brief, and He left earlier than was usual. This short visit and lengthy stay on the balcony outside caused the friends to feel shame. Everyone knew that the smoke from the hookahs and the impure air in the room deprived them of the good-pleasure of His company, and from being uplifted by His talks. Everyone there expressed regret. Following this incident,

I went on pilgrimage many more times, but never again saw either Bahá'ís resident there or pilgrims smoking cigarettes or puffing hookahs.[25]

Azízí made at least two more pilgrimages. In 1912, he was able to meet 'Abdu'l-Bahá at Lady Blomfield's home in London and then followed Him around through England and France.[26]

Hooper Harris and Harlan Ober, and others

Other pilgrims who arrived late in the year included Charlotte Bingham, Edith Sanderson and Aline Shane Devine, who reached 'Akká on 13 October; Hooper Harris and Harlan Ober, who came in December; and Maryam Thornburgh-Cropper, who had been on pilgrimage with Phoebe Hearst in 1899, and now came with three others. One of the questions Charlotte, Edith and Aline asked the Master was if it was permissible to pray to 'Abdu'l-Bahá. He replied strongly, 'No, not to Me, but to the Glory of God, Baha O'llah, whose light I reflect.'[27]

Hooper Harris and Harlan Ober came to 'Akká in December on their way to teach the Faith in India at the behest of the Master. As they passed through Egypt, they visited Mírzá Abu'l-Faḍl specifically to ask about teaching in India because of his experience there. The famous scholar, however, refused to give them advice, saying that 'Abdu'l-Bahá would tell them all they needed to know. When his visitors persisted, Mírzá 'Abu'l-Faḍl said, 'When the sun shines, the candles go out.'[28]

Because of the dangers of the time, 'Abdu'l-Bahá instructed Hooper and Harlan to come to 'Akká in a carriage with the window shades drawn, so their trip was one of sounds rather than sights: the swish of the waves as they rode along the beach and the rumble of the wheels as they regained dry land. A peek through a narrow gap in the curtains showed them little more than 'the dim outlines of the great wall' of 'Akká. Then the carriage stopped and a voice carefully spoke the English word 'welcome'. They were escorted to their room out of which they could see soldiers on watch. Laura Barney soon arrived and said that she would be their interpreter. While they chatted, 'Abdu'l-Bahá suddenly appeared. With a warm welcome and a strong embrace, He told them that they had 'arrived at an opportune time, for tonight we are having a feast of farewell for forty pilgrims from Persia and you will be present at that feast'.[29]

As opposed to Julia Grundy, who wrote almost exclusively about the answers 'Abdu'l-Bahá gave to her questions, Hooper wrote only about his feelings after having been in the Master's presence. 'How shall I write so as not to feed the fires of superstition on the one hand, or fail to do justice to the greatness of the subject on the other?'[30] Hooper was trying to communicate what George and Rosa Winterburn called the 'greatest test': how can an apparently ordinary man have so much spiritual power? Like many others, Hooper found the physical description of 'Abdu'l-Bahá the easiest:

> I will try and give you an outer description of the Master. First, it must be remembered, that he is 63 years old and that he has lived a life of imprisonment, of constant anxieties and of hardship. He looks His age. But no sign of physical weakness is apparent; on the contrary He impresses you as being full of strength and energy, an example of splendid manhood at that age. His hair and beard are gray, and the thoughtful lines on his face are in keeping with his years. His beard is not very long nor full, but of silvery, fine quality. His hair which is the same color as the beard, he wears about level with his shoulders. While the hair, like the beard, is inclined to thinness, there is, as I remember, no sign of baldness. His nose is large, slightly aquiline and finely moulded. His mouth is large and firm, but without, in the slightest degree, being hard, indicating a combination of firmness and kindness. His forehead is high, broad and full, giving the impression of great intellectual power. The wonderful thing about the Master's physical personality is his eyes . . . I must confess my inability . . . to tell . . . whether they are black or blue or gray, or a combination of colors, I cannot say. In fact, they seemed to change even as I looked at them and into them, as I did more than once. Of this, however, I am quite certain, that I cannot think of Abdul-Baha, nor say my prayers, without seeing these indescribable eyes, and more than once since I left Acca they have looked love at me in my dreams.[31]

Then Hooper moved beyond the physical and into the spiritual;

> But one tires of physicalities. The important matter is to try to realize the fragrances of the Spirit that are being wafted from that

white spot and from that pure heart. Truly, there is that at Acca which cannot be seen with the physical eye, heard with the physical ear, nor understood with the intellect; a something which the heart can feel and the soul alone apprehend and which cannot be reduced to the physical symbols we call words.

When the Master speaks a something is set in vibration over and above the physical words, a something which is Spirit and Life, and which bestows Spirit and Life; and it would seem that outer words are merely a means of contact, or a physical medium of connection between the soul and this Spirit of Life which is imparted to the soul. That which the soul receptive receives from the words is far more than the mere outer form of the words would seem to warrant. For instance, I asked the Master for the answer to a question which had troubled me for a year or more. He answered me in a few words, without apparently any particular effort at explanation, yet his simple statement conveyed to me immediately an understanding of the whole matter that perfectly satisfied. Perhaps the same words spoken by another would have made no impression, for his answer was a simple statement without proof. Uttered by him, however, they seemed to change the whole current of my thought, create a new consciousness in me, and supply me with the power of comprehension, so that a matter which had puzzled me for more than a year was cleared up in an instant.[32]

Hooper also tackled the problem of how to describe a human being who has spiritual powers:

I would to God that all the people of the world could see and know Abdul-Baha as I saw Him and know him! Then indeed would war, strife and conflict cease, the fire of hell and hatred cease to burn, and peace and good will reign on earth.

But if we write of Abdul-Baha as a personality, as a man, we must describe him as the simplest and most humble and most natural man in all the world. He indulges in no poses, makes no pretensions, asserts no superiority, claims no special privileges and in no way whatever seeks to impress you with his dignity and importance. He will eat with you, walk with you, talk with you, ask about your health, discuss the simplest matters with you, and answer your most trivial questions. In every sense of the word he is natural, and in every sense of the word simple. The physical eye will observe no halo, see no sign of supernatural power, detect nothing, in fact, that might not be noticed in any really good, simple minded and naturally dignified man ... We will find it difficult at first to realize that this simple, dignified, kindly and lovable man is the Centre of a spiritual power, of a knowledge and inspiration which is re-creating the world; and is the object of a love and devotion which no man in the history of the world, except Bahá'u'lláh, his father, ever received in his life-time. And this love and devotion is not confined to his followers, but is seen in those who know nothing of the Religion of which he is the Centre. We will see high Turkish officials (his jailors), Turkish women of high rank, and people of all classes and conditions come to consult him on their most important matters, to seek consolation and advice from him in their domestic troubles and to ask for his prayers. Twice a week we will see the poor gather around him to receive gifts at his hands, their only benefactor, their only real protector, in this prison city of squalor and wretchedness. We will plainly see, even with the physical eye, that there is something in this simple, unpretentious man which causes all around him to lean upon him in all things ... What is it in this man that conquers all who come in contact with him? This man to whom all about him go in their troubles, but who himself, if he has any troubles, never mentions them, except to rejoice over them as victories! ...

... I, whose heart has often seemed to him like a stone, a man hard-headed and combative by nature, accustomed to indulging in plain speech, and in argument to giving and receiving blows, one who has never been regarded as sentimental or emotional – I ... am obliged to confess that my heart melts like wax, that the tears blind my eyes, and that all desire for controversy and argument, except as God may will, is taken out of me. What, I repeat, is the strange power of this man, so simple, so natural, so unassuming, who asks for himself no special consideration or reverence whatever, but continually points us to the things of the spirit and to God? ... There are some things which the heart can comprehend, but the tongue can not utter.[33]

Harlan thought that he understood 'Abdu'l-Bahá's station as the Centre of the Covenant, but witnessing the dictation of a letter and its aftermath convinced him that his understanding had been very shallow. A Bahá'í woman worried about her non-Bahá'í sister's apparent mental imbalance and, to Harlan's surprise, the Master dictated a reply that said that the woman 'should not worry, but that she should become mad like her sister. The disciples in the time of Christ had been considered insane by many people, but while others were engaged in selfish pursuits they were "busy with the affairs of the Kingdom".' He promised to pray for her. By the time Harlan returned to America, the woman's sister was much better and was soon completely recovered.[34]

Hooper and Harlan kept asking when 'Abdu'l-Bahá would tell them what He wanted them to do in India. Finally, He came and said, with Laura Barney translating: 'In India people believe that God is like the sea and man is like a drop in the sea, or that God is like the warp and man is like the woof of this coat. But the Bahá'ís believe that God is like the sun and man is like a mirror facing the sun.' He then began to repeat the statement and when Laura protested that she had already translated it, He said, 'Tell them again.' Then He said, 'Whenever difficult questions or problems come to you, turn your hearts to the heart of 'Abdu'l-Bahá and you will receive help.' When they travelled through India, they did as they had been instructed and their answers often astonished their listeners.[35]

Hooper and Harlan were very active Bahá'ís. After teaching in India, Hooper returned to America, became the chairman of the National Teaching Committee for the northeastern states and served on the Spiritual Assembly of the Bahá'ís of New York until his passing in 1934.[36] Harlan served as president and secretary of the Bahá'í Temple Unity Board and then was a member of the National Spiritual Assembly. In 1956, he pioneered to South Africa where he was appointed an Auxiliary Board member.[37]

Sometime during 1906, Mr and Mrs Osborne, also on their way to teach the Faith in India, visited 'Abdu'l-Bahá. 'Abdu'l-Bahá was under more close scrutiny when they arrived and He apologized, saying, 'I am sorry that it is so that you may not visit the Tomb or go out for exercise. I fear you feel somewhat a prisoner here. These are difficult times for believers to come. Had you not been on your way to India, I would not have granted you permission to come just at this time.' The Master's primary topic for them was imprisonment and freedom:

Outwardly I am a prisoner, considered as one, but no one is as free. I rejoice evermore. Much do I prefer to be absolutely free, at one with GOD, fearing nothing, wanting, desiring nothing, but that all shall know the fullness of GOD, than to possess the material wealth of the world. To be free and yet to possess mind and heart bound to the world and a slave to self, must not, cannot be compared with being a so-called prisoner yet possessing supreme happiness, perfectly sound in mind and body and in loving relation to the universal order.

It is possible to overcome the world, the flesh and all evil by walking constantly in the path of GOD, by burying all negation, weakness, fear, selfishness, and all doubt under a mountain of positive, intense living Truth. Few attain this station.

The more obstacles one has to overcome, the more difficulties one meets successfully, the stronger one will be. Never become discouraged . . .

One may call one's self a Bahai, and in no way live the life, on the other hand one may live the life, and never be known as a Bahai. It is not so much by what name you are called, but what you are in your heart. Are you loving and serving GOD? Love and service are the greatest requisites of a good life. Endeavor in every possible way to do some favour, some service for some one else, do this daily, no matter how small or trivial the act of kindness may be. Even a smile counts for much.

I am the most humble servant of GOD. I would rather be a doormat, a door-keeper in the house of GOD than to be the ruler of nations . . .

I am not bound by the chains of appetite, passion, impulse, custom, creed, fashion, necessities, politics, traditionalism or the animal nature. I am in absolute perfect freedom. My body may be in restraint, I am kept in Acca by law, but my spiritual self is free.[38]

1907

Edwin Woodcock, and Edith and Joseph de Bons

Sometime in late January or early February, Edwin Woodcock, his wife and mother-in-law, Mrs J. C. Chapman, were in Egypt waiting for permission to continue to 'Akká. While there they encountered Dr Joseph de Bons and his wife, Edith (McKay), who had also received permission for pilgrimage. After some consultation, it was decided that Edwin would go to Haifa with them and await his permission there. When the three pilgrims left Port Said, they were joined by Aḥmad Yazdí and Mírzá Núru'd-Dín. Edwin fell ill in Haifa, but through the aid of Dr de Bons he recovered sufficiently so that when permission came from 'Akká they were able to depart together.[1]

Edwin and the de Bons were together when they met the Master on 5 February. Edwin wrote:

> He almost seemed to glide into the apartment, and, as he approached and welcomed me in his gracious manner, I gazed into his great, luminous and kindly loving eyes. He first took my hand and then instantly seemed to enfold me in a loving embrace. I seemed to immediately feel at rest and peace with all the world, although tears, which I could not repress, filled my eyes and I almost sobbed. In fact, it was some minutes before I could regain control of myself. He then sat down on a divan and motioned me to come and sit beside him, which I humbly and gladly did. Holding one of my hands, he entered into a general conversation, through the interpreters, of which I can remember but little, as I was trying to analyse the sensations of joy and gladness which seemed to possess me. Gradually he directed his conversation to me, at the same time throwing one arm over my shoulder. As I nestled more closely against him, and as he spoke of the wondrous love of God, everything for the moment

seemed clear to me, and all doubts that I may have had vanished instantly. I did not need any verbal arguments, or assurances, to convince me that divine love was the ruling and saving force of this world. I experienced it then and there, and the desire to so live as to radiate even a slight reflection of this love to others, was newly born, and, before leaving Acca, became greatly intensified.

During the remainder of my stay, which was cut short owing to my illness, 'The Master' gave us table talks during meals and several times came to my room where such talks continued, and he, seemingly, to answer many unasked questions which I had in my mind.[2]

Edith de Bons, who had made her first pilgrimage in 1901, also described that meeting:

Presently I heard the voice! Oh that voice, so well known, the memory of which had never left me! My feelings were stifling me . . . At last He was before me, speaking words of welcome. I threw myself at His feet and kissed His hands which he stretched out to me in His loving kindness. We passed to our room, where my husband was waiting. The Master came forward, while my husband prostrated himself and the Master embraced him with ineffable kindness; the emotion of the believers was indescribable . . .

February 8th. This morning after breakfast, the Master came for a moment into our room. He spoke of the tests which we would have to face in the Cause, saying: 'God will prove the believers in such a way that those who are not entirely sincere will not be able to stand the tests. A believer is like gold which is tested by fire; the more he is burnt, the more beautiful and pure he will become . . .'

February 9th. Alas, today is the last day! . . . This morning I was permitted to come to the Master's room very early; the family and the servants gathered there for morning prayers. The Master was sitting on the divan in the corner of the room, showing with kindness their place to each new arrival. Being placed almost directly opposite Him, I dared surreptitiously to lift my eyes to His countenance. No words are able to render the beauty, the holy radiance of that unique Being. The eyes especially were extraordinary: now penetrating and as piercing as steel, now of ineffable sweetness . . . Of medium height, the Master's deportment had an extraordinary, superhuman majesty which strikes all those who see Him for the first time. He usually passes suddenly from absolute immobility to the highest point of activity . . . Five years ago I had never heard the Master laugh, though He always smiled when His eyes met mine. But this year He laughed frequently, especially when talking to my husband and Mr. Woodcock.[3]

After being in 'Akká for a few days, Edwin noticed that though 'hemmed in by poverty' and 'restricted by every condition that ignorant humanity can ingeniously devise and contrive', pilgrims came from all over the world for enlightenment. He noted:

These pilgrims are not ignorant and superstitious worshippers – they comprise some of the brightest and most enlightened minds of the world, and the majority of them have passed through the various and highest grades of intellectual and educational accomplishments. They come in the spirit of scepticism, bringing to bear all of their greatest guns and batteries of the accumulated learning of centuries. But when they come within the influence of that powerful, spiritual aura which seems to surround 'The Master' in his lowly prison, their carefully prepared logical shafts of learning and argument fall broken and harmless against the shield of divine truths presented and taught by him, and they become speedily disarmed.[4]

When Edwin left Haifa, he met nine new pilgrims coming from China, India, Japan and other countries.

Corinne and Arna True, and Mary Scaramucci

Later in February 1907, Corinne True and her 16-year-old daughter Arna made their first pilgrimage. Before leaving for the Holy Land, Corinne had been involved in getting people to sign a petition calling for the construction of the House of Worship in Chicago, a Mashriqu'l-Adhkár. Eight hundred signatures had been collected and Corinne's husband, Moses, had glued all the pages together into a long scroll which had been put in a metal tube. Initially, Arthur Agnew was supposed to have delivered the scroll, but when his son fell ill, delaying his pilgrimage, the task was given to Corinne. In addition to the scroll,

VISITING 'ABDU'L-BAHÁ

she also ended up with a large suitcase filled with gifts from American believers for the Master.[5]

Corinne was not a good traveller and was uncomfortable with unknown people and places. In Naples, when all the others had gone ashore, Corinne had remained on board the ship. Changing ships in Alexandria had frightened her when a group of Arabs had scrambled aboard. Her adventurous daughter, however, was a great help on the trip.[6]

They paused briefly in Port Said where Aḥmad Yazdí boarded the ship with the English Bahá'í Mary Scaramucci, who was also on her way to see 'Abdu'l-Bahá. Disembarking at Haifa on 25 February was another traumatic time for Corinne. Ships still had to anchor offshore and passengers had to be ferried to shore in boats rowed by eight to ten Arab oarsmen. But to enter the rowboat required a couple of Arab sailors and good timing, with the small boat rising and falling with the waves. The passengers were first lowered to a small platform from which the sailors would abruptly grab a passenger when the rowboat was at the right position and haul them bodily into the small craft.[7] Finally, the pilgrims were ashore in Haifa.

Corinne and Arna stayed for the first two days at the Hospice of the Little Child below Mount Carmel. After dinner, they received a note from Cook's Travel Bureau in Haifa asking them to walk up the road a few blocks where they would be met. This they did and Corinne described their welcome:

> Such a night as this was; it was full moonlight, the weather was as balmy as May with flowers blooming everywhere! We met our two Bahá'í escorts and they quietly guided us to 'Abdu'l-Bahá's residence where first, as was the Oriental custom, we met a number of Bahá'í men. They questioned us concerning the progress of the Cause in America and of our visit with the Egyptian Bahá'ís who we had seen in Alexandria. In a short while these gentlemen excused themselves in order that we might meet the Ladies of the Holy Household of 'Abdu'l-Bahá. At this time one of the daughters of 'Abdu'l-Bahá, Rúhá Khánum, was living in the Master's Haifa house because the enemies had stirred up fresh trouble for 'Abdu'l-Bahá in Constantinople, causing Him to be re-confined within the old Penal Colony of 'Akká . . .
>
> How thoughtful of our beloved Master to send His wife, the

revered Munírih Khánum, and the little grandson, Shoghi Effendi, together with some other members of His Household, from 'Akká to Haifa to welcome us! Those Bahá'ís of today who may have known the Master as a free man, can scarcely comprehend the emotions of the early pilgrims going to Palestine to visit the World's Greatest Prisoner, who for forty years had been confined in that terrible Penal Colony of 'Akká, drawing not one breath of freedom! Had the local authorities known who we were, our safety might have been in jeopardy. But God mercifully protected us from any harm, and bestowed upon us the boundless favors of His shelter. We were permitted to have six days of indescribable joy associating with the members of 'Abdu'l-Bahá's Household, with His wife and with His family. Words fail to depict to those who read what I write, the emotions of our hearts! Scarcely had our feet walked upon the soil of the sacred Mount of God when we found ourselves the recipients of 'Abdu'l-Bahá's fatherly love and tenderness and were made the associates of His Holy Household. His wife had driven all the way from 'Akká to Haifa to greet us and to extend to us her most cordial welcome.[8]

The next morning, Mary Scaramucci took the excited young Arna on a sight-seeing trip. Soon after their departure, Corinne was taken to the home of Mírzá Asadu'lláh where she met Munírih Khánum and Rúhá Khánum. When Arna returned, Rúhá took them to what would become the Shrine of the Báb. Corinne was impressed with the Tomb, writing:

> Not only is its architecture very remarkable, but its location is positively commanding, built upon the solid rock of the great mountain, very high up from the sea and looking down the main avenue of Haifa, which leads direct to the sea; a stone pier or landing having been built a few years ago for the Emperor of Germany, who visited the Holy Land, entering by way of Haifa because here is a large German settlement . . .
>
> A great interest existed in our hearts to see thoroughly this wonderful Tomb . . . After seeing its massive walls and solid masonry, we did not wonder that the Turkish Government had conceived the idea that The Master was building a great military fort . . . There is quite a flower garden in front of this building and the wife of the

keeper gathered a lovely bunch of red roses and brought them as a gift to us . . . After Rhooah Khanum had explained the inner rooms . . . we came out of the building to find this dear little keeper's wife had placed four chairs in front of the building and was waiting to serve us a cup of Persian tea . . .[9]

Early the next morning, a messenger arrived saying, 'The Master has sent word from 'Akká that the three pilgrims are to hire a carriage and drive around the bay to His prison home in 'Akká.'[10] At 10 o'clock, they boarded a carriage and headed for 'Akká. Anxiety struck Corinne as the horses splashed through the surf, sometimes completely submerging the carriage's wheels. She focused on something the Master had told an earlier pilgrim: 'Love knows no fear.'[11]

Once in the Master's house, Corinne and Arna shared a small room that contained two small beds, straw matting on the floor, a table with a vase of flowers and a wooden bench. From their window, they could see the sea wall and the Mediterranean. They had barely settled into their room when Munavvar Khánum, 'Abdu'l-Bahá's youngest daughter, arrived with roses from her Father. Then He Himself arrived with a bouquet of pink and purple hyacinths, which He divided into three parts, one for each of the new pilgrims. Corinne was overpowered by the Master and instinctively bent her knee and kissed His hand. She then realized that the scene with her daughter and 'Abdu'l-Bahá was the fulfilment of a dream she had after becoming a Bahá'í. Corinne only knew of 'Abdu'l-Bahá's appearance from the photo of Him as a young man and when He entered her room, He looked

> absolutely nothing like the picture in America. Once, when first I came into the knowledge of the Revelation, I dreamed of attaining the great meeting and of bringing one of my daughters. The personage I saw in my dream was not like the picture, so for several years I had fancied it must be Baha'u'llah. To-day, when The Master entered, there was the One whom I had seen in my vision.[12]

Corinne wrote:

> I really was not prepared for such a Manifestation of Power. I expected the Love but pictured Abdul Baha as the Christian does the

meek, humble Nazareen. I found Him to be a powerful Dynamo – a Lion – as well as the Most Majestic Personage I ever hope to see.[13]

Mary Scaramucci's mind went blank when she first met 'Abdu'l-Bahá:

> I, myself, felt so much awe when first entering his presence that I was unable to ask the many things which I had intended; but the questions in my mind have been answered by him in his talks to us all together without my having asked them. This has been the experience of many beside myself. His explanation and knowledge seem to flow endlessly as water from a fountain, and if one leaves Acca with one spiritual hunger and thirst unsatisfied it will be from the unworthiness of one's own soul to receive and not from any limitation of his power of explanation or enlightenment.
>
> I would wish all pilgrims who come here to look for Divine virtue and example and not for any supernatural experiences or astonishing visible signs, and to remember that in looking for the extraordinary or supernatural, the clouds of the human body will most surely veil such from their sight and prevent their eyes from being opened to the true essence of Light and Teaching . . .[14]

On the second day of their pilgrimage, Corinne and Arna were taken into the Master's presence along with the trunk of gifts and the scroll. The scroll Corinne placed behind her while she began to present the gifts from the trunk to 'Abdu'l-Bahá. Suddenly, the Master stood and walked over, picking up the metal container with the scroll, raising it high and pronouncing, 'Mashriqu'l-Adhkár! This . . . this is what gives me great joy. Go back . . . go back and work for the Temple; it is a great work, the best thing you could do, Mrs True.' He then told Corinne that she was His own daughter, 'an event she would never forget. It wasn't the words alone she would remember, but the expression of His total acceptance.'[15]

Though spiritually soaring, Corinne was practical enough to ask what it was that she should do about the House of Worship. 'Abdu'l-Bahá sketched out the design: nine sides, nine avenues radiating outward with gardens and fountains between.[16] The temple was of great importance to the Faith, He told her, and would cause her to suffer and be misunderstood. She would have to pray for the strength to do it.[17]

Being given the

responsibility for the Temple was extremely challenging, particularly as a woman in a country where women did not yet have the opportunity to vote. Because of the marked individualism of those days in the Bahá'í community, there were many 'philosophical' differences. The Bahá'ís of that time were immature in the ways of the Faith and 'Abdu'l-Bahá used Corinne True to begin a transformation of the Bahá'í community . . .

Corinne True wanted a nation-wide committee to develop the Temple plans so that it would not be just Chicago's Temple, but America's (which at that time also included Canadian believers). When 'Abdu'l-Bahá enthusiastically approved of this plan, things moved forward. The next thing 'Abdu'l-Bahá did was send the Americans a Tablet in which He stated that women should be on the new national committee.[18]

The next day, 1 March, was Friday and from her window, she watched 'Abdu'l-Bahá giving help to 'Akká's neediest. There were about 200 desperate people in the courtyard, men, women and children, many clothed in rags, some blind or crippled. One man wore a patched quilt while a woman was dressed in a gunny sack. Corinne watched as the Master passed from one to the next, giving a coin or two plus some encouraging words. Not all received 'Abdu'l-Bahá's munificence. Two men he turned away, twice, because He had told them where to go to find work and they had not done so. He gave to those who needed help, not those who refused to help themselves.[19]

Afterwards, Corinne passed the Master's door and saw Him exhausted on His bed. He called her in and said

'These are my friends; my friends. Some of them are my enemies, but they think I do not know it, because they appear friendly, and to them I am very kind, for one must love his enemies and do good to them.' The Master explained that there really was not work for the poor of Acca, only two avenues being open to them to earn, one by fishing and the other by carrying heavy loads. Yesterday, and for two or three days, the sea has raged madly so that no fishing could be done, and it requires great strength to carry heavy loads. He knows the impostors and will not encourage mendicancy, and as he passes them he rebukes them for laziness and idleness and tells them where they can go to obtain work.[20]

Though Corinne was sailing on a spiritual sea, teenaged Arna was restless. On the fourth day of pilgrimage, 'Abdu'l-Bahá suddenly asked Arna if she was happy. The teenager replied, 'Yes, but not very.' Corinne was aghast, but the Master simply smiled and asked if she would prefer to be with the Persian children of the household. Neither understood the other's language, but that didn't slow the exuberant Arna and she soon had them all, including 10-year-old Shoghi Effendi, who was home from school in Haifa, doing every American game she could remember. One day as Arna and the children played jump rope, the Master came to watch and ended up turning the rope Himself for the delighted children.[21]

Arna became one of the household. One of 'Abdu'l-Bahá's daughters dressed her in Persian clothing, including a veil, and took her thus disguised around 'Akká, even to the mosque. Corinne knew none of this. One day Corinne, who was still a bit uncomfortable in situations where she did not know the language, heard a knock at the door to her room. She opened it to find a veiled Persian girl who she motioned to come in. They sat for a while in, for Corinne, an uncomfortable silence. The girl suddenly laughed and removed her veil, revealing, to her mother's consternation, her own daughter Arna.[22]

Every day Corinne spent considerable time with Munírih Khánum and the Greatest Holy Leaf. She wrote:

> Very early in the mornings we were permitted to meet in the large reception room where the beloved 'Abdu'l-Bahá and His Family would gather together for an hour of communion. The Master would ask different members of the family to chant the Holy Utterances of Bahá'u'lláh and always the motherly presence of Munírih Khánum filled the atmosphere of that room with the benediction of her great mother heart. She seemed the personification of Universal Motherhood – indeed the 'Holy Mother.' When I was standing beside her one morning the dear Master came and placed my hand in hers, and looking into my face said in English: 'She is your Mother.'[23]

After six soul-stirring days, the time came to leave. On the last day, Corinne asked 'Abdu'l-Bahá what He wanted her to do. 'I wish you to live in Chicago. I wish you to work for the Mashriqu'l-Adhkár, and if you do that you must live in Chicago.' Then He took her hand and she felt a great power pulsing through her, a 'most unusual thing', she said.[24]

Separation was very difficult:

> When the hour for leaving this sacred prison home of 'Abdu'l-Bahá came and we had to return to America, it seemed as if our hearts would break to have to say 'good-bye' to these divinely precious members of the Holy Family! We wept, and they wept with us – because of this parting. Through this sacred visit we had found a Heavenly Father in 'Abdu'l-Bahá and a Heavenly Mother in His wife, Munírih Khánum.[25]

Knowing of Corinne's trouble with strangers, the Master told her, 'Mrs True, when you go back I want you to look at every human being and say to yourself, "You are a letter from my Beloved, and I must love you because of the Beloved Who wrote you. The letter may be torn, it may be blurred – but because the Beloved wrote the letter, you must love it."'[26]

After leaving the Holy Land, Corinne wrote:

> We had spent six memorable days under His blessed roof as His guests, and each day we loved it more and more until, when the six days were up, it just seemed as if we could not say good bye and go away from the kind, loving Master, whose very footsteps and tones of voice we had learned to listen for on the stone pavement of the court upon which our room opened. It is a remarkable thing how all these little things weave a golden network of love about the heart, and you forget the world and all its burdens and cares, and think only of the beautiful Master and His Holy Words, every one carrying a marvelous lesson with it which expands and expands in meaning as you apply its heavenly significance to the objects of life. We felt our littleness all the time while there, not because we were made to feel this but because in the Presence of so great a Light our capacity dwindled to a mere atom. Our Lord only tells us how good we are, and how we have served the Cause, and how much He

thinks of us because we are sincere and faithful; but all the time you feel your lips are sealed for some reason.[27]

In March, Richard Brooks and his mother visited the Holy Land. They spent most of their time visiting the Christian holy places, but were one day offered the opportunity to meet 'Abbas Effendi', 'a holy man whose strange religion was beginning to spread into all parts of the world'. Though they looked forward to meeting Abbas Effendi with 'much curiosity', unfortunately, 'Abdu'l-Bahá 'was being examined & questioned by the magistrates, a custom or precaution which took place, we understood, once a year'. It was 'bad luck & a real disappointment'. The visitors did manage to see 'Abdu'l-Bahá's home, 'though we were narrowly watched'. Though Richard was not able to meet 'Abdu'l-Bahá on this visit, he was present in the audience at the City Temple in London in 1911 when the Master gave His first public talk in the West.[28]

Thornton Chase, Arthur and Mary Agnew, and Carl Scheffler

Thornton Chase, Arthur and Mary Agnew, with their young son Ruhullah, and Carl Scheffler, a 17-year-old, arrived in Haifa at 5 p.m. on 8 April. They had joyfully encountered the Trues and Mary Scaramucci in Naples and learned of their experiences.[29] Like all other Haifa ships, theirs anchored well offshore. Thornton Chase watched as a

> fleet of boats came racing toward the ship. They represented different landing Companies, the Hamburg-American, Clark's, Cook's, etc. Each was manned by eight to ten swarthy, sturdy, red-fezzed boatmen handling as many long, heavy, square-handled oars. The race was in earnest, all eager for passengers and backsheesh. As they came nearer, at a signal from the leader of the crew, each rower placed one bare foot on the cross seat before him, leaped up as high as he could, pulled back his oar with a long, powerful sweep, sinking down to his seat, and then sprang up again for another mighty pull, accompanying each effort with a quick, strong call of encouragement: 'Haley! Haley! Haaa! Saleh!' It was an exciting welcome, the crews rising and sinking, the boats lifting through the waves and almost in collision, the stirring cries keeping time and becoming louder and more intense as they approached.

'Cook's' arrived first and took our party to the landing place. When entering the boat the passenger has to submit entirely to the crew. One goes down the slippery steps on the ship's side to the little hanging platform and as the light boat rises on a wave to meet it, one or two of the Arab sailors seizes him (or her) in his arms, holds him as the boat sinks and bears him to a seat.[30]

As they arrived at the dock, they spotted Mírzá Asadu'lláh, and Thornton managed a clandestine handclasp before they were taken to the Hospice of the Little Child. When the pilgrims had settled into the Hospice, Mírzá Asadu'lláh and two other Bahá'ís came and welcomed them, much to the curiosity of the other residents, who spoke both English and Arabic and who were trying to learn what business Americans and Persians had together.

The next morning, they walked up to Mírzá Asadu'lláh's house, passing through the German Templer Colony, some of whose doorways were inscribed, 'Der Herr ist Nahe' (The Lord is near). Later that afternoon, while Thornton was sitting at a table on the hotel veranda, he saw a rainbow that began in Haifa and ended right on the gate of 'Akká. The rainbow lasted for a full half hour, connecting the two cities.[31]

The next morning, the Agnews went to 'Akká and Thornton and Carl moved to the Hotel Pross on the top of Mount Carmel. Several American and English tourist women were also at the hotel and one of them talked about her visit to the 'New Prophet'. She said He was 'a man of striking and attractive appearance'; as they met, 'Abdu'l-Bahá had presented her with a rose. The woman had asked a number of questions 'which he answered in a courteous and gentle manner, and she could see no difference in what he said from the teachings of Jesus'. Another woman, who had not met Him, said 'she had heard that Americans sometimes came all the way there expressly to visit him and receive his teachings and she wondered how they could be such fools. She also supposed they brought much money to him.' Thornton and Carl had a difficult time holding their tongues.[32]

The next day, the pilgrims stumbled down to the Shrine of the Báb on a donkey trail that was 'very steep and all of loose, crumbling stones'. The slope they descended was terraced and cultivated with the fields separated by stone walls. When they reached the Shrine being built by the Master, Thornton described it as a square of brownish yellow limestone with white iron paneled doors, simple in architecture and with little outside ornament. A considerable space was cut out from the side of the mountain and leveled around the tomb. A portion of it is a stone surface in which is the mouth of a large cistern for water. Another portion is a flower garden, beyond which is the house of the caretaker, a Persian Bahá'í. He lives there with his wife and baby and has an Arab assistant.[33]

Then two Bahá'ís from Cairo, Muḥammad 'Alí Yazdí and Ḥájí Muḥammad Schushtari, arrived. They knew no English, but had been told to let Thornton know that a carriage would come for him and Carl the next morning. To tell them, the Egyptians talked with the custodian's wife, who knew a little English, and told them, 'Tomorrow morning, go Acca.'

At 7 a.m. on 12 April the three-horse carriage arrived and they were off to the goal they desired more than anything else. Like most other pilgrims, Thornton added his description of the trip to 'Akká:

> Then began the nine mile drive along the beautiful curve of the Mediterranean shore, most of the way in the water where the sand is hard and the surf plays 'tag' with the carriage wheels, while the horse hoofs clatter and splash a quick tattoo through the gliding water. Higher up the beach are mounds of loose sand with long, wiry bunch grasses and occasional tall date palms. When we crossed the two rivers that run into the sea, we rode out forty or fifty yards from the shore so as to follow the sand bars formed by the breakers as they meet the outflowing rivers. Sometimes the water was up to the box of the carriage and the horses had to strain to pull us through. We passed carriages coming from Acca, pack-trains of asses and camels, flocks of little, black, lop-eared goats, foot travelers, fishing boats and fishermen standing far out in the surf, casting their round nets as their fathers have done for decades of centuries. Ever before us was the walled city, rising clearer and larger from the water by which it is nearly surrounded . . .
>
> When within a half mile of the city lying on the point of land out in the sea, we left the beach and entered a roadway between fine shade trees, leading to the gate in the wall. We passed through the gate into a market place filled with men and animals, and through the inner

gate curving under the second wall, and so into the prison city. Mirza Assadu'llah had left us, and we went on with Cook's driver as tourists do who visit Acca; yet we were probably recognized as Americans and as we entered the city we were greeted with a shower of stones which rattled harmlessly against the carriage. Possibly they were thrown in a spirit of mischief. A rabble of youths and boys ran after us all the way across the city to the entrance of the house of Abdul-Baha. There the driver got down from his seat and drove them away. Our progress had been slow as the three horses filled the ways and crowded the people against the walls, and the turns in the alley like streets were sharp and narrow and made with difficulty.

We did not know we had reached our destination until we saw a Persian gentleman, and then another and another, step out at the entrance and smile at us. We alighted and they conducted us through the arched, red brick entrance to an open court, across it to a long flight of stone steps, broken and ancient, leading to the highest story and into a small walled court open to the sky, where was the upper chamber assigned to us, which adjoined the room of Abdul-Baha. The buildings are all of stone, whitewashed and plastered, and it bears the aspect of a prison.[34]

Thornton then described the setting of the house in which 'Abdu'l-Bahá lived:

Our windows looked out over the garden and tent of Abdul-Baha on the sea side of the house. That garden is bounded on one side by the house of the Governor, which overlooks it, and on another by the inner wall of fortification. A few feet beyond that is the outer wall upon the sea, and between these two are the guns and soldiers constantly on guard. A sentry house stands at one corner of the wall and garden, from which the sentry can see the grounds and the tent where Abdul-Baha meets transient visitors and the officials who often call on him. Thus all his acts outside of the house itself are visible to the Governor from his windows and to the men on guard. Perhaps that is one reason why the officials so often become his friends. No one, with humanity, justice, or mercy in his heart, could watch Abdul-Bahá long without admiring and loving him for the beautiful qualities constantly displayed.

Five days we remained within those walls, prisoners with Him who dwells in that 'Greatest Prison.'[35]

Three Persians who spoke English made them welcome until 'Abdu'l-Bahá arrived: 'he came into the room with a free, striding step, welcomed us in a clear ringing voice – "Mahrhabba! Mahrhabba!" (Welcome! Welcome!).' The Master embraced them 'as would a father his son'. 'Abdu'l-Bahá asked about their health and their trip, then told them to be happy and expressed His own happiness that they were there. Then He left. Thornton and Carl had said nothing more than yes and no, finding it next to impossible to speak, but both were full of joy because they felt that they were 'home'. It was then that Thornton understood what George Winterburn had told him: 'The world seemed miles and centuries away.'[36]

Thus, Thornton Chase, whom 'Abdu'l-Bahá would declare to be the first American Bahá'í, met the Master. And like many before him and many after him, he attempted a pen portrait of the man he had travelled so far to see:

> I saw a strikingly handsome man, tall and kingly. He wore a white fez with the small turban-kerchief wound around. This, the symbol of wisdom and learning among Mohammedans, was the only outward insignia of his station. A long, dark coat or cloak was worn over a dove colored undercoat. He is not thin or anaemic, but has the appearance of strong health. Although of medium height he is commanding in appearance and I can never think of him as less than six feet tall. His bright, fair face, light brown in complexion, was framed in silvery white beard and moustache. Usually his hair, or much of it, was tucked up under the fez. His nose was large, straight and strong. The mouth was rather full and very gentle. Deep under the broad forehead, and shaded by white, thick eyebrows, shone the wondrous eyes, large, prominent, brilliant, penetrating and kind. Around the dark pupil and brown iris is that wonderful blue circle which sometimes makes the eyes look a perfect blue. Any description of them is only an attempt, no more. In repose the face expressed a dignity, intelligence and nobility which none would dare to disrespect. Conscious power and authority were there enthroned. He assumed nothing; his powers were natural, his sincerity thorough,

his affection pure. His smile charmed and attracted friends to him.

He had the stride and freedom of a king – or shepherd. My impression of him was that of a lion, a kingly, masterful Man of the most sweet and generous disposition. I had formed an idea of Jesus as very meek, humble, lowly, gentle, quiet, soft and sweet, and I looked for such another one. I have revised my idea of Jesus and now, as I read his Words, I see in that one of the past a Man of Authority, whose words were clear and forceful, penetrating the hearts as with a two-edged sword. I found in Abdul-Baha a man, strong, powerful, without a thought as to any act, as free and unstilted as a father with his family or a boy with playmates. Yet each movement, his walk, his greeting, his sitting down and rising up were eloquent of power, full of dignity, freedom and ability.

In his presence all are small and they are conscious of this. They show a deference to him that could not be excelled before the most absolute monarch, hesitating to approach him unbidden, humbly bowing when he passes, and halting afar off when coming into his presence. This was not of his doing or will, but purely from their recognition of the Spiritual Power proceeding from him and through their intense love and respect for him. He seemed utterly unconscious of their deference. He extends love to every one; he draws near to them; he invites them; he loves to serve them, even in little things. He demands no awe, no reverence, no separation, but is an elder Brother of affection and sweetness. He is gentle but not weak; sweet and powerful; humble and mighty; no bar of restraint is there, but winsome love and attraction. His work accomplished daily is very great, and yet much time is given to social and official affairs. He is abrupt in manner, the abruptness of power, but most courteous and charming. There is no aloofness in him; he invites all to be prisoners of love and fellow-servers of humanity with him. He spoke in brief, pithy expressions, intoned in medium pitch with a clear vibrant voice. No words were wasted.[37]

Interestingly, Thornton had come to the same conclusion about the reputed meekness of Jesus as had Corinne True.

Mary Agnew, like Corinne, was surprised to discover that 'Abdu'l-Bahá looked nothing like the young man in the photo. She noted,

We have the photographs in America of Abdul-Baha taken when a youth – his hair looks dark, also his eyes and his features somewhat sharp. But when Abdul-Baha came into our room shortly after our arrival, we saw an elderly gentleman with white hair, blue eyes, and a face full of love and tenderness, which far exceeded our expectations, and which bore no likeness to our photograph.

And how could a face full of the expression of Spiritual Life ever be photographed on paper and do credit to GOD'S Love. Impossible! It is to be demonstrated in the Life, both by the Everlasting Words and by His Deeds.

It was really not these outward signs of a physical man that we were to discover and become acquainted with, while in Acca; it was a spirit which before we left, so enveloped us that we discovered we had breathed from Abdul-Baha's Life a new life, and by coming in contact with His Spirit had inhaled a new spirit.

The Spiritual Face of Abdul-Baha was a face which was and will be through all ages to come, one of perfect patience, perfect resignation, and perfect humility before the throne of GOD'S endowments. This Spiritual Face in Acca is that Face severed from all else save GOD.

In that city of Acca in the Life and Heart of Abdul-Baha dwells that wonderful Spirit of GOD'S power that makes the heart of man move by It's flow, for from this Point comes the WORD OF GOD to the world to create within men Eternal Life.

How could one hear a beautiful musical composition without becoming charmed; if the impression is perfect, it will remain with the senses a long time. If this is so with sound, how much greater will it be with a spirit whose soul is listening for a note from the Real Musician who sings but the Words of GOD.[38]

Arthur Agnew described his room in the house of the Master as being 'neat, but very plain and simple' with straw matting on the floor. In the middle was a Persian rug on which stood a table. The room contained two iron bedsteads and a divan covered with white muslin. Hooks in one corner were for hanging clothes, and an iron wash stand with towels occupied the other. Each day, fresh flowers would adorn the table and at night a lamp was lit.[39]

At lunch that first day, there were a dozen at the table including

Arthur, Mary, Carl and Thornton. After the meal, 'Abdu'l-Bahá began talking about the necessity of decomposition, a topic that startled Thornton and Carl because just that morning they had been talking about the crumbling rock and soil on Mount Carmel and how the rock had to decompose before it could be 'transmuted into the higher kingdom of plant life'.

That evening, the American pilgrims gathered in the Agnews' room for a visit of the Master. When 'Abdu'l-Bahá entered He was very tired and sat on the divan, with Carl and Thornton sitting on either side, holding their hands with a 'rapid, strong, vibrating grip' while He talked. 'Abdu'l-Bahá told them that He had been 'sorely tried that day by strangers' and that He was very happy to be in the company of friends.[40]

Arthur Agnew found his expectations scattered after meeting 'Abdu'l-Bahá:

> I cannot say that my ideals were realized in the Holy Presence in that White Spot; in truth it was quite different from my anticipation. The first meeting with Abdul-Baha was like being shaken severely and made to stand up squarely upon my feet; shaken, that is from my preconceived ideas and stood up squarely to lift my head into the sunlight of the Truth of God and take a deep breath of the true atmosphere of the Spirit of God. We met not our ideals but the will of God. His ideas are not our ideas. It is well when we can set aside the ideals born of our own imagination, limited to our imperfect grasp of Truth and take for our own the ideals set before us by one who has the perfect knowledge with which God endows His Manifestation. May all the sincere and earnest people of the world come into oneness of ideal with Baha'o'llah, the Manifestation of God.[41]

The next morning, Sunday, the pilgrims were awakened before dawn by the Muslim call to prayer. A little later, the bells of the Syrian Church called the Christians to do the same. These spiritual sounds were followed by the call of a military coronet, reminding them that they were in a fortified city. At 7 o'clock, they saw Asadu'lláh Kishani sweeping the steps with obvious care, earnestness and pleasure, making it 'evident there that service is esteemed a privilege and is a cause of happiness'. Half an hour later the Americans breakfasted on bread, honey in the comb, eggs and tea. During the morning they watched 'Abdu'l-Bahá's activities. He and Mírzá Asadu'lláh walked back and forth, deep in conversation for a while, then a soldier with his rifle came to deliver a message. At other times, they watched the many visitors, tourists and officials pass in and out of the courtyard. One afternoon, three nuns, a portly woman with no headdress, and several unveiled ladies came to see the Master in His tent.

Later that Sunday morning, the pilgrims were allowed to see the photograph of Bahá'u'lláh. Thornton wrote simply, 'I will not attempt to describe it, nor the solemnity and influence of that visit. No word was spoken. It was a time for silence.'[42]

Thornton wrote that the one great lesson that was impressed on them while they were in 'Akká

> was the waste of time and strength in observing and struggling with the little things, the annoyances, the actions or efforts of opposers, the disagreeables which crowd against us in life. Rather should we look only at the good, strengthen and encourage the good, sure in confidence that the worthless will fade away and that it is powerless against the valuable. To look at things in a larger way than some of us have done; to take our point of view from the mountain of the Holy Spirit, and with full reliance thereon, to devote ourselves to those things which are its servants. Resolved into daily life, this means to overcome evil with good, to heed not personal desires and ambitions, but rather endeavor to serve others, make our lives useful, to serve the good in others and veil the evil in them; to judge not, but, looking keenly for the good, to encourage that good by wise and loving service.
>
> Service is the key to unity, and Unity is the one great theme of the Teacher of Acca. Without unity nothing can be accomplished. As the unity of the world is the aim and purpose of this Bahai Revelation, that unity must begin at home; unity of the few, the assembly, many assemblies, the country, many countries, the world. As the family is the symbol of the home and its peaceful unity, so must the Bahá'í assemblage be the type and foundation of the whole. And unity which is confined to the society or assembly alone is not unity; it must be open armed unity, seeking oneness of will, or purpose and of work with all other groups and assemblies. Each individual

strengthens his individuality, not by maintaining it alone, but, on the contrary, by joining himself, his powers and abilities with others. Thus his own efficiency is enlarged and multiplied by cohesion with others. As a single letter is of small worth compared to its value in a word and greater value in a sentence, so the individual man must enter into combination with all that he possibly can for the strengthening of the Cause of God and humanity, and this means the increased worth of himself.[43]

On their last night in 'Akká, 'Abdu'l-Bahá held a feast of fellowship with all the pilgrims, American and Eastern. About forty people filled the upper balcony room, including the five Americans and about ten Persian pilgrims wearing red fezzes. In addition to the pilgrims, there were 'aged men with white fezzes, green and white turbans, flowing robes, full beards, faces of dignity, sweetness and rare intelligence . . . Many of them were old believers who had passed through the fires of persecution . . .' Mary Agnew was the sole woman, though there were a few children at the table. Thornton suspected that the ladies of the household were nearby and listening, though not seen.[44]

The Master went around the table handing each person a napkin and a plate. With all seated, He said,

It is a good gathering. Thank God that believers are gathered around this table from every part with utmost sincerity, unity and friendship. I beg of God that, as we are gathered in this contingent world around this table, we may also be gathered in the world of the Kingdom and be united. I hope that the gathering together of the believers may be the source of unity and harmony of all the people of the world; that this physical table may be a symbol of the heavenly table.[45]

After dinner, Carl, Arthur and Thornton spoke to the gathering. They were followed by Mírzá Ḥaydar-'Alí, who spoke 'wisely and pleasantly'.

The Americans' pilgrimage, unfortunately, was suddenly cut short when the Governor in Beirut learned of their presence by telegram. Thornton was particularly devastated by this. On the morning of the last day, 16 April, 'Abdu'l-Bahá called each pilgrim for a private interview, telling them that it was best if they departed. He said, 'If you go now it will make it easier and possible for those coming after you to come.'[46]

A devastated Thornton wrote:

> I did not say good-bye. Soon after the noon meal Abdul-Baha met me in the little upper court. He embraced this servant, and, moving away a few feet, he turned, looked steadily and pronounced a promise that is a precious memory and hope. Then he went into the apartments of the household. A little later we were called to go. We descended the old, stone stairway, with friends watching us from the grated windows, crossed the lower court, passed through the archway and out to the carriage awaiting us.
>
> As we entered the world again it was with a sort of chill as when one steps from a warm room into a cold night air. Curious eyes watched us as we rode again through the city, the cramped streets and crooked ways, to the outer gate where we waited for the third horse of the team. There we were surrounded by vendors and beggars calling out the names of the loved one we had left, evidently hoping thus to extract money from us. We had descended from a realm of happiness, peace and light to an underworld of greed and strife. Never before had we so perceived the ignorance and animalism which possesses men, and at first we shrank from them, but when we noted their condition, their sickness, their burdens and griefs, a longing tenderness welled up in our hearts toward them and to all creatures, a great wish to pour out on them the fragrances of peace, good-will and love, to lift them up from darkness to light, from ignorance to knowledge, from hell to heaven – and to serve them, even to extinction of self. The contrast between the world and that 'Prison' we had left was so strong that it intensified the consciousness of that heavenly condition in which we had dwelt during those blessed days and nights.[47]

The American pilgrims softened their departure by visiting both the Shrine of Bahá'u'lláh and the Garden of Riḍván on the way. At the Shrine, each pilgrim entered the inner chamber alone, 'communing with God and remembering the friends far away before the Presence which unmistakably was there. It was the culmination of our pilgrimage.' At the Garden of Riḍván, the gardener, Mírzá Abu'l-Qásim, served them tea beneath the mulberry trees.[48]

Carl Scheffler recalled that 'Mr Chase was so moved by this departure that he spoke no word during the entire journey and not until he again entered the Hospice of the Little Child in Haifa were his tears dried'. It was the last time Thornton Chase was to see 'Abdu'l-Bahá – he passed away on the very day that the Master entered California, his home state, on His epic journey across America in 1912.[49]

Wellesca (Aseyeh) Allen-Dyar

As the Chase group departed through Haifa, they encountered Edith Sanderson who had just arrived for her pilgrimage, and then while passing through Port Said on 19 April they met arriving pilgrims Roy Wilhelm and his mother, Laurie. In addition, in Cairo, they met 'Mrs. Allen and Miss Moore' (Lua Getsinger's sister)[50] who were about to begin their own pilgrimage.

'Aseyeh' Allen became a Bahá'í in 1901 and later married Harrison Dyar. She was reportedly given her name by 'Abdu'l-Bahá.[51] She now found herself to be very happy, so much so that one morning she 'bubbled over,' much to the enjoyment of 'Abdu'l-Bahá. She noted that

> He was able to be to us a loving father, a companion and friend, and we could enjoy ourselves socially because we did not continually keep Him answering questions, at which time He would at once assume a different attitude and a distance would come between us and one would feel His Kingship, His Greatness, the unlimited depths of His Wisdom. He is indeed as a 'well of living water springing up into everlasting life,' and knowledge and wisdom come from His lips as does water from a fountain, giving life to every thirsty heart and all who will may come and take the water of life freely.[52]

She noted that some who came were attracted by the majesty of the Master, but blind to the source of that majesty:

> A visiting Pasha from Damascus, who had lost his position, prevented our dining with the Master, for this Pasha is not a believer, though he loves the Master and comes to see Him for a week at a time. It is strange how those people who live near the Master recognize that He is extraordinary; they come to Him for counsel and

enjoy being in His presence, and yet they seem to be veiled. They are so near to the Light they are dazzled and cannot appreciate it, while we who are far away and maybe never have seen Him personally, have been blessed with a discerning, spiritual sight, and we see the Light which is shining to the uttermost parts of the earth, quickening all mankind into spiritual life, causing an awakening such as will soon move the hearts of all and change this selfish world into a veritable paradise of love, peace, harmony and joy.[53]

Aseyeh was evidently a prolific writer of long letters and one day she showed 'Abdu'l-Bahá a pile of seventeen Tablets He had written to her in response to her questions. She then asked Him, 'Now that you have seen me, do you mean all the beautiful things you said in these Tablets?' He replied saying, 'Part is what you are and part is what I hope you will be.' He then counselled her to 'write briefly, and I will understand the rest'.[54]

One day Aseyeh asked 'Abdu'l-Bahá for two stones, one to be the corner stone and the other to be the keystone of the American House of Worship in Chicago. Just before they left, He sent a block of limestone a foot square and two inches thick, with instructions to cut it in two so it would serve both purposes. Aseyeh even asked the Greatest Holy Leaf to bless the stone, and she 'put her hand on it' and said she 'would pray that the Temple would be completed during the years when our Lord was on this earth'. The stone had originally come from India for use in construction of the Tomb of the Báb.[55] Though Aseyeh carefully guarded the stone, when the temple ground was dedicated by 'Abdu'l-Bahá in 1912, the only stone available was a broken block of limestone contributed with deep devotion by a poor seamstress from Chicago.

After a six-day stay, Miss Moore, Mrs Allen and Edith Sanderson departed.

Roy and Laurie Wilhelm

Roy Wilhelm and his mother, Laurie, reached Haifa on 21 April, arriving in the bay shortly before sunset, but it wasn't until after dark that they had made it to shore and the Hotel Carmel. They had letters of introduction from the Bahá'ís in Port Said, but they learned that the recipients were then in 'Akká. The next morning, they contacted another believer who warmly welcomed them to Haifa.[56] That afternoon, they were to go to the Shrine of the Báb. Roy went early in order to take some photos:

> Upon reaching the Tomb I found only one room open and within were several Persians sitting about a table. They did not understand English, but by tapping my camera and making signs I made my wishes known and received permission to take some pictures.
>
> I saw upon the finger of one of them, a venerable man with flowing white beard, a ring such as is worn by many of the believers. As he was close to me, I whispered in his ear in Arabic the universal Bahá'í greeting; he immediately cried it aloud, and as he grasped me in his arms and kissed me on both cheeks the tears came into his eyes. Then they all crowded round, pressing my hands, and I knew that I was among friends. In the meeting of the West with the East is fulfilled the prophecies of the Books.[57]

The next day, Roy and Laurie received permission to go to 'Akká. Like many other pilgrims, the carriage ride from Haifa to 'Akká was remembered by Roy:

> The smooth hard sand at the edge of the Mediterranean is the road, and as we drove along, the waves would frequently wash up against the horses' feet. The little horses knew that the sand was hardest at the water's edge, and they followed the waves as they washed up and receded, traveling in scallops, as it were. It is a low sandy coast and the outline is broken only by an occasional clump of date palms and tall cactus plants. We passed here and there an Arab on horseback, usually with a long rifle pointing above his shoulder; also a number of natives with their flowing garments girded up into their belts to give greater freedom and to offer less resistance to the wind, which at times blew with considerable force. Above the water line the sand seemed to be constantly shifting into irregular mounds, some of them as much as fifteen or twenty feet in height.[58]

Roy described the arrival in 'Akká in the early afternoon, driving 'through narrow winding streets, the driver cracking his long whip to warn people at the turnings' until they reached a house with an arch and a heavy swinging door. They were immediately welcomed and their baggage carried away. They were helped down from the carriage and stepped into the courtyard 'the end of our seven thousand miles' journey'.

> We passed through a courtyard and up a long flight of stone steps into an upper court from which we were ushered through a dining room into a large square room facing the Mediterranean and overlooking the three crumbling walls that remain of the once strong fortification. Here the welcome was repeated and we now realized that we were guests of 'Abdu'l-Bahá. The young man who had been our escort, after inquiring if we were well and if we had had a pleasant journey, informed us that this would be our room and said he would leave us that we might rest.[59]

An hour later, a young man announced, 'The Master is coming,' and in stepped 'Abdu'l-Bahá, saying 'Welcome! Welcome!' 'Abdu'l-Bahá took Laurie Wilhelm's hand in His own and put his other arm around Roy, again repeating His welcome.

> 'Welcome! Very Welcome! I have been waiting long for your coming. It is with God's help that you have reached 'Akká. Many leave their homes to come to 'Akká but do not arrive. This is a good day; this a good season of the year because it is Spring. The Cause of God is like a tree – its fruit is love . . . Thank God that you came.' We replied: 'We do thank God and hope to become worthy,' and He answered: 'You will become more worthy.'[60]

Roy was immediately struck by the unity between all those present from different backgrounds and countries:

> That which most impresses the pilgrim to the 'Most Great Prison,' at 'Akká, is the spirit of sacrifice. Nowhere have I witnessed such love, such perfect harmony. The desire of those in that prison is to serve one another. In our western liberty it is difficult to realize the bitter antagonism and hatred which exists in the East between the followers of the several great religious systems. For example, a Jew and a Muḥammadan would refuse to sit at meat together; a

Hindu to draw water from the well of either. Yet, in the house of 'Abdu'l-Bahá we found Christians, Jews, Muḥammadans, Zoroastrians, Hindus, blending together as children of the one God, living in perfect love and harmony . . .

At the house of 'Abdu'l-Bahá, in 'Akká, we met many of these peoples, but they had lost all trace of discord and hatred which has been inbred and cultivated for centuries, and now they are as members of one Household. They sacrifice their lives for one another. To what shall we attribute this miracle of unity?[61]

Roy and his mother stayed in 'Akká for six days with a number of other pilgrims. During their last meal with 'Abdu'l-Bahá, the Master broke bread into His bowl, then served a portion to each pilgrim. When dinner was finished, He told them, 'I have given you to eat from My bowl – now distribute My Bread among the people.' Finally leaving the Master's presence, they were taken to the Shrine of Bahá'u'lláh where the gardener filled their arms with roses and carnations. From there, the party went to the Garden of Riḍván and Abu'l-Qásim, the gardener, gave them more flowers. Three days later they left Haifa, visited Jerusalem and Bethlehem, then sailed to Port Said and, at the request of 'Abdu'l-Bahá, to Paris and London via Italy and Switzerland.[62]

In 1922, immediately after Shoghi Effendi became the Guardian, Roy was one of those called to Haifa for consultations. After his death in 1951, he was named a Hand of the Cause.

Mason Remey and Frances Phelps

Mason Remey, making his second pilgrimage, and Frances (Frank) Phelps, from Washington DC, arrived in Beirut on 6 July, but due to illness on board their ship, they had to go through quarantine and have their clothes fumigated. It was quite an ordeal according to Frances:

> . . .we got ashore with our baggage and climbed up the hill to the fumigation plant. This was a great experience, we had to take off all our clothes and our under clothes were wrapped up in old bags and put into a large cylinder to be steamed for half an hour. We were given gowns to wear while this was being done. We were all huddled there together, arabs and all classes of people and you can

imagine what our clothes looked like when they came out, with the dirty smell and then the scramble to find our own. I was pulling and hauling at an arabs clothes [sic] thinking they were mine, but he was stronger than me so he picked them up and took them elsewhere and then I looked a little further and found mine in a mess. I put my other clothes on without them and after we secured a room Mr R and I washed them all out. This was very fortunate that they had running water. I thought sure the clothes I was claiming were mine, but it was hard for any one to tell from the looks of them. The only way I could tell was by the belt that I wore. They all smelled and looked alike.[63]

Mason and Frances had left Mr Wells, a travelling companion as far as Beirut, watching the baggage. An Egyptian Bahá'í who had been with them on the boat encountered Mr Wells and through some conversation with the men running the fumigation facility and the exchange of some coins, Mr Wells was able to avoid the fumigation. Later, Zia Bagdadi treated them to ice cream of 'assorted colors and tastes'.[64]

Mason and Frances arrived in Haifa at 6:30 on the morning of 10 July. They had arranged for the Cook's travel agency to get them ashore, which cost them $1.25 each, but saved the trouble and confusion of bickering with the rowboat owners. Being with Cook's also allowed them to pass through Customs without having their baggage examined. The two men stayed in the Hotel Carmel that night.[65]

On 11 July, Frances walked up to the Shrine of the Báb, where he met Mírzá Núru'd-Dín, one of 'Abdu'l-Bahá's English-speaking interpreters. At that moment, Mírzá Núru'd-Dín was translating a Tablet to the Assembly in Washington and he asked Frances to check the spelling of the names. Mírzá Núru'd-Dín took Frances into an outer room of the Shrine where they talked about the Faith, then took him reverently into the inner chamber.[66]

The next day, Mason and Frances went to 'Akká, but were only allowed to stay for a few hours because of the dangerous conditions. Mason was initially disappointed because he had hoped for a full nine days, but even this short visit had been difficult to arrange.[67] About fifteen minutes after being shown to their room, 'Abdu'l-Bahá entered. Mason was closest to the door and therefore was the first to greet the Master, kneeling at His feet before being raised up and embraced and kissed. Frances was likewise embraced and kissed. After a few minutes, He left. Later, the Master came and escorted them to the midday meal and gave Frances the bounty of sitting next to Him. There were a dozen people there to eat and the meal consisted of 'soup, meat, potatoes, pilau and watermelon'. After the meal, Frances took nine watermelon seeds from the Master's plate to take home. Later, 'Abdu'l-Bahá spent two hours with them in their room talking about the American believers.[68]

Mason noted that 'Abdu'l-Bahá ate in the Persian manner, with His fingers. The Master told him that 'In the East there are many peoples who never use a knife or fork. To eat with their fingers is the custom . . . We must each view with respect the customs of the other.' He then added that spiritual food required neither knives, forks or fingers and brought peace and contentment. Another pilgrim asked why 'Abdu'l-Bahá didn't say Grace or a thanksgiving before meals. He replied that His heart was always in a state of thanksgiving, adding that in many cases, Grace was said solely with the lips while the hearts were 'far from thanksgiving'. He later gave Mason Bahá'u'lláh's prayer 'O My God! Make Thy Beauty to be my food . . .' as a Grace for Americans.[69]

Mary Hanford Ford

Mary Hanford Ford made her first pilgrimage in 1907, possibly later in the year, five years after she had become a Bahá'í. She arrived blithely unaware of the dangers 'Abdu'l-Bahá faced or the increased persecution at that time, or that for several years He had been confined to 'Akká, denied even the opportunity to visit His Father's tomb at Bahjí.

Mary was particularly worried about how she would react when she met 'Abdu'l-Bahá. She had heard about the extreme emotional experiences of others, how some had fainted while others had fallen at His feet weeping uncontrollably. She wanted to avoid 'such calamitous exhibitions'. 'I decided when I came into the presence of 'Abdu'l-Bahá, if my lips began to tremble and my knees to shake, I would mentally repeat the little word Iron and become unimpressionable as its black substance.' So, when the Master appeared in the doorway and her knees began to quiver, she

> gazed upon Him, squaring my shoulders, while my mind fastened itself purely upon the black little word Iron, Iron! Can I ever forget

how He looked at me with laughing eyes, and began to relate all the tortuous journey that had brought me to 'Akká, meeting plague and quarantine at every port, and pouring out the contents of my thin pocket book, until it seemed as if nothing would be left in it if I ever reached the bleak walls of the ancient town.

He laughed at me saying: 'Many people come here in a gala journey. They stop at the best hotels. They come here when they have nothing to fear, they travel in a company of friends and are a gay crowd! They do not realize they are on a pilgrimage to a holy place – and that they must pray much before they can understand it. If they do not pray before arriving, they must pray after they come here, but you have been forced to pray for guidance during the entire route, and so you are filled with the sense of prayer. You have lived and attained only through prayer.'[70]

'Abdu'l-Bahá continued telling amusing stories until Mary's knees had stopped quivering and she felt at peace. But then, into this tranquillity came the feeling that she could never ask this centre of wisdom and love a question. She wondered how could she get answers if she couldn't ask the questions? And one question burned in her mind. When she had been in Paris en route to 'Akká, she had heard from the Bahá'ís there about the most recent martyrdoms in Iran in searingly gruesome detail. Finally, she had been unable to take any more of the horror and she blurted out, 'but don't you realize that the blessed martyrs are in a state of bliss from the moment the torture begins, and feel none of the pain inflicted upon them?' The group instantly reproached her saying, 'How dare you say such things! You are taking away all the glory of martyrdom!'

This question was in Mary's mind, but she never asked it. That first morning when the Master had come into her room, He paced back and forth, then started speaking:

'There are many kinds of martyrdom. How many times have I prayed for it, but instead of that I have lived on in prison as if with the sword of Damocles suspended by a hair over my head! Each morning as I waken I feel that before the day ends I may be dragged to the public square and shot to death. But nevertheless I have been very happy in this long martyrdom, for no victim suffers from the cruelties inflicted upon him. The instant the torture begins he is in a state of bliss, and feels nothing but the joy of Heaven which surrounds him.'

He paused, looking out through the wide windows at the blue Mediterranean, the view of which beyond the huge walls seemed to eliminate their imprisoning power. Then he added: 'So Christ never suffered upon the cross. From the time the crucifixion began His soul was in Heaven and He felt nothing but the Divine Presence.'[71]

Describing the house where she and the family of 'Abdu'l-Bahá lived, Mary noted that it had a little gallery that ran all around the second story onto which each room opened. Strangely, every door was painted a different colour. There were pink, yellow, green and white doors. When she asked why this was, she was told that it was because the family never had enough money to buy paint for more than one door at a time. Her room had a narrow iron bed on a floor covered with matting. There was an iron wash stand with holes for a bowl and a pitcher that were rat-proof. There was also a divan that the Master would sit on. In addition to its simplicity, everything was 'scrupulously clean, and there was an abundant supply of sparkling water for bathing and drinking.' Her window looked over the city wall at the blue Mediterranean.[72]

Mary spent much of her time with 'the ladies of the household' and they made a deep impression on her.

> They make all their own simple wearing apparel, by the aid of a sewing machine from the western world. They oversee the production of the kitchen for their many guests and are thoroughly hygienic in the cleanliness of their environment. They typify the modern saint, the conception of whom obliges us to revolutionize our entire spiritual cosmogony. A fashionable woman of the western world, as helpless as are some of these artificial dames, and so eager for spiritual culture, was caught in the gentle household without a trunk, and so handsomely garbed that she felt disgraced in the presence of the lovely simplicity that reigns there. The Greatest Holy Leaf thereupon made her a print dress with her own beautiful hands, which was a model for grace and adjustment. The western woman is still puzzling perhaps over the problem of how such profound spirituality can be associated with such excellent practical skill and sense, but in reality they are always found side by side.[73]

1907

One day, some of the pilgrims decided to make a ceremony out of the ablutions taking place at 'Abdu'l-Bahá's reception of the pilgrims. They had a young boy carry in a beautiful and highly-polished pewter bowl, with a bronze pitcher and a clean damask towel, scented with attar of rose. Their intention was to make a noble ceremony that all could enjoy. However, the moment 'Abdu'l-Bahá saw the advancing procession, He crossed to the water trough with a pipe for watering the flowers of the garden. There He did His ablutions, using the much-used towel that hung nearby. Then He 'rushed back to love the dusty pilgrims, and pass them most hospitably the beautiful pewter bowl, and the rose scented towel. So there was no function except the spiritual meeting which he always delights in, and he had the pleasure of seeing others enjoy the pretty bowl, the clear water, and the fragrant towel.'[74]

Mary's most memorable times with 'Abdu'l-Bahá were when He talked about the economic future of the world and the effect on 'permanent unemployment' of the increasing use of labour-saving devices, which in 1907, were beginning to make an appearance. Years later, she reported that the Master had said:

> 'Today the dynamic energy of the Holy Spirit has poured in such volume through the Messenger of God that even the masses of men have received it, and that was not possible before. Always in the past specially sensitized souls received the influence and acted upon it. But today for the first time the minds of all people have been touched by the spirit, and the result is that the designs of labor saving machines have been clearly revealed to them. It may seem strange to you that the Holy Spirit should give designs for labor saving machines . . . but in reality every creative impulse of the brain can arise only through contact with the spirit. Without that the brain is merely capable of conventional and traditional action.'

> 'The civilizations of the past have all been founded upon the enslavement of mankind and the poor working class has suffered every oppression for the sake of the enrichment of the few. This limited wealthy class has alone had the privilege of developing individuality. The down trodden worker after laboring long hours each day, has not had sufficient mental capacity at the conclusion of his task to do anything but eat and sleep.'

> 'That all mankind might have opportunity, it was necessary to

shorten the hours of labor so that the work of the world could be completed without such demand of strain and effort, and all human beings would have leisure to think and develop individual capacity.'

'The labor saving machines were given to create leisure for all mankind.' 'Abdu'l-Bahá repeated this several times. He was so deeply impressed with this fact that as He spoke He arose and walked back and forth in the little room, His face and eyes shining with joy over the happy future into which He gazed.

'The first decided shortening of the hours will appear,' He declared, 'when a legal working day of eight hours is established,' and this of course took place in 1917 when Woodrow Wilson enacted the legal day of eight hours for all federal workers, and really for the workers of the United States.

'But this working day of eight hours is only the beginning,' went on 'Abdu'l-Bahá. 'Soon there will be a six hour day, a five hour, a three hour day, even less than that, and the worker must be paid more for this management of machines, than he ever received for the exercise of his two hands alone.'

Speaking in 1907, 'Abdu'l-Bahá said, 'You cannot understand now, how the labor saving machines can produce leisure for mankind because at present they are all in the hands of the financiers and are used only to increase profits, but that will not continue. The workers will come into their due benefit from the machine that is the divine intention, and one cannot continue to violate the law of God. So with the assurance of a comfortable income from his work, and ample leisure for each one, poverty will be banished and each community will create comfort and opportunity for its citizens. Education will then be universal at the cost of the state, and no person will be deprived of its opportunity.' All these eloquent words and many others which I have not time to note here, were spoken to me by 'Abdu'l-Bahá without the asking of a single question. His utterance, as always, was directed toward the inner urge of the mind He addressed, and He was perfectly aware that the mentality seeking Him at the moment was deeply interested in the problem of banishing poverty.[75]

Whenever Mary sat with 'Abdu'l-Bahá, she commonly felt a growing lightness of body. When this happened on one day, she thought to herself, 'if He stays much longer, I shall not be able to keep my feet on the floor, I shall float up to the ceiling!' The Master then left abruptly 'with that rapid gliding movement which made one feel He was flying rather than walking'. This happened again on the last day of her pilgrimage. As He left, she thought, 'I have been here, I have seen Him, and everything is just as I knew it would be.' At that moment, 'Abdu'l-Bahá paused on the threshold, looked back at her 'with His eyes full of laughter' and said, 'You have been here, you have seen me and everything is just as you knew it would be.'[76]

As she was leaving 'Akká and speaking to 'Abdu'l-Bahá for the last time, she was struck by emotion and cried out, 'O 'Abdu'l-Bahá! Why cannot all the world come here to see You as I have done and receive this understanding of life and its meaning, this light of the Spirit!' He looked at her sadly and replied,

> 'Dearly beloved, many people cross the ocean and cross the desert and come here to see me. They stay sometimes a week – a month – a year and then they go away. They have not seen me at all.' He paused a moment with a far away look in His eyes and added, smiling as He took my hands – 'It is better to meet me in the worlds of love!'[77]

After returning home, Mary wrote in her book *The Oriental Rose*:

> All the travelers have come back like pilgrims of a new hope, bubbling and overflowing with the ideas, impressions and suggestions drawn from their visit to this inspiring spiritual center, and their contact with Abdul Baha. Each has illustrated the reply given by the Servant of God to the questioner who asked him: 'Why do all the guests who visit you come away with shining countenances?'
>
> He said with his beautiful smile; 'I cannot tell you, but in all those upon whom I look, I see only my Father's Face.'[78]

Mary became a well-travelled Bahá'í speaker in both America and Europe, and contributed many articles to *Star of the West*.

Other visitors

Another pilgrim, who was there that year at the same time as a group of women from Ashkabat, wrote:

> Outside the sea is raging and the wind howling, which it has done since we came – and it is as if this were to show us the perfect contrast of Serenity and Gentleness in the spiritual atmosphere of The Master's Home.
>
> Our Beloved Master holds in this home an absolute reign of Love and Peace, and those who visit here can but realize more and more that they must help in sending out over the different countries to which they return the rays of that love, kindness and courtesy.
>
> I, myself, felt so much awe when first entering His presence that I was unable to ask the many things which I had intended; but the questions in my mind have been answered by Him in His talks to us all together without my having asked them.[79]

Mason Remey wrote that some pilgrims in 1907 sought to extend their stay by proposing to dine with 'Abdu'l-Bahá in the name of a different person each day. When they proposed dining one night in the name of the Council Board of Chicago, 'Abdu'l-Bahá replied, 'Not only in remembrance of the Council Board but also of all the believers.' When asked if He would soon visit America, the Master said no because His enemies would claim that he had fled. 'Then he said in English, "Very well", and was so happy that He repeated it in French, "Très bien", in Italian . . . and in Turkish, Persian and Arabic.'[80]

Troubles and the threat of exile

In 1914 'Abdu'l Bahá related a story about the schemings of the Mutasarrif of 'Akká, that may have taken place about 1907. The Mutasarrif, Abdu'r-Raḥman Páshá, continually tried to find a way to punish or exile the Master.

> One evening he [the Motosarraf] called upon the Mofti, and told him he had received a cablegram from the Sublime Porte which stated that Abbas Effendi's power had become so paramount in Acca

that the influence of the local authorities had been negligible. Therefore some practical steps must be taken to stop the further spread of his power. The first thing to be done the next day would be to close the shops of all the Persians, arrest them and throw them into prison; then arrest Abbas Effendi himself. In short, he boasted of the many dire punishments that he would mete out to us on the morrow. That very night I was invited to the house of Beem-Bashi, and while I was there they brought this – what they termed distressing news. They were very much agitated, and wished me to send a cablegram to the Governor-General begging him to withdraw his threatened orders. I told them this was quite impossible; that they should not be worried, and that God knows best how to deal with these treacherous people . . .

Early in the morning, we heard someone knocking at the door of the house, and the Telegraph Manager was ushered into my room, with beaming face. 'What is the news?' I asked. 'I have just received a telegram,' he answered, 'from the Governor-General, deposing the Motosarraf, stating that a Commissioner is on his way to investigate his affairs and kiss the hand of Abbas Effendi.'

On the other hand, Adbor-Rahman Pasha left his house very early and taking with him several guards went to the bazaar and stood in a corner. He was waiting for the time the believers would open their stores, that he might order their arrest. While he was thus waiting never realizing that his doom was already sealed, the Mofti passed by. No sooner did he see him than he flew off in a rage, flared up and stormed. 'What is this secret?' he cried out. 'I hear that the Manager of the telegraph office has called on Abbas Effendi early this morning, and that thou hast called at the house of the Judge, at an unusual hour . . . What is this intrigue and conspiracy?' The Mofti said, 'Your Excellency! There is no plot. Only I hope, God willing, you will be promoted to a higher Government position.' 'Oh!' the Motosarraf cried out in astonishment, understanding his situation. Cowering and cringing with fear, he beckoned to his guards to leave the market, and hurried back to his home. Thus in this miraculous way he was defeated . . . That evening I was walking in the street and I saw a tall man covered with a counterpane and a shawl was wound over it . . . When I approached him I was surprised to see the Motosarraf in this fantastic disguise . . . When he saw me, he began to plead and implore in order that I might . . . mediate in his behalf. 'You are the only person in the world,' he said, 'who does not dream of any retaliation, but these many persons to whom I have done evil, now that they have heard I am deposed, will do their utmost to vilify my character and ruin my reputation. You are forgiving. I beg you to come to my assistance!' All the friends know how well I treated him, and he left Acca very happy.[81]

Marion Jack was in 'Akká late in 1907 and wrote about the efforts of the Mutasarrif to enrich himself. She wrote that one day 'Abdu'l-Bahá

> received the beautifully clad deputy of the Governor General of Syria who offered him a much greater liberty than he had hitherto enjoyed in return for a big sum demanded of him. From the window of the room of the Greatest Holy Leaf we saw the Beloved gesticulating vehemently so when he came upstairs a little later we asked what had been the matter since the Master was always so calm and poised. He told us saying, 'I told him the Governor could do as he liked with me, but that I never either gave or received bribes.' This took place near the end of my stay when the whole town was alive with drastic rumours as to what should be the fate of the Beloved. They said that he should be taken and hanged at the gates of the city or taken to sea and drowned or other horrible things should be done to him, least of which was a further exile, probably to Tripoli where [we] should have to travel on the backs of camels.[82]

In the winter of 1907/1908, 'Abdu'l-Bahá was subjected to another investigation of some sort. Mírzá Munír Zayn wrote to Thornton Chase in March 1908: "'Abdu'l-Baha is in great danger; a commission has come to Akka. 'Abdu'l-Baha has never been so calm, though. All pilgrims have been sent home'.[83] Marion Jack wrote about the tension amongst the Bahá'ís during that time and the Master's efforts to cheer everyone up: 'The Master . . . was even more gay than usual at this time . . . He used to frequently make jokes or tell funny stories at this time to cheer them up. He certainly was indifferent himself as to these threats.'[84]

One month before Mary Hanford Ford arrived, the Muhammadan priesthood, frustrated at their continued failure to rid themselves of the magnetic Presence in their midst, had sent the police to the Master's house, 'commanding every guest to leave the place instantly, and forbade 'Abdu'l-Bahá to receive any western friends henceforth'. A special committee drew up a questionnaire.

> According to its plan if 'Abdu'l-Bahá filled out the questionnaire His answers would be so incriminating, that there could be no difficulty in obtaining the Sultan's signature for His death sentence. All the danger threats were in the background of my rendezvous with 'Abdu'l-Bahá, but I knew nothing of them.[85]

'Abdu'l-Bahá ignored the questionnaire.

Mírzá Ḥaydar-'Alí told a story about Mírzá Badí'u'lláh that may have happened during this time:

> Mírzá Badí'u'lláh gave a promissory note of 1200 liras to Yahya Bey, the Damascene, known as Tabur Aqasi, for him to arrange 'Abdu'l-Bahá's exile to Fizan [Fezzan, Libya]. However, after their plans fell apart. Yahya Bey enforced the payment of the note. Mírzá Badí'u'lláh was compelled to sell two pieces of land for six hundred liras and to sell the ownership of one-third of the Mansion of Bahjí to Tabur Aqasi for the remainder of the debt.[86]

One of the Bahá'ís noted that a few years later 'Abdu'l-Bahá 'travelled with the utmost majesty to Europe and America to demonstrate that "God is the best of plotters".'[87]

There were many rumours during this time that 'Abdu'l-Bahá was to be exiled to the Fezzan and these were not exaggerated. Proof that this threat of exile had been real came in 1914 when the former Governor of Tripoli, who was then the Governor-General of Beirut, visited 'Abdu'l-Bahá. During their conversation, he told the Master that in 1907 he had received a telegram from Sultan 'Abdu'l-Ḥamíd informing him that 'Abdu'l-Bahá would be arriving in just a few days on His way to exile in Fezzan, deep in the Sahara. The Sultan told him to be ready to take Him to Fezzan with a strong escort of horsemen. The Governor waited, but the only thing that happened was the Sultan being forced by the Young Turks to reinstate the Constitution and form a Parliament, which greatly reduced his power. Exile was forgotten.[88]

During this time of trouble, a number of pilgrims were in Egypt waiting for permission to come to Haifa, a permission which did not come. After waiting for two months, 'Abdu'l-Bahá sent word that they should return home. But not all was gloom in 'Akká. At the height of the tension and danger, 'Abdu'l-Bahá performed a marriage between Mírzá Enayatu'lláh and Zia Khánum, a descendant of both the King of the Martyrs, Mírzá Muḥammad-Ḥasan, and the Beloved of the Martyrs, Mírzá Muḥammad-Ḥusayn. Commenting on the event, 'Abdu'l-Bahá said, 'When in trouble we shall have our marriage, for in time of trouble do we Bahá'ís have our peace.'[89]

1908

Helen Goodall, Ella Cooper and Marion Jack

At noon on 4 January, Helen Goodall and her daughter, Ella Cooper, arrived in 'Akká from California. After their carriage pulled up, Munír Zayn and another believer silently escorted them through the narrow streets until they reached the gate of 'Abdu'l-Bahá's house, where they were met by Mírzá Asadu'lláh and others and conducted to their third-storey room. 'Abdu'l-Bahá quickly arrived, 'the joyous ring of His voice reaching us even before we saw Him, calling, "Welcome! Welcome! I am glad you are here!" and adding to His warm, strong handclasp the greater welcome of His wonderful eyes and heavenly smile.' The first thing He asked about were the believers in America. Then He asked about their journey saying, 'Those who go in search of the North Pole count as nothing the hardships endured, and although you have come here in the winter when it is cold and the way a little difficult, yet you count the journey as nothing. Those having this Visit as their goal will bear hardship for the sake of attaining.'[1]

The two women noted:

> One can only feel but never hope to describe the spiritual atmosphere which surrounds Abdul-Baha and the members of His Holy Household. The favored visitor is so quickly enveloped in this subtle Harmony that he is conscious of living in a new element, of breathing a different air from that of the outside world, of being immersed in a perfect Ocean of Divine Love which submerges all his human selfishness for the time being, calling forth and sustaining every spiritual quality of which he is possessed . . .
>
> Although each individual, from the youngest servant to the Greatest Holy Leaf, is constantly on guard, no parade is made of their watchfulness. Not even the creak of a distant door or a strange footfall escapes their attentive ears, yet the visitor is never reminded

that he is the cause of anxiety. When it becomes necessary to move the whole supper table suddenly into another room to escape the observation of the Turkish callers, it is done with a quiet smile and no hint of inconvenience. How obvious and easy it would be to impress the sensitive pilgrim with their daily martyrdom and the constant strain of their precarious position. That they do just the contrary is another lesson to us!

Were it not for the close proximity of the barracks and its guards, one would never realize that he was visiting a Turkish prison . . .

Every day Abdul-Baha came to our door and called us to His table, which was bountifully spread with material and spiritual food, saying in English, 'Come here, come here, sit down, sit down. How are you – very well?' and when we answered, 'We are very well,' He said in Persian, 'Very good, very good; it makes me happy to sit at table with you, because you are the servants of Baha'o'llah.' We replied that He made us happy. He said, 'Very good, I am glad you are here. It makes Me rejoice when I see you, for I love you very much' . . .

When emotion is shown, Abdul-Baha says, 'No, no, not that, not that; be happy, be happy,' and when one shows enthusiasm and happiness, it seems to lighten His burdens.

The pressure of life there is very great, and sometimes, Abdul-Baha is very weary, but a quick response to His greeting or incidents related that show the activity and steadfastness of the believers, will cause His eyes to shine instantly, and His step to become more buoyant. He listens intently to every word, no matter how trifling.[2]

Ella noted that the ten years since her first pilgrimage had had their effect on 'Abdu'l-Bahá:

But it smites one's heart to see how the years increase His great Burden, and the strongest thought that comes and comes instantly is, O! if our believers could only realize that it is not by weeping at His feet they can best show their love for Him, but by promptly obeying His Command to unite in love and harmony, so that this Cause shall spread as it should, in America, before He has to leave the world. If they could only hear His voice as He asked so tenderly after their welfare; if they could only see that Beloved Face light up when we tell Him of the splendid service of some faithful one; if they could only hear Him say that nothing in the Prison makes Him sad, no matter how great the turmoil here, no matter how great even the fact of His own death – nothing has the power to sadden Him for an instant – except the inharmony among the believers, and nothing can give Him such happiness, He adds, with that wonderful, patient smile, 'as to hear of their love and unity'.³

Helen and Ella spent much of their time with the ladies of the Holy Household. These women included 'Abdu'l-Bahá's sister Bahíyyih K͟hánum, the Greatest Holy Leaf; Muním K͟hánum, His wife; and His four daughters, from oldest to youngest, Ḍíyá'iyyih K͟hánum, Rúhá K͟hánum, Ṭúbá K͟hánum and Munavvar K͟hánum. Shoghi Effendi was Ḍíyá'iyyih K͟hánum's son. 'Abdu'l-Bahá's three eldest daughters were married and had children. In addition to His family, there were scores of others who were dependent on the Master, including orphans and spouses of some of the Persian martyrs.⁴

Each morning, Helen and Ella joined the ladies for the morning devotional. 'The children came, and leaving their sandals outside, knelt near the door, listening quietly. Even the sparrows were welcome, and they flew in and out at their own will (picking up bits of sugar thrown to them by the young girl at the samovar). Tooba Khanom, Monerva Khanom, and sometimes the visiting ladies chanted.'

Once morning, 'Abdu'l-Bahá greeted Ella and Helen by shaking their hands, after which He turned to the Persian ladies present and said, 'This looks strange to you, for this is the first time you have seen a man and a woman shake hands. After a while all will adopt this custom.' He then asked the Americans if Persian chanting sounded strange to them. When they replied that it did, He noted that 'the Persians did not like the "part" singing of the Americans when they first heard it'.⁵

Since it was dangerous for people to know that Americans were visiting 'Abdu'l-Bahá, Helen and Ella spent most of their time indoors. On occasion, however, they were allowed to walk on the rooftop for fresh air and exercise. The women remembered:

The view from there was superb. Toward the West lay the blue Mediterranean, South of us was the Bay of Acca, Haifa, and beautiful Mt. Carmel. To the North and East was the rolling country where the shepherds were tending their sheep as in the olden time, in the same flowing garments, and carrying their shepherds' crooks in the same old way.

From the minarets was heard the call to prayer. How we longed to shout to the muezzin that a 'New Call' had been 'vociferously raised' and to the shepherds – The 'True Shepherd' hath appeared!

At table one day Abdul-Baha asked:– 'If the people here should not let you leave Acca, what would you do – how would you feel?'

We answered:– 'We would stay here always and be perfectly happy.' He smiled at this and said, 'Suppose they should ask you why you came here? They might say, These prisoners are Persians. What have Americans and Persians to say to one another?'

We answered that we should like nothing better than to mount the house-top and shout to all the people the reason of our coming. He smiled again and said:– 'You are shouting although you are silent; but your words will be heard in the future. The words of Christ were not heard until three hundred years after His death.'[6]

Marion Jack arrived in 'Akká a short time after Helen and Ella. Marion had learned about the Faith from Mason Remey on a dance floor in Paris. Mason remembered that it was at a

> fancy dress dance, that I met Marion. She was dressed in a fiery red costume that she had made herself of crinkled tissue paper topped by an enormous 'Merry Widow' hat . . . It was as we danced and sat out between dances that I told Marion of the Bahá'í Faith.[7]

Earlier in 1907, Edith Sanderson had returned from pilgrimage and said that 'Abdu'l-Bahá needed an English teacher for His daughters. Marion Jack was asked to go and found it impossible to refuse. Marion and the Master shared a sense of humour from the start:

> With a merry twinkle in His eye He would ask Miss Jack how she liked being on the roll of prisoners . . . When she answered that she would like to be written down as 'the woman who had just found her freedom', He laughed with the rest, and was highly pleased that she responded to Him in the same tone.[8]

> . . . the Master . . . hardly ever came to the table without beginning

to chaff Miss Jack about being now on the roll of the prisoners ... and asking what she would do if they should surround her with Turkish soldiers; and one day Monever Khanum came in to lunch a little late and greeted us, for we had not seen her before on that day and He immediately turned to her with a twinkle and asked how it was she was saying 'Good morning' at that hour, and why she had not seen us earlier. We explained that Miss Jack was to blame, having given her a long, strenuous English lesson. He laughingly said to Miss Jack: 'If you keep her away from our guests I shall have to punish you.' At which Miss Jack asked, 'How?' And He promptly brought His hands smartly together with great glee as He said, in English: 'Slap! Slap!' He was pleased when we responded to Him in the same spirit and told us, over and over again, that He wished to see us always smiling and happy.[9]

Marion loved to paint and her new job gave her ample time to do so. She really wanted to paint a portrait of 'Abdu'l-Bahá, but He was not keen on the idea so, at the suggestion of Rúhá Khánum, she began painting the places 'Abdu'l-Bahá visited. He asked her to paint a view of the Shrine of Bahá'u'lláh and though she offered Him all her work, it was the only one He took. Marion did have one problem in her painting and that was that she had to do much of it hidden from public view, since the Bahá'ís were very carefully watched by the authorities.

As many did, Marion wrote a pen portrait of the Master:

Such a saintly man I have never expected to meet. Such a kind loving unselfish being I had never expected to meet. Words fail one in speaking of this Great One ... Whenever anyone heard His wonderful voice in the court or in the garden there was a rush for the windows. It seems as if the family, servants or guests could never see enough of Him, and I was just as keen as anyone else. It was as if just catching a glimpse of this heavenly being was like a benediction ...

Abdul Baha's life as I saw it day in & day out for about six months was one of absolute selfless beauty. He slept little, he ate sparingly; he would not accept of a multiplicity of garments. If his wardrobe contained more than one it was immediately given to the poor. He loved them, as if they were his flesh & blood children, and they adored him ...

The Governor of Akka, a very fine upright Mohammedan, was one of Abdul Baha's most ardent admirers. He called frequently & asked for advice from the one whom he recognized as being infinitely his superior . . .

In Acca there were no hospitals, no soup kitchens, no charitable institutions. Abdul Baha was the one vitally interested in the needs & wants of this dreary unhealthy town. Then when people were consumptive the members of the family shrank back in fear from them. These were Abdul Baha's special care. He arose very early in the morning, and when the poor were sensitive about accepting his attention he quietly slipped a basket or bowl of food into their dwelling, for the doors were often not locked . . . He also helped other missionaries, all were servants of God to him, whether in service as Protestants, Catholics or Mohammedans. So when they came to him, he helped them. I saw a loving letter of a Protestant missionary who had been his neighbour. It was filled with loving gratitude for Abdul Baha's kindness and help. He said never in his life could he ever forget the days when they had lived side by side and that he would never cease to pray for his beloved friend . . .

So often it was ten at night before the Beloved One had His little supper which the Greatest Holy Leaf his dear sister would try to keep warm on the brazier in her room . . .[10]

'Abdu'l-Bahá hosted a Feast for a group of Persian pilgrims from a Jewish background, inviting Helen, Ella and Marion as well. The event was held in a large hall containing a table 'laden with fruits and cakes, and nine large platters of pilau, and beautifully decorated with flowers'. The three American women were placed at the head of the table, after which the male pilgrims came in. 'Abdu'l-Bahá greeted each one and poured water over their hands. His attendant, Bashír, held a towel on which they could dry their hands. When all were seated, 'Abdu'l-Bahá served everyone a plateful of pilau. When dinner was finished, The Master said:

'In this Great Day, God has manifested One Light, and to this Light are attracted these pilgrims from three great religions – Mohammadan, Christian, and Jewish. We must all thank God for the privilege of sitting down at this table, for this gathering is a symbol of unity of the Kingdom when all nations, all creeds, all races, and all religions will gather in unity under one Tent, under the shade of one Tree, at one Table to partake of spiritual food.'

Then Abdul-Baha stood close behind us (three women) and said, 'In the olden time it was not possible for women to sit at table in equality with the men, but in this Day it is different, and the change has been largely brought about by the position given to women in free America.'

'It is the power of Baha'o'llah that made it possible for these American women to sit at this Table with these pilgrims. This is to show that in the Kingdom of Abha there will be equality established between women and men. They are equal.'[11]

After the Feast was finished, 'Abdu'l-Bahá and His helpers sat at the table and Helen, Ella and Marion were given the great privilege of serving them. Toward the end of her stay, Ella fell ill, but didn't complain, commenting:

> It would be worth a good deal of suffering to experience, in that Holy Place, the tender care, the cheerful service and devoted attention, all lavished with such infinite love, as a simple matter-of-course. Our Lord came in to see me at least twice a day. On the third day, as I was not better, He sat by my bedside, holding my hand, and said, in that tactful, sweet way of His: 'We are commanded by the Blessed Perfection to consult a physician when we are sick.' Of course the doctor came, and after one day of following his advice, I was well enough to get up and travel. But I was delighted at the way in which the doctor was suggested.[12]

On 19 January, Helen and Ella left 'Akká to carry back 'Abdu'l-Bahá's inspirational words to their fellow Californians.

Marion spent a lot of time in the Greatest Holy Leaf's room. She particularly remembered seeing the schoolboy Shoghi Effendi in that room. She described him, as well:

> And I shall never forget our beloved Guardian when as a little boy home for his holidays from the Monastery school on Mount Carmel was graphically describing to her [the Greatest Holy Leaf] whom he

so loved all his experiences during his absence from her . . . As there was a dramatic element at the Monastery School so he felt there should be in the holy household, and he drew up a poster which was placed in the hall. I never saw the theatricals but I can imagine that they were stage-managed. Then he held a banquet or feast rather in the servant's quarters for all the young people, and I am told it was beautifully arranged with little paper napkins and flowers at each place.[13]

When it came time to leave, in July or August, Marion remembered the grief and copious tears of other pilgrims and vowed not to do the same, telling herself, 'Well, that is something I certainly will not do.' But when the moment of departure came, she said that she

> started weeping so much that I was a perfect fountain of tears. Nor could I often keep them back. It was awful, but it taught me a lesson not to be so cock-sure of myself . . . I shall never forget the miserable show I made of myself in the presence of a whole room full of the Holy family and friends when He told me before them all how I must be a comfort for the sorrowing and all sorts of lovely things I must be. My own handkerchief was wringing wet, and I believe it was sweet Monaver Khanum who gave me hers to fill with tears too – finally I was forced to get up & run to my own room I was so overcome . . . That condition went on for days . . . He said in English in His sweet sympathetic way, 'Not cry Jack, not cry Jack.' Can you imagine what a lesson all this was to me? I who gave up crying years before! And was so sure that, I at least, was going to spare the glorious one such scenes?[14]

'Abdu'l-Bahá first called her 'General Jack' during this time. Marion later travelled with Emogene Hoagg in Alaska and the Yukon, then pioneered for many years in the Balkans. Shoghi Effendi later said that she was an example of a true pioneer.

Jean Stannard

During all of this intrigue and rumour, and while Marion Jack was still there, Jean Stannard arrived in 'Akká from England unexpectedly and without the Master's permission. Jean was unhappy and combative, but 'Abdu'l-Bahá treated her gently. 'Abdu'l-Bahá allowed her to stay long enough for an interview and dinner, but said she should stay no longer because of the situation at the time. Marion Jack's youngest English pupil, Munavvar Khánum, was the interpreter. Marion remembered that Jean told 'Abdu'l-Bahá:

> She had had such severe experiences in her search after Truth and in psychic matters that her faith had been sadly shaken . . . He ['Abdu'l-Bahá] seemed then just like the All-Wise Physician dealing with a very sick patient . . . he told her to read the words of Baha'u'llah, the Hidden Words. She like a rebellious child said, 'I have read and read so much that I don't feel I can read any more.' He said, 'Just try, try for one month and see how you will be helped.' Also he said, 'I want you to return to the West.' Her idea had been to live in Eastern countries . . . When he left the room she said to me, 'Abdul Baha advises me to return to the West but I am not going to do so.'[15]

After dinner, Jean went back to Haifa and waited for 'Abdu'l-Bahá to give her permission to return. A month later 'Abdu'l-Bahá gave her that permission and sent Marion to dress her in Persian clothes for the trip. This time her interview with the Master was much nicer though she was still 'obstinate & little eager as before to return to the West'. In spite of insisting that she wasn't going to read anything, Jean evidently did because the next time she visited 'Abdu'l-Bahá, she stayed for three days and had some very informative talks with Him. When she left, Marion told 'Abdu'l-Bahá that Jean was a very changed woman. He replied, 'Yes but I worked very hard over her, very hard.' The fruit of this work was displayed at the World Congress of Nations in London in 1931 where Jean 'best set forth the real purport of the Cause and in the clearest manner. No doubt the Beloved foresaw her true nature, and realized that this woman was a woman worthy of his effort.'[16]

Stanwood Cobb

In February 1908, Stanwood Cobb was in Egypt trying to recover from a difficult time at Robert College in Constantinople (Istanbul), where he taught English and Latin. He had become a Bahá'í in 1906 after talking with Mary Lucas for a half hour at Green Acre. She had just returned from pilgrimage and her stories brought Stanwood into the Faith. The next year, he took the job at Robert College.[17]

One day he unexpectedly ran into Lua Getsinger on the steps of the Shepard Hotel in Cairo.

> 'What are you doing here?' asked Lua in great surprise.
> 'What are you doing here?' I asked, in equal surprise.
> It seems that Lua was on a pilgrimage to 'Akká, and she urged me to leave off my travels in Egypt and join her. I explained that I had written 'Abdu'l-Bahá for permission to visit, but had been answered that at that time it was not advisable.
> 'But I have standing permission to take anyone with me,' urged Lua.
> 'But I have arranged a trip up the Nile with my friend Hussein.'
> 'What is a trip up the Nile compared with the privilege of visiting the Master?'
> Lua's logic was convincing and her ardour compelling. Twenty-four hours later saw me ensconced in a room adjoining 'Abdu'l-Bahá's in the historic 'prison of 'Akká'.[18]

For their first meeting with 'Abdu'l-Bahá, Stanwood Cobb and Lua Getsinger were taken into a long room with large French windows at the far end. Stanwood wrote that 'I saw a large desk there, but no person sitting at it. Only a radiance of light. As we approached the end of the room, a majestic figure in Oriental garb became evident to me. It was 'Abdu'l-Bahá.' Lua immediately 'fell to her knees and fervently kissed His robe' with what Stanwood called 'the devotion of a Mary Magdalene'. He, however, was at a loss as to what to do. Following Lua's example would be insincere and simply shaking hands awkward. 'Abdu'l-Bahá solved his dilemma by embracing him in a bear hug saying, 'You are welcome!'[19]

As with most pilgrims, much of the time they had with 'Abdu'l-Bahá was at meals. The Master did not eat with them, however, but helped serve, piling food onto their plates. Oriental custom was that the host should serve the honoured guest with his own hands. This was the height of Oriental hospitality.

The time after dinner was when 'Abdu'l-Bahá gave talks. Stanwood didn't remember much from the talks except that a desire had to be followed by action, and the need for loving patience. Most people, 'Abdu'l-Bahá said, will endure an exasperating person as long as possible. Bahá'ís, He said, 'must endure people even when they are unendurable!' This pronouncement was not stated with ponderous solemnity. The Master 'beamed upon us delightfully, as if to suggest what a joy to us it would be to act in this way!' 'Abdu'l-Bahá was joyful in everything He did and had 'the joyousness with which [He] always depicted the spiritual life as He enjoined it upon us. Stanwood Cobb's response was 'And why not? Is man's spiritual life not in reality more joyous than any other kind of life that he can lead?'[20]

One day, 'Abdu'l-Bahá came to Stanwood's room without a translator, sat beside him and took one of his hands in both of His. Though Stanwood had not mentioned it, he had been under a great strain at his college and also suffered from deep depression, which was why he had been in Egypt when he encountered Lua. But the Master knew, and from that moment his troubles evaporated and 'No matter how hard the going, I have always since then been glad to be alive.'[21]

After only three days, it was time to go. Stanwood didn't describe his parting feelings, but he did Lua's:

> I shall never forget how Lua Getsinger sobbed as if her heart would break as she slowly descended the long flight of steps, looking back frequently at 'Abdu'l-Bahá Who stood benignly at the top.
>
> And I shall never forget how joyously 'Abdu'l-Bahá smiled at Lua's tears, knowing that they were more precious than pure gold. For they were the complete offering, at that moment, of Lua's heart and soul to the Master – the instinctive expression of her great love. 'Abdu'l-Bahá knew that these were not tragic tears. They were like the vernal showers that prelude the rich blossoming of spring.[22]

Stanwood later became a prolific writer of Bahá'í books and was the editor or co-editor of both the *Star of the West* and *World Order*.[23] In 1952, the Guardian told a pilgrim that the best English Bahá'í writer was George Townshend, while the best American Bahá'í writer was Stanwood Cobb.[24]

Mason Remey and the Revolution

Mason Remey was in 'Akká visiting 'Abdu'l-Bahá in June, just a few weeks before the exciting events in Istanbul during which the Young Turks forced a constitutional government on the Sultan. That meant, however, that upon his arrival 'Akká was still a dangerous place to be; the Sultan was wounded and defensive. Because of the uncertainties, Mason had to wait for five days in Haifa before he was able to travel to 'Akká. 'Abdu'l-Bahá told him that He

> had received threatening messages from a very high official . . . to which he had replied, saying that he was Abdul-Baha (the servant of God), that were that official to exalt him, he would still be Abdul-Baha, were he to oppress him he would still be Abdul-Baha, and were he to kill him, yet would his station ever be the same, Abdul-Baha.[25]

Some American pilgrims had been unable to meet the Master and had only been able to see from a distance as He stood on His balcony, reminiscent of the time Bahá'u'lláh was in the Most Great Prison.[26]

While Mason waited for his call, four new Bahá'ís, who had been confined in 'Akká because of their declarations of Faith, were released and the guard removed from 'Abdu'l-Bahá's house. Even so, when permission arrived, Mason had to travel clandestinely, dressed as a Syrian wearing a fez and Arab clothing, in order to enter 'Akká, because the Master's house was still being watched. Mason did not stay at the Master's house but in the house of Ḥájí Mírzá Muḥammad-Taqí, a cousin of the Báb who had been charged with building the first Bahá'í House of Worship in Ashkabat. Mason only remained there for two days and two nights, but the Master visited him twice each day. Mason noted:

> Despite the agitated conditions – for his followers had been almost panic-stricken – Abdul-Baha was calm and evidently very happy. The strain of many years of trouble had left its imprint upon the physical man, but his soul, so emancipated, was brimming over with the love and joy of the Lord.[27]

He also noted that this was quite different from his first visit in 1901, at which time he was comparatively free from worldly troubles, being allowed by the governor of Akka to reside temporarily in Haifa. Our party of nine American and European pilgrims were in his house. Then the approach of a Bahai was an easy matter: we went about the town mingling freely with people, and meeting them socially as one would have done in any place. But as I recall those days I remember that our leader often looked distressed. Then the cause in the West was not united spiritually as it is now. While many were attracted and the movement was growing, yet the believers were in danger. They were as young trees enveloped by the blast of the winter's gale. This Abdul-Baha knew and realized while we did not, and, notwithstanding his own ease, it weighed upon him. Now all was reversed. He was in trouble, but those over whom he had so diligently watched and prayed had, through his labor and sacrifices, grown strong in spirit and were uniting in serving humanity as he by his example had taught them to do.[28]

The Master spoke about the Nineteen Day Feast:

of the necessity of the believers coming together – only the believers – to read the Holy Verses and to speak of and discuss the Holy Teachings . . . There are two types of meetings. One for receiving spiritual guidance and one for giving the same. One when the beloved meet together for strength and enlightenment and one when they call the seekers together to share the heavenly blessings. Undoubtedly, Abdul-Baha saw the necessity of the believers coming together in the close communion of a meeting essentially for those of the Faith, when he spoke to me as he did.[29]

Mason's visit was very short and he found the Persian hours to be difficult. It was up at 5 in the morning and to bed at 11 at night. He had a difficult time getting up for his departure. 'Abdu'l-Bahá came by at 7:30 to say goodbye, but when He found Mason still asleep He would not allow anyone to wake him, but stood guard at the door, walking up and down the narrow corridor. After half an hour of this, the Master was called away briefly, giving one of the resident Bahá'ís a chance to 'enter the room and give me a necessarily vigorous poking'. A half hour later, having received 'Abdu'l-Bahá's 'fatherly embrace and parting blessing',

Mason and an Eastern pilgrim were 'being driven through the canyon-like streets of Akka on the way to Haifa'.³⁰

Mason soon learned about the influence of 'Abdu'l-Bahá on people who had never met him. With a companion, he went to Nazareth. His companion told him of Sheikh Youseff, who had known Bahá'u'lláh. When they arrived in Nazareth, they called on the Governor of the town, who happened to be a son-in-law of the sheikh. The Governor received them very warmly and said that he held 'Abdu'l-Bahá in high esteem. He was unsurprised that the Master now had followers in the West. The Governor placed a servant to guide them in the town. He was their friend because they were friends of 'Abdu'l-Bahá.³¹

Mason and Sydney Sprague spent the next several months travelling in Persia. When they returned to 'Akká in September, a tremendous change had happened. The Young Turk Revolution resulted in Sultan 'Abdu'l-Hamíd II being forced to reinstate the constitution on 24 July. Because of this, on 31 August, 'Abdu'l-Bahá was a free man.³² So when Mason returned from Persia, instead of having to wait in Haifa for permission from 'Abdu'l-Bahá to come at a safe time, he drove directly from the dock to the house of the Master in 'Akká.

The resident Bahá'ís were all extremely happy about their new-found freedom, but 'Abdu'l-Bahá, though happy about the freedom of the friends, indicated that the change really did not make any difference.³³ He even said that with freedom, things were worse, contrasting the time as a prisoner and His new 'freedom':

> For some time now the pressures have been severe, the restrictions as shackles of iron. This hapless wronged one was left single and alone, for all the ways were barred. Friends were forbidden access to me, the trusted were shut away, the foe compassed me about, the evil watchers were fierce and bold. At every instant, fresh affliction. At every breath, new anguish. Both kin and stranger on the attack; indeed, one-time lovers, faithless and unpitying, were worse than foes as they rose up to harass me . . .
>
> Affliction beat upon this captive like the heavy rains of spring, and the victories of the malevolent swept down in a relentless flood, and still 'Abdu'l-Bahá remained happy and serene, and relied on the grace of the All-Merciful. That pain, that anguish, was a paradise of all delights; those chains were the necklace of a king on a throne

in heaven. Content with God's will, utterly resigned, my heart surrendered to whatever fate had in store, I was happy. For a boon companion, I had great joy.

Finally a time came when the friends turned inconsolable, and abandoned all hope. It was then the morning dawned, and flooded all with unending light. The towering clouds were scattered, the dismal shadows fled. In that instant the fetters fell away, the chains were lifted off the neck of this homeless one and hung round the neck of the foe. Those dire straits were changed to ease, and on the horizon of God's bounties the sun of hope rose up. All this was out of God's grace and His bestowals.

And yet, from one point of view, this wanderer was saddened and despondent. For what pain, in the time to come, could I seek comfort? At the news of what granted wish could I rejoice? There was no more tyranny, no more affliction, no tragic events, no tribulations. My only joy in this swiftly-passing world was to tread the stony path of God and to endure hard tests and all material griefs. For otherwise, this earthly life would prove barren and vain, and better would be death. The tree of being would produce no fruit; the sown field of this existence would yield no harvest. Thus it is my hope that once again some circumstance will make my cup of anguish to brim over, and that beauteous Love, that Slayer of souls, will dazzle the beholders again. Then will this heart be blissful, this soul be blessed.[34]

Mason had extensive contacts with 'Abdu'l-Bahá and many people wanted to know how the Master impressed him:

I should hardly use the word 'impress' in connection with him. An impression is something which is imprinted upon one from without. His influence is not that of one personality upon another. Through contact with him the soul responds, is quickened and refreshed by his spirit of love, humility, service to humanity, and all other kindred virtues. This soul-quickening then produces its regenerating effect upon the character and soul of the individual, working from within outward.

Each time I have gone to Akka I have naturally carried with me a conception or a mental picture of Abdul-Baha, and each time I have been obliged to lay this aside in order to find a larger and higher one. He has remained unchanged, while my vision has been a changing and growing one. Surely, if one were to go to him twenty times, each successive time he would appear different . . .

Abdul-Baha is a physician, who is healing the spiritual diseases of man. He sees and understands all conditions of the soul and gives to each just what that soul needs. His teaching is simplicity itself. The gospel of love he makes very real through living the life of God's servant among men. His words and explanations are so simple that oftentimes people may at first feel a pang of disappointment, expecting abstruse theories and explanations, but, when they begin to realize the force of the spirit which characterizes Abdul-Baha's life, then they see the real power of his teaching, realizing how much greater is this than philosophizing.[35]

After a short visit to tell 'Abdu'l-Bahá of his trip through Persia, Mason returned to America.

The Knobloch sisters

Two of the three Knobloch sisters, Fanny and Alma, came for pilgrimage from America on 7 November. Their other sister, Pauline, and her husband, Joseph Hannen, made their pilgrimage early the next year. Fanny left America accompanied by Ida Finch from Seattle. Upon arriving in Naples, the two women were joined by Alma. When their ship docked at Alexandria, they looked down on a sea of faces looking up. Alma said, 'Notice the man almost in the middle of the fifth row with a green scarf around his turban. Now count seven to the right. What do you see?' Ida replied that she saw 'a very friendly face'. They noted three more 'friendly faces' then descended from the ship into the crowd. Soon one of the friendly faces was at their shoulder softly whispering 'Alláh'u'Abhá'. Thrilled, the women replied with the same greeting, though also quietly since it was dangerous to be recognized as a Bahá'í at that time.[36]

The three women were taken to the home of Muḥammad Yazdí. A meeting was held with the local Bahá'ís where the women were given a supplication to carry to 'Abdu'l-Bahá asking that He visit Egypt.

Arriving in Haifa soon afterward, the three women faced that daunting journey from the ship to the shore on a day when the weather was not pleasant. Looking down from the deck of the ship, Fanny wrote:

> Below us were large flat-bottomed boats – Orientals making much noise – men in some of the boats loading bags upon the backs of others to carry up on deck, others at the same time carrying quantities of freight down to boats below. These boats, because of rough water, were swaying and crashing against each other. Looking down upon this noisy, picturesque scene, we wondered how we, ourselves, would ever reach one of those boats. But there had been no need to worry, for suddenly a huge oriental unceremoniously grabbed us like a bag of meal, with our heads facing frontward and bodies hanging, carried us down the steps between the freight carriers and dropped us into the arms of waiting boatmen. There were eleven men in the boat to row three little women with hand baggage to shore! Again, when landing at shore, we were picked up and carried in the same manner over a pile of coal. We heaved a sigh of relief when we felt the cobblestone of the road beneath our feet.³⁷

When they arrived in 'Akká, Fanny noted that

> In our small hotel we occupied a second story front room, one door of which opened on to a small balcony. That night the glorious rays of a full moon revealed the white crested waves of the sea, rolling upon the sands of the Valley of Achor. The minaret of the mosque gleamed white above the walls of the prison city. In the distance was Mt. Carmel, illumined, while close at hand great rows of tall palms cast weird shadows upon the road.³⁸

Fanny, Alma and Ida soon met Munírih K͟hánum, 'Abdu'l-Bahá's wife, and Bahíyyih K͟hánum, the Greatest Holy Leaf. They were greatly impressed with the two women. Fanny wrote:

> A strange and unknown feeling possessed me while in the presence of Bahíyyih K͟hánum the Greatest Holy Leaf. Possibly it can be described as a feeling of awe, a feeling very unfamiliar to me. However, later, I realized that I had been in the presence of the greatest, the most holy woman in the history of the world – the Greatest Holy Leaf! The daughter of the Manifestation of God, Bahá'u'lláh.³⁹

When they met 'Abdu'l-Bahá and His family in the tea room at 7 o'clock on the morning of 8 November, He told them,

> 'The Catholics believe that when they die they go to a place between Heaven and hell, called purgatory, to become purified, where they suffer, and then they are prepared to enter Heaven.' Looking and referring to us three pilgrims, he said: 'That is your condition while here in Acca, you suffer some bodily discomforts, you do not have the food you are accustomed to; troublesome and long journeys, etc.
>
> 'Every one who visits here should make progress. I hope you, too, will make progress day by day; each day as I see you I hope that you will have made more progress. As a father who loves his children; as a teacher who loves his pupils and desires that they make progress, so I hope that you will make progress. As I love you very much, I hope that you will advance rapidly, and when you leave here you will be changed so that you may become like refreshing water to the thirsty ones, brilliant stars in the Assemblies, and firm trees in the garden of the Kingdom of God. Each one of you, like the light of a lamp, shall be the light of an Assembly.'[40]

One day, Munírih Khánum spoke about the people of 'Akká and how they were unable to appreciate the Master or even understand why He was there in 'Akká. She recalled a conversation she had with a young Christian woman.

> Moneera Khanum asked her, 'Have you ever thought why we were sent here?' The reply was, 'No!'
>
> Moneera Khanum, said: 'You know us, that we neither steal, nor do we kill any one.' The lady replied: 'I have heard some of the natives speak of of [sic] you, saying, "These Persians were exiled because they have a faith, a religion, which is contrary to the religion of Persia."' Moneera Khanum then asked, 'What is religion? Is it not the expression or form of worshipping God? You are a Christian, can you prove to me the truth of Christ's teaching?' This young lady could not. She was then asked if she was certain that Christ's teachings are true? She replied, 'I do not know!'[41]

1908

On 10 November, 'Abdu'l-Bahá asked them why none of the other Manifestations of God had united the world and then answered His own question:

> Although the former Manifestations have come from God, the means of unity for mankind was not prepared in their time. It was as though there was nothing, and conflicting conditions were still remaining in the world; there was no transportation and railways, no joining of Europe, Asia and Africa. People could not meet each other, the means were not ready. If a man should travel some distance from his country, he could not let it be known where he was. Because of this the teachings of Moses were confined to Palestine. The cause of Jesus Christ was spread over some parts of Europe, Asia and Africa, and the cause of Mohammed over some parts of Europe, Asia and Africa; none were universal. The unity of mankind was not realized, perfect connection was not produced amongst mankind, for there was no means for this; they could not meet each other. But in the Cause of the Blessed Perfection, Baha'o'llah, the greatest preparations are in evidence. The means for the unity and harmony of mankind is found in the most complete way. Communication is so easy that in a single moment the East can communicate with the West. A hundred days can be passed in a single day. Ships, in other Manifestations, could only sail near the shore, and if sometimes they did go far they would be missed and could not be traced. Now they cross the ocean.
>
> In the days of the Prophets, Christ and Mohammed, there were many plains and deserts on which no one had traveled, now the trains can go directly and pass over them easily, and the land and sea are so connected with each other that the globe can be traversed in one month.
>
> Hence the world has received the capacity for the unity of mankind. These preparations, these capacities, are all made ready for the spread of the teachings of this Great Cause; and it is possible that the teachings and instruction of Baha'o'llah can be given to everybody in the world; therefore, the hope is great that the tent of unity will soon be pitched, and there is great probability that war and strife will be annihilated, and it is possible that the trades, professions and arts of the earth shall be diffused, therefore it is possible that the Teachings shall be spread throughout the world.

Were it not for this preparation it would be impossible for you to have heard of this Cause in your country. This is a self-evident proof that the world has received the capacity for the Cause, and what Cause in the world is greater than this?[42]

The next day, the Master talked about the qualities needed for teaching, comparing them to what most people in the material world thought was needed:

In the world of existence one must look in everything to the capacity and ability.

For instance, if a man wishes to attain the art of writing, he must look to himself to see whether he has the ability or not. If a man wishes to teach, he must feel sure that he has the ability. So it is with a captain; he must first realize in himself whether he is fitted for that work or not. In short, every work depends upon capacity and ability, that is man must first see whether he has the ability for working in some profession, or not; without regarding this matter he would at last be disappointed. But in the work of the Kingdom of God, that is exceptional: In this place or station one should not consider capacity or ability; the confirmation of the Spirit will descend; because we hold that the weakest souls through the confirmation of the Holy Spirit become the most powerful. Some souls who were outwardly ignorant, through this gift become learned ones. The weakest souls become the strongest. Many times a woman has surpassed a thousand men, or, rather, through this help could withstand all the people of the world.

His highness, Moses, was apparently a shepherd, but through the Divine Power, he overcame Pharaoh and his armies. Likewise, the disciples were the weakest souls, but through the Breath of the Holy Spirit and the assistance of the Kingdom of God, they became the strongest ones. The object which I wish to convey to you is this, – you should not look at your capacity or ability, nay, rather, rely upon the confirmation of the Holy Spirit, – do not doubt. (after a long pause) Be confident and sure. It will help you.[43]

Ida, Alma and Fanny spent nine days with 'Abdu'l-Bahá and as they left, tears streamed down their faces. 'Abdu'l-Bahá said, 'You are not weeping? Do not weep! Many friends weep because they wish to remain longer.' Fanny, however replied, 'No, we have received so many blessings and are eager to go out and share them with all who are ready to listen.' It was a novel response and 'Abdu'l-Bahá happily noted that 'The general does not love most the man in the back of the ranks. He loves most the man in the front. If you but knew the value of these days, you would not eat, you would not sleep, you would not walk. You would run and give to all the Glad Tidings!'[44]

Fanny, Alma and Ida travelled back through Cairo, where Mírzá Abu'l-Faḍl gave Fanny his prayer beads, his most precious possession, saying, 'My Lord gave them to me.' Fanny and Alma spoke at a large meeting in Germany after which Fanny visited both Paris and London to share her experiences.[45] Alma was in Germany when the First World War began and, instead of escaping to America, she stayed and suffered what the German people suffered. Fanny was one of the early teachers of the Faith in South Africa.

1909

Ethel Rosenberg again visited 'Abdu'l-Bahá in January 1909. One of the questions she asked was what could be done to increase the number of believers and make the work more effective. The Master's answer was simple – the Bahá'ís 'should love each other very much and be devoted friends. The more they loved each other, the more the meetings would attract and draw others, and the more they loved, the more their influence would be felt.' But they must also love everyone, not just the believers: 'I say this for you in English. I do not often do that; but I say also in English, that you may understand how much I mean it, that love is the foundation of everything, and that all must be good.'[1]

'Abdu'l-Bahá's new status as a free man was solidified on 28 January when the Military Governor, the Mayor as well as judges and several prominent men of 'Akká came to the Master's house for a banquet. Though all had visited individually, this was the first time such a gathering of important men had happened.[2]

May and Sutherland Maxwell

There was a significant pilgrimage in late February when Sutherland and May Maxwell (formerly Bolles) arrived with Louise Stapfer. It had been a decade since May had first visited 'Abdu'l-Bahá and been transformed, and now, a married woman, she and her husband stayed there for six days. Two significant events happened while they were there. The first involved Sutherland and was later recounted many times by Rúḥíyyih Khánum:

> One day at table, Sutherland said to 'Abdu'l-Bahá:
> 'The Christians worship God through Christ; my wife worships God through You; but I worship Him direct.'

'Abdu'l-Bahá smiled and said: 'Where is He?'

'Why, God is everywhere,' replied Sutherland.

'Everywhere is nowhere,' said 'Abdu'l-Bahá. He then went on to demonstrate that such worship was worship of a figment of the imagination and had no reality; we must worship God through something tangible and real to us, hence the role of the Manifestations. Sutherland bowed his head in acceptance. The real seed of his faith germinated from that hour.[3]

This was the beginning of a life that led to Sutherland being named a Hand of the Cause of God by Shoghi Effendi. May also had a moment that changed not only her life, but had an important impact on the future of the Faith. May described it herself:

> We were there only a few days, and one evening, in the twilight, with a white veil the Beloved had wrapt around my head and shoulders, I had the little babe of Rouha Khanum in my arms. As I passed the Master's door on my way to show the child to my husband I saw in the gathering darkness the blessed Form standing at His threshold, and He called to me in a clear tender voice and motioned me to come – Rouha was at my side and the Master said: 'You like that baby? I will give him to you.' I said, 'But he belongs to Rouha Khanum,' and she replied, 'If our Lord gives him to you, he is yours.' Then I told the Master that twice I had had the opportunity to adopt lovely children but my husband would not. With that swift motion combined of love and action, the Master bade me enter His room, and setting all the waves of life in motion by His walk, He asked me if I would like to have a child – if I knew why I had never had a child – if I wanted one now! . . .
>
> I told Him I could not have children but I was content with the Will of God. In ringing tones He said, 'This is not true; you can have children,' then suddenly half laughing half eager – yet with underlying gravity He said: 'do you want a child – shall I give you a child?' I replied, 'Whatsoever you desire for me – this is all I wish.' In a moment I found myself, Babe, and all, clasped in His Holy Arms – His hands passed tenderly over my head. He said: 'That is the reply of my own daughter – be assured – be happy – I will pray for you.[4]

Mary Maxwell, who would become Rúḥíyyih Khánum and the wife of Shoghi Effendi, was born a year and a half later.

Joseph and Pauline Hannen

Two things happened on 20 February: 'Abdu'l-Bahá availed Himself of His newly acquired freedom to host a Feast in Haifa, and Joseph and Pauline Hannen arrived from America. Although their ship dropped anchor in the bay at 10 a.m., the Hannens were unable to leave the ship due to rough seas until 5 p.m. Settling into their hotel, they were surprised to be told that 'Abdu'l-Bahá was in Haifa and would meet them after dinner.

At 7:30, they were escorted to the house of the Master. Pauline wrote: 'The Heavens seemed to be a mass of stars, shedding their light upon us and [as] though even the stars were happy for us. But how did I feel. Like a timid little bird, expecting I knew not what.' When she entered 'Abdu'l-Bahá's room and heard His voice,

> I flew at Him, my arms about His Blessed neck my head on His Shoulder . . . and the uppermost thought was Father, Father, Father. I seemed like a weather beaten birdie having passed through storms and at last had reached the Heaven of rest. Just as I began to feel that I was losing consciousness, this wonderful Father led me to a chair then I was quiet and more composed . . .
>
> His wonderful wonderful eyes. They express as no other eyes can unspeakable love, sympathy, power and authority, submissiveness and oh the merry twinkle I never saw anything like it.[5]

Joseph's reaction was more muted: 'Words cannot describe the scene which followed. If the soul could speak its language might by being a million times richer than that of the mind – feebly convey our emotions.'[6]

After talking about the dedicated service of Pauline's sisters, Alma and Fanny Knobloch, who were to pioneer in Germany and South Africa, respectively, the Master took Pauline to meet the ladies of the household, then returned to Joseph to whom he said, through the interpreter, 'You are my own son,' then repeating in English, 'My son, my son.'[7]

The next morning, 'Abdu'l-Bahá Himself went and collected the Hannens, giving Pauline a bunch of violets, and took them to the Tomb of the Báb for the Feast. As they drove up, the Master told Pauline that what she would see would be what she had seen in a dream two years before. At first Pauline didn't remember the dream, but when she arrived it came flooding back.[8] There were about two dozen Bahá'ís from Russia, Iran and India, mostly from Jewish backgrounds. 'Abdu'l-Bahá explained that Christian missionaries had been striving for years to convert them to Christianity without success, but that through the power of Bahá'u'lláh they now believed in Christ. After following 'Abdu'l-Bahá into the Tomb and listening to Him chant the Tablet of Visitation, all of the pilgrims gathered for the feast of 'rice, bread, cheese and clabber'[9] (a yogurt-like substance with a strong, sour flavour). Afterwards, the group scattered through the gardens and the Master went to rest in the gardener's house. Pauline and Joseph were sitting with a Jewish Bahá'í and a Muhammadan Bahá'í on the platform in front of the tomb. Pauline said 'we were being instructed from our own Bible – given marvelous truths beyond our ken. The wonder of this was that the Jew was teaching, the Mohammedan was interpreting, and we two Christians were listening!'[10]

Pauline wrote that sometimes the spiritual power of 'Abdu'l-Bahá threatened to overwhelm them and they thought their hearts would burst. The moment they had that thought, the Master would stop and tell them stories. When they were relaxed, He would continue with His instructions.

Joseph was quite sensitive about his bald spot. One day when they were with 'Abdu'l-Bahá in Haifa, Pauline suddenly remembered that she had promised to supplicate the Master for a believer in America. Immediately, she fell to her knees in front of Him. Unexpectedly, she realised that Joseph was on his knees just behind her. She pulled him forward then stood up and backed away. Joseph then added his supplication. Suddenly, 'Abdu'l-Bahá bent over and planted a big kiss on Joseph's bald spot. Afterwards, Pauline told her husband that 'Abdu'l-Bahá had 'kissed great capacity into that head of yours'.[11]

'Abdu'l-Bahá made many interesting comments to the Hannens. One day He pointed out a party of nuns walking by in their religious habit. The Master said, 'See these women, they have severed themselves from the world, and given all to serve God, and to know Him. Consider how blessed you are to have what is nevertheless denied them.' On another occasion, when the Hannens presented Him with letters from America, He told them that, 'You are in yourselves a long and interesting letter from all the Believers. You are a present from the Friends in the Occident. When a merchant wishes to sell any grain he sends a handful as samples. You are the samples of the American Believers.' One evening, 'Abdu'l-Bahá stepped into their room and said, in English, 'Goodnight', followed by 'Good evening'. He then explained that 'Arabs greet each other when meeting, by saying: "Good night," whereas in English the term is Good evening'.[12]

A lot of 'Abdu'l-Bahá's instructions centred on racial unity. The Hannens had opened their home in Washington DC and were teaching both blacks and whites, but it was very difficult and potentially dangerous and they wondered if they should continue. Pauline noted:

> At that time the colored people were not so fond of my husband . . . When the boys of the neighbourhood knew that colored people were coming to meetings at our house, they would throw bricks and stones and overripe tomatoes and vegetables in our vestibule, and also unhinge the front gate. I would sit by the door in the hall and quietly hide these things back in the vestibule door, so that the friends never knew. My husband would unhinge the gate and put it in a place of safety until the meeting was over, replacing it later. All these happenings really brought joy to my heart and I believed, contrary to the others, that Abdul Baha would understand it all when I saw him . . .
>
> . . . one morning Abdul Baha came to our room very briskly and said, 'How are you? Are you happy? Are you well?' He then made several other remarks, after which he turned to my husband and said, 'Tell me about the race question in Washington.'
>
> After having spoken at length on this subject, he suddenly left the room and walked in the large circular central room. Hearing him walking briskly, we followed him and stood close to the wall, together with several Persians, and watched the majestic figure pace back and forth. The power of the holy spirit was almost too much for us. We practically shrank against the wall, overwhelmed, when suddenly like a bow from an arrow [sic], he came towards us. We did not know what was going to happen. Placing his hand on my

husband's shoulder and looking into his eyes with great power, he said, 'May you be the means of uniting the colored and the white races.' Then he walked out and left us . . .

My husband did all in his power to obey the command of Abdul Baha, and eventually became much beloved by the colored people.[13]

Joseph Hannen was destined to play an important part in the preservation of 'Abdu'l-Bahá's talks while He was in America, taking notes from about 30 of them which were later included in *The Promulgation of Universal Peace*.[14] This future was suggested one day in 'Akká when 'Abdu'l-Bahá began a lesson and Joseph jumped up, grabbed paper and pencil and began to take notes.

> 'Abdul Baha stopped speaking for a second and watched my husband's hand, writing rapidly. Then he said, 'You are a rapid writer,' and smiled beautifully. We both felt that this was a baptism for much greater speed and opportunity for writing in the cause of Baha'u'llah.[15]

On 24 February, 'Abdu'l-Bahá left the Hannens and went to Tiberias on the train, the first time He had ever travelled by rail. Munír Zayn later described the trip to Joseph,

> recalling the Master's pleasure in the new experience of His desire to stand during the trip so as to see the panorama of desert and verdure. The trip on the railroad occupied about 3 hours – then they proceeded on horseback to a nearby Arab village where [they] dined. Thence followed by about 30 Arab sheikhs, who recently followed the Master (though themselves Mohammadans) the procession proceeded impressively to another village about 2 hours journey, opposite and in sight of Tiberius in Galilee. Here prayers were said for the departed, using the Mohammadan Ceremony, the Master led and all followed Him and reverently kissed His Hand.[16]

The Hannen's last day of pilgrimage was 28 February. Pauline said that she had to use every effort not to cry. He allowed Pauline to lay her head on His shoulder and kissed Joseph, then they were off.

Placing the Báb's remains in His Shrine

The remains of the Báb had been in the possession of 'Abdu'l-Bahá since 31 January 1899, when they secretly arrived from Iran. For a decade, only 'Abdu'l-Bahá and the Greatest Holy Leaf knew about them and where they were hidden. But 21 March 1909 was a momentous day, the culmination of a decade of work by 'Abdu'l-Bahá: the remains of the Báb were placed in a marble casket and lowered to their final resting place in the Shrine of the Báb. Shoghi Effendi described the decade-long construction of the Tomb for the Manifestation of God Who announced the coming of Bahá'u'lláh:

> The long-drawn out negotiations with the shrewd and calculating owner of the building-site of the holy Edifice, who, under the influence of the Covenant-breakers, refused for a long time to sell; the exorbitant price at first demanded for the opening of a road leading to that site and indispensable to the work of construction; the interminable objections raised by officials, high and low, whose easily aroused suspicions had to be allayed by repeated explanations and assurances given by 'Abdu'l-Bahá Himself; the dangerous situation created by the monstrous accusations brought by Mírzá Muhammad-'Alí and his associates regarding the character and purpose of that building; the delays and complications caused by 'Abdu'l-Bahá's prolonged and enforced absence from Haifa, and His consequent inability to supervise in person the vast undertaking He had initiated – all these were among the principal obstacles which He, at so critical a period in His ministry, had to face and surmount ere He could execute in its entirety the Plan, the outline of which Bahá'u'lláh had communicated to Him on the occasion of one of His visits to Mt. Carmel.
>
> 'Every stone of that building, every stone of the road leading to it,' He, many a time was heard to remark, 'I have with infinite tears and at tremendous cost, raised and placed in position.' 'One night,' He, according to an eye-witness, once observed, 'I was so hemmed in by My anxieties that I had no other recourse than to recite and repeat over and over again a prayer of the Báb which I had in my possession, the recital of which greatly calmed Me. The next morning the owner of the plot himself came to Me, apologized and begged Me to purchase his property.'[17]

1909

Nine years previously, the Bahá'ís of Rangoon had sent a large marble casket to Haifa. On each side were three gilded Greatest Names in relief, designed by Mishkín-Qalam. A few weeks before Naw-Rúz 1909, 'Abdu'l-Bahá had the casket pulled up to the Tomb by twenty men. At the Master's command, the men lowered the casket down into its receptacle. Munír Zayn wrote that the work 'must have been performed with the help of the Hosts of El Abha, for though the work presented great difficulty and was done by inexperienced men, every one wondered at the ease with which was all done'.[18] A week before Naw-Rúz, 'Abdu'l-Bahá sent two Bahá'ís to Haifa to prepare everything at the Shrine of the Báb.

On 21 March, before pilgrims from both the east and the west, 'Abdu'l-Bahá placed the small wooden casket in the large marble one, and Zayn wrote:

> The shrine under the ground was lighted with but one lamp. Abdul Baha waited until all was well finished.
> He threw off His turban and hat,
> He removed His shoes,
> He took off His coat, but what followed was so impressive that it is useless for me to attempt to picture it. I will simply relate what happened. Our beloved Lord with His hair waving around His beautiful head, His face shining with light, looking inspired, tragic and majestic, rushed down and threw Himself on His knees. He placed the remains of the Báb in the large coffin (placed in the marble casket) and leaning His blessed head on the border of the coffin, He wept, wept, wept and all wept with Him!
> That night the Master did not sleep.[19]

May Woodcock and A. M. Bryant, who were in Haifa for a month, were also there when the Báb's remains were placed in the tomb:

> It is beyond me to depict the beauty and solemnity of that scene. Our Lord was indescribably grand. We saw Him for the first time without His fez (head-dress), His beautiful white hair falling in picturesque disorder upon His shoulders. He had thrown off His dark outer garment and was robed in a flowing garment of neutral blue. When the huge sarcophagus was finally placed in position our

Lord with the men believers grouped about Him, made a picture never to be forgotten. One of the believers held aloft a lamp, the light of which fell like a radiance upon the beloved Master's form as He stood in the sarcophagus, and with tears streaming down His blessed Face, changed with His own Hands the Sacred Ashes from the casket which had held them many, many years, to the magnificent white marble sarcophagus which is a loving gift of the believers of India. When the marble cover was placed, our Lord threw Himself on the sarcophagus and wept aloud.

The believers who were with Him, as well as the ladies who were standing or kneeling about the entrance to the Tomb, wept with Him, and for Him too who made such a pathetic figure beside the Tomb of the One Who had proclaimed His Glorious Advent. Such a tumult of thoughts and emotions surged through our minds for it seemed as if all the miraculous happenings of the Cause from its earliest Dawn passed before our vision, flooding our souls with awe and wonder at the mighty works of God. When at last our dear Lord walked out of the Tomb He had an expression on His Face which is indescribable. The Power of the Spirit was so intense that we stood as if petrified until He had passed into another part of the building where a room was prepared for Him to rest in. In the meantime the believers who had been working with the Master came out and stood in groups speaking together in hushed tones while they waited to accompany 'Abdu'l-Baha back to Haifa. Such a wonderful picture they made, especially the white haired, saintly looking believers in their Oriental costumes. One believer had given up business and came and camped with his family near the Tomb for some weeks, during which time he had worked with pick and shovel to dig a hole in the foundation of the Tomb through which the sarcophagus had been passed. They could not employ skilled laborers for fear of drawing the attention of the Nakazeen.[20]

According to one report, the young Shoghi Effendi was down in the tomb when the coffin was lowered.[21] While this happened on Mount Carmel, in America the believers were holding the first 'Mashrak El Azkar Convention' in Chicago.[22]

Within weeks of the Báb's remains being placed in the Shrine, Sultan 'Abdu'l-Hamíd, who had survived the revolution of the Young

Turks by granting their demand for the restoration of the constitution, overthrew the cabinet in what was called 'the counter-revolution' of 13 April 1909. Shortly thereafter, when the government retook control, 'Abdu'l-Hamíd was deposed and his brother declared to be Sultan.[23]

Juliet Thompson, and Edward and Carrie Kinney

On 25 June, Juliet Thompson, Alice Beede, and Edward and Carrie Kinney with their two sons, Sandy and Howard, arrived in Haifa. It was the second pilgrimage for Edward and Carrie, but the first for the rest. Juliet was strongly affected just by being in Haifa:

> I am sitting in the hall, looking through the wide window at the end, across twelve miles of the bay to the Holy City. 'Akká, dreamed of for nine long years – the Mecca of my prayers – is before my bodily eyes! I am absolutely inarticulate. What I have felt, what I have seen, is too vast to be expressed in human language. I can find no words great enough to convey the impressions of these last three days – or two days, I lose track of time! And as yet, I have not seen 'Akká! In His infinite mercy and wisdom and love the Master is preparing us; in his gentleness. Yet even the preparation has been almost too much for the human heart.
>
> That first sight of Carmel, with its Mystery, the Holy Mountain, 'the Mountain of the Lord,' broke me down. I am still overpowered when I look at it, and as I grow more sensitized I will surely feel it more and more. Here the Divine Spirit breathes and reveals itself. I know now. Ah, the poor human hearts to whom that Spirit is not revealed, to whom the material is everything, who cannot know of the Spiritual Kingdom surrounding them, who have not rent the veil! Will they believe me when I return to testify? I would 'ascend to the cross' for them! To breathe this Truth into the world I would give my own last breath with joy. I can now understand the ecstasy of the martyrs. I pray to be one of them, to be worthy of their destiny. I know now what the Master means by the Holy Fragrances. I have come to the centre of their emanation. The air is laden with the Divine Incense – verily, the Breath of God. It is almost unbearable. I am immersed, lost in it. My prayers used to grope through space. Now I am conscious of a close communion with a heart-consuming

Spirit of Love, a Spirit more intensely real than the earth and all the stars put together, than the essence of all human love, even than mother-love.[24]

On the afternoon of their first day in Haifa, Dr Fareed, who later went with 'Abdu'l-Bahá to Europe and America and then broke the Covenant, took the pilgrims to the Shrine of the Báb where they met Mírzá Asadu'lláh, Fareed's father, and Asadu'lláh's wife and daughter. After some enlightening conversation, they descended to the house of the Master where they met the ladies of the Household:

> we went to the Holy Household to visit the Holy Leaves. I shall never forget that little procession as they entered the room with the dignity of queens, led by the Greatest Holy Leaf. She was all in white: the Greatest Holy Leaf, the daughter of the Blessed Perfection. Her face had the look of one who had passed through crucifixion and was resurrected in another world. In it shone great blue eyes, eyes that had looked upon many sorrows and now were ineffably tender. Behind her came Túbá Khánum, Munavvar Khánum, and Edna Ballora.
>
> Ah, what can I say? Nothing but this: As a bud that was little and hard opens in the sunlight, so my heart opened to a wealth of love inconceivable to the human mind.
>
> That night we went again to see the Holy Leaves. They are staying in the house that Madame Jackson built. We sat on the broad marble steps, Mount Carmel looming, a dark mass, above us. Above the mountain hung the moon. Down in the village the little white dice-like houses, each with its pointed black cypress tree, were a pale blue in the moonlight. The bay to our right splashed its waves on the beach.
>
> I whispered to Munavvar Khánum: 'What is that – it cannot be imagination – what is that breathing from Mount Carmel? It is too strong for me. It is unbearable!'
>
> I covered my face with my hands. Munavvar pressed close to me. 'Ah, you feel it too?' she whispered back.[25]

Carrie Kinney became ill on Sunday 27 June with what Dr Fareed and a British doctor diagnosed as typhoid fever, tossing restlessly on her bed and having an extremely high fever. The next morning, they were all supposed to have gone to 'Akká to meet the Master, but plans had to be changed. Juliet ran to the Master's house and informed the ladies of Carrie's illness:

> Immediately Túbá and Munavvar returned to the hotel with me and we all went up into Carrie's room, where she lay tossing on her bed with a terrifically high fever. Munavvar and Túbá, standing by the bed, bent over it with the tenderest love. 'We will all pray for you, Carrie,' they said. 'Our Lord will pray for you. His prayers are always answered.'
> As Túbá bade me goodbye at the door of Nassar's hotel, she said, 'Tonight this will pass.'
> Munavvar too whispered, 'Tonight.'
> At midnight it 'passed.' I was with Carrie when she woke up free from fever.[26]

Early on 1 July, Juliet heard a knock on her door. She opened it to find Caroline Rodgers, who had arrived in Haifa unexpectedly and without the permission of 'Abdu'l-Bahá. Juliet remembered that she had long prayed that Caroline would be with her when she met the Master and now that prayer had been answered. But first, Caroline had to get permission to go to 'Akká so she had to wait in Haifa while the other pilgrims went to the old city.[27]

For pilgrims going to meet 'Abdu'l-Bahá for the first time, the carriage ride from Haifa to 'Akká was a time of great anticipation. Juliet's feelings were laid bare in her description:

> Never shall I forget that afternoon's journey. I was dazed, numb, unable to realize – yet, afraid. For one thing I did realize – and that was my own unworthiness. But the scenes through which we passed should have helped me to realize, to sense, some of the divine joy toward which we were traveling.
> We were in the Holy Land. We were in a bygone age. We drove along a wide white beach, so close to the sea that its little waves curled over our carriage wheels. To our right, a long line of palm trees. Before us, its domes and flat roofs dazzling white beneath the deep blue sky: 'Akká, the Holy City, the New Jerusalem. Camels

approached us on the sand, driven by white-cloaked Bedouins, their veils bound by circlets; or sheep, led by shepherds in tunics and carrying crooks, striped headcloths framing their faces. And once there came a family, the woman riding a donkey, a child in her arms, while a man walked beside her. The woman was wrapped in a dark blue veil.

We forded the river Kishon, then Hebron, and at last reached the walls of the Holy City, the City of Peace. Walls: walls within walls, menacing walls. Tall, prison-like, chalk-white houses, leaning together as they rose toward a rift of sky, slits of barred windows set here and there in their forbidding fronts. Streets so narrow that our carriage wheels grazed the buildings on either side, streets sometimes bridged over by houses that met in an arch at their second stories.

Suddenly a wide expanse before us. A garden. The seawall. The sea. Our carriage stopped. I knew we were at the door of the Master. My heart almost ceased to beat. I felt we had arrived too soon, too suddenly, that I was too unprepared.

The curtains of the carriage were raised. In front of a great stone house, very picturesque and rambling, stood a group of men in turbans, long white robes, and dark *'abás* (cloaks) with faces miraculously pure – shining, smiling – whose hearts seemed to welcome us. Then one with a very tender face: Siyyid Asadu'lláh, an old man, led us through an arch to a great inner courtyard open to the sky, where two giant palm trees stood in the midst of flower beds. Two stairways of old worn stone, one on either side of the courtyard and diagonally opposite each other, led directly to the third floor, on which the Holy Household lived. The railing of the stair leading to the Master's room was vine covered.[28]

Then came the moment of meeting the Master, 'Abdu'l-Bahá:

As I entered the court, a great spasm of feeling convulsed me. My unworthiness overwhelmed me. The light of the inner court was too strong. I sobbed and bowed my head.

The Kinneys and Alice had gone ahead of me. I followed them up the stairs with the vines, across a small open court with low white walls, to a room next to the Master's. This room I was to share with Alice.

Soon Edna Ballora came in. She took me to the window. Outside was a large square of bare ground, four trees in a row at a little distance; beyond these a street of tall houses, and to the right, at the foot of the double sea wall, a long, narrow garden.

'The Master is in the garden,' said Edna.

He was in white, seated at the side of a wall in the center of the garden, surrounded by guests.

My first thought as I saw that Figure was God Almighty! – such was the majesty and purity. I then thought: King of men! Lion of the tribe of Judah!

Soon He came into our room. He burst into it like the sun, with His joyous greeting, 'Marhabá! Marhabá!' (Welcome! Welcome!) And His effulgence struck me blind.

Alice fell at His feet. I could not kneel. I could not do anything. At last, I knelt for a moment. Then He led us to the divan by the window and, speaking formally to me, placed me at a distance from Him; while to Alice, again at His feet, He spoke with smiling tenderness.

Sitting in the corner of the divan, now surer than ever of my unworthiness, I prayed: O God, remove this thing which separated me from my Lord!

Suddenly He changed His seat. 'Bíyá!' (Come!) He called to me lovingly, drawing me close to His side.

He asked me many questions, answered by Alice, for still I could not speak . . .

The great overwhelming Spirit in Him, the Divinity of His Being deprives one of all one's powers, even the power of sensation, for a time. Yet He makes Himself so simple: in the mercy of His Love, in His great God-tenderness, bends so close to us.

Suddenly my heart burst open to the outpouring from His Heart, like a rose beneath strong sunbeams. A beam seemed to pierce my heart. At that instant He flashed a lightning glance at me. When He left the room, as He did almost at once, my breast dilated as if a bird were spreading wings in it. I went to the window. Just as I did so, Munavvar appeared in the doorway. 'The Master is calling you, Juliet,' she said, and she led me to His room.

That dear little room, wood paneled, with its white-canopied bed, its divan, its simple little dressing table, and on the windowsill two stone water jars: nothing more. He was sitting on the divan at the end nearest the door, and when I entered, He beckoned me to His side. As I passed Him to take my seat I wanted to kneel at his knees – my own knees almost drew me down. But, fearing to be insincere, I would not yield. He took my hand in His – His so mysterious Hand – so delicately made, so steely strong, currents of life streaming from it.

'Are you well? Are you happy?'

But my lips seemed to be locked. I was helpless to open them.

'Speak – speak to Me!' He said in English.

A sacred passion had been growing in my heart: my heart was almost breaking with it.

'Is not my heart speaking to Thee, my Lord?'

'Yes, your heart is speaking to Me and your spirit is speaking to Me. I hear, I know.'

Then he inquired for the two believers I cared for least.

Of one I could honestly say when he returned from 'Akká he was on fire.

'And he remained but a few days,' said our Lord. Then: 'Do not think your services are unknown to Me. I have seen. I have been with you. I know them all. Do not think I have not known. I have known all. For these you are accepted in the Kingdom.'

My 'services' – and He knew them all! He had 'seen': seen their pitiful smallness and the lack of real love with which I had tried to serve. I bowed my head with shame.

'Forgive my failures.'

'Be sure of this.' After a moment He said again, 'Be sure of this.' Then He dismissed me.

As I passed Him the second time, my knees did draw me down; my heart drew me down to His feet.

Later that evening He came to our door, a blue door in the whitewashed wall, leading out into the open court. We knelt in the doorway, Alice and I.

'We are at home, Lord,' I said, 'at home, for the first time.'

'Yes. Home, home. It is your home.'[29]

That evening, the pilgrims gathered around 'Abdu'l-Bahá at the table for dinner, Juliet on His left. Edward Kinney told the interpreter, 'We have no questions to ask. We wish Him to fill our spiritual needs.' So, 'Abdu'l-Bahá told them:

> Without firmness there will be no result. Trees must be firm in the ground to give fruit. The foundation of a building must be very solid in order to support the building. If there be the slightest doubt in a believer, he will be without result. How often did Christ warn Peter to be steadfast! Therefore, consider how difficult it is to remain firm, especially in the time of trials. If man endure and overcome the trials, the more will he become firm and steadfast. When the tree is firmly rooted, the more the wind blows the more the tree will benefit; the more intense the wind the greater the benefit. But if weak, it will immediately fall.[30]

The pilgrims were called for tea at six the next morning. When they arrived, they found 'Abdu'l-Bahá in His usual seat, the right-hand corner of the divan by a high window, correcting Tablets with His secretaries. The Holy Family sat around Him, and along the divan and on the floor were the families of the martyrs, whom He had taken under His care. A samovar rested on the floor by the entrance. Juliet noted one 'beautiful, happy-faced woman' with deep dimples and black braids, serving tea. She learned that the woman was the wife of a martyr:

> Her story was this: Years before in Persia, when she was a bride fifteen years old, she was with her mother-in-law in a room of their house on the ground floor when suddenly they heard a howling mob outside. And then a severed head was thrown through the window and rolled to the young bride's feet. It was the head of her husband, a boy of nineteen. The girl fainted, but the mother quietly rose, took the head of her son to the washstand and washed off the blood, then carried it to the window and threw it out to the mob. 'What we have given to God,' she said, 'we do not ask back.'[31]

'Abdu'l-Bahá greeted the pilgrims as He greeted everyone, asking if they were happy. Then He noted that they couldn't have slept very comfortably, saying 'In New York it is better and more beautiful than here. There it is beautiful. You have parks and trees. But here the heart is good.' Then He told them that 'since the Cause is established in Persia and America, the East and West are united, happy, and in perfect love with one another.'³²

Juliet had a private meeting with 'Abdu'l-Bahá on 2 July when she presented Him with letters and petitions from the friends back in America. For Lua Getsinger, May Maxwell, Howard MacNutt, Laura Barney, Ellen Beecher, Agnes Parsons, Bernard Ginzig, Mr Barakatu'lláh, Claudia Coles, Mabel Rice-Wray, Mary Little and Bertie Warfield, the Master gave responses. Then Munavvar Khánum brought in Caroline Rodgers, thus fulfilling Juliet's prayer. The Master called for Alice Beede and Carrie Kinney and declared that He wanted a great love to develop between them for 'the more you love one another, the nearer you get to Me'.³³

On 4 July, 'Abdu'l-Bahá took the pilgrims to Bahjí and the Shrine of Bahá'u'lláh. They stopped first to have tea in a 'cool, whitewashed room, its door and window-trimmings painted blue'. On a table was a photograph of Lua Getsinger. When the tea arrived, 'Abdu'l-Bahá served it Himself in clear glasses, after which He called the four children, Howard and Sandy Kinney and His own grandsons Shoghi Effendi and Rúhí Effendi, to Him and

> with a lavish tenderness, a super abundance of overflowing love, such as could only have come from the very Center and Source of Love, He drew all four to His knees, clasped them in His arms, which enclosed them all, gathered and pressed and crushed them to His Heart of hearts. Then He set them down on the floor and, rising, Himself brought their tea to them.
>
> Words absolutely fail me when I try to express the divine picture I saw then. With the Christ-love radiating from Him with the intensest sweetness I have yet witnessed, He stooped to the floor Himself to serve the little children, the children of the East and the children of the West. He sat on the floor in their midst, He put sugar into their tea, stirred it and fed it to them, all the while smiling celestially, an infinite tenderness playing on the great Immortal Face like white light. I cannot express it! In a corner sat an old Persian believer, in a state of complete effacement before his Lord, his head bowed, his eyelids lowered, his hands crossed on his breast. Tears were pouring down his cheeks.³⁴

Then 'Abdu'l-Bahá turned to the parents and prepared them to visit the Shrine of Bahá'u'lláh.

> '. . . one of the gifts of God is to be able to pay a visit to the Holy Tomb, but man cannot fully realize it while in this world. But when he enters the World of the Kingdom, there the blessings and gifts will become evident and clear.
>
> 'Is this clear to you?'
>
> Then, giving us each a handful of jasmine, He led us one by one to the jasmine-strewn threshold of the Holy Tomb. As He led me, His hand quickened me. Never can I forget its vital, tingling pressure.
>
> We knelt at the Divine Threshold. Suddenly, He was beside us: luminous, silent. Bending, He anointed our foreheads with attar of rose. Then He lifted each of us to our feet. And then, in a voice which struck across my heart, causing my entire being to quiver, the memory of which even now pierces and wrings my heart, He chanted.
>
> When He had finished He asked Mr. Kinney to chant. I could scarcely bear the thought of a human voice following His. Yet Mr. Kinney sang beautifully: 'O Lord, make us pure and without desire.' My whole being echoed this prayer.
>
> Our Lord then requested us all to sing, and the hymn we chose was 'Nearer, My God, to Thee.'
>
> While our Lord was chanting I could not look at Him, but during the singing that followed, I kept my face turned toward Him. I still see Him standing by the window, the translucence of that majestic profile, the grandeur of that luminous head, white turbaned against the white wall.[35]

Before they had gone to the Shrine, Juliet, Carrie, Alice and Caroline were talking together in Juliet's room. The topic became contentious and the women began to disagree. Suddenly there was a tap at the door which, when opened, revealed 'Abdu'l-Bahá standing there with His hands full of jasmine. After returning from the Shrine, one of the ladies said something 'off-color. It was carried on by someone else. Remembering our sacred morning, my soul rebelled.' Again came 'Abdu'l-Bahá's tap at the door.[36]

On 5 July, Caroline departed for Iran. As she left, 'Abdu'l-Bahá told her:

> This is the third time you have been here. It has been a great pleasure for you to have been with your friends each time. Now a long trip is before you. If throughout this trip you are always sincere in your intentions you will enjoy it very much. This ought to be a spiritual and not a physical journey. You must always do your best to behave spiritually, not physically, so that everyone who meets you will know that your intention is to do good to mankind and your aim to serve the world of humanity. Whatever you do, let the people know you are doing it for good, not only to earn your own living. By doing thus you will be able to serve every city to which you go. Now associate with good people. You must try to associate with those who will do you good and who will be the cause of your being more awakened, and not with those who will make you negligent of God. For example, if one goes into a garden and associates with flowers, one will surely inhale the beautiful fragrance, but if one goes to a place where there are bad-scented plants, it is sure he will inhale an unpleasant odor. In short, I mean that you will try to be with those who are purified and sanctified souls. Man must always associate with those from whom he can get light, or be with those to whom he can give light. He must either receive or give instructions. Otherwise, being with people without these two intentions, he is spending his time for nothing, and, by so doing, he is neither gaining nor causing others to gain.
>
> You must keep these words very well. This is the third time you have come here. Fruits must be the results of these visits. Patients go to a hospital. Some leave but slightly improved. Some leave more ill than when they entered. And some leave entirely cured. I hope you will be of those who are entirely cured. You must be very thankful that you have come.[37]

One problem that plagued Juliet at this time, and would continue to bother her for years, was love and marriage. She was very much in love with a charismatic Unitarian preacher named Percy Grant. Grant, however, was vehemently against the Bahá'í Faith and 'Abdu'l-Bahá tried to guide Juliet to a different path. On the evening of 8 July, the Master came to Juliet and talked about Mason Remey, at that time one of the leading and most active Bahá'í teachers. The Master said He would like to see Mason and Juliet marry. Juliet immediately bowed to His suggestion, but 'Abdu'l-Bahá asked what her inner feelings were, saying that inner feelings could not be forced. The Master knew about Percy Grant, so asked if she could love Remey as much as she loved Grant. When it became obvious that she was unsure, 'Abdu'l-Bahá said, 'But your marrying the other [Grant] is good,' but then He added the caveat, 'if you can make him a believer'.[38] Though Grant did become very attracted to 'Abdu'l-Bahá, Juliet could never make him a believer.

The next day, when He was with Juliet, 'Abdu'l-Bahá returned to the subject of Percy Grant. He told Juliet about one of the first Western pilgrim women: 'she came here and was full of love and aglow. Then she returned and married [a man who was not attracted to the Faith] and her love for the Blessed Perfection grew cold . . . I want to tell you not to marry this man until you have made him a believer. Because afterward it would be more difficult. First make him a believer.'[39] Juliet never managed to open Grant's spiritual eyes, so remained unmarried.

Sydney Sprague and Mason Remey were in 'Akká on 9 July, having just returned from their teaching trip to Persia. 'Abdu'l-Bahá asked Sydney to speak to the pilgrims, but Sprague demurred, saying, 'It is impossible to speak when our Lord is here.' When the Master encouraged him, he talked about a meeting attended by a Zoroastrian, a Jew, a Christian, and a Muslim. Because the meeting lasted so long, the four stayed the night sharing the same bed. 'Abdu'l-Bahá trumpeted, 'Consider what the power of the Covenant has done! It was an impossibility for a Zoroastrian to unite with a siyyid and a mullá with a Jew. And for these to assemble with a Christian was an absolute impossibility. But the power of the Covenant has even so gathered them that they are accounted as one spirit.'[40]

'Abdu'l-Bahá called Carrie, Juliet and Alice in separately on 10 July to experience His dictation of Tablets. Juliet wrote:

> I sat on the divan, my eyes upon His white-robed figure – I could scarcely raise them to His Face – as He paced up and down that small room with His strong tread. Never had the room seemed so small; never had He appeared so mighty! A lion in a cage? Ah no! That room contain Him? Why? As I felt that great dominant Force, that Energy of God, I knew that the earth itself could not

contain Him. Nor yet the universe. No! While the body, charged with a Power I have seen in no human being, restless with the Force that so animated it, strode up and down, up and down in that tiny room, pausing sometimes before the window, below which the sea beat against the double seawall, I knew that the Spirit was free as the Essence itself, brooding over regions far distant, looking deep into hearts at the uttermost ends of the earth, consoling their secret sorrows, answering the whispers of far-off minds.[41]

Then the Master called all three women together and showed them the pile of correspondence He had to reply to. He showed them one letter that was illegible, saying 'The man could not write. But he wished to supplicate to His Master, so he simply made marks.' Then 'Abdu'l-Bahá handed to Carrie a Tablet he had written to one man, saying, 'This is for you too.'

O thou who art firm in the Covenant!
Though thy father was not kind to thee, praise be to God thou hast a Heavenly Father. If the earthly father forsook you, it was the cause of your obtaining the mercy and kindness of the Spiritual Father. All that father can do is to be kind to you, but this Father confers upon you eternal life. That father will become angry for the slightest disobedience, but this Father forgives the sins, overlooks the faults and deals with Bounty and Favor. Thank thou God thou hast such a Heavenly Father. And I hope thou mayest attain, through the Divine Mercy, to the greatest Bounty.

The three women were shocked. Carrie had never mentioned it to the Master, but her own father had driven her out for becoming a Bahá'í and would 'not even speak to her'.[42]

On the morning of 11 July, 'Abdu'l-Bahá called for Juliet:

I knew what was coming!
'How many days have you been here? Nine is the utmost. How many days have you stayed?'
'Twelve, my Lord.'
'Three more than the utmost!' Then He told me we must go tomorrow.[43]

Finally, the last night came for the pilgrims and the Master hosted a feast. There were also seventy Persian pilgrims who had walked on foot for three months to visit 'Abdu'l-Bahá. They came from Zoroastrian, Jewish and Muslim backgrounds, but all were now united under the banner of Bahá'u'lláh. As He usually did, the Master served His guests. The Persians all sat in humble silence with heads bowed, a reverent devotion of a different style than the Americans. When the meal was finished, 'Abdu'l-Bahá, 'His tread the tread of a conquering King, His white robe, His white hair, His white turban in the soft candlelight enhancing His ethereality', gave His final talk to the combined group:

> Tonight . . . is a beautiful night because, *al-ḥamdul'illáh* (Praise be to God!), the believers of America and Persia are joined here at one table. This is one of the great fruits of the Word of God.
>
> In the future the East and the West shall become one. They shall be united. I have said in My letters that the East and the West will become as two lovers. That each is beloved of the other. That the East and the West will take one another in their arms will give one another their hands, each as the beloved of the other, each embracing the other.
>
> The unity of mankind will be the beginning of the radiation of this Light. Our gathering tonight around such a table is one of the evidences of the human unity. Generally speaking, such a gathering would have been impossible, that is, that Persian and Americans should sit around the same table. Praise be to God, such things have taken place through the power of the Word of God.
>
> Verily, since the early days of childhood I have devoted Myself to the Word of the Beauty of Bahá'u'lláh, and have forborne every difficulty and calamity, among these imprisonments for all My life, to lay the foundation of the oneness of mankind.
>
> All the different sects of the world hate and antagonize one another. Were it possible, they would kill one another. Each of these sects pretends that it is established and is acting according to the law of God. Exactly the opposite is the fact. All the Divine Words lead the people to unity, because they were spoken for life, not for death! And the Divine Teaching is a Power that attracts the hearts, through which all the different sects and nations will be attracted.
>
> You find that the different sects are in hatred toward one another.

But you should be lovers of all sects and nations and all the different parties of people. You should love them and consider them as of your own families. Do not look upon them as separated from you. Bahá'u'lláh has said that all of you are as branches of one tree, leaves of one branch. That is, all the people are of one tree. Therefore, all things that cause opposition should be removed. Consider everyone, of every nation or sect, as one of your own family. Deal with them with love and harmony. Never be the cause of any sorrow to anyone, neither the cause of any embarrassment. Bear all sorrow, for yourselves and to please all hearts, even the hearts of your enemies. Be true to all the different parties or nations and act toward them with faithfulness. Take care of the properties of others more than you do of your own, and never do any harm to those who show animosity. If you do thus, you are a true Bahá'í. Be submissive and try to control self. Follow the ordinances of God – do not follow your own desire – that ye may be ready always to be helped by God.

Be sure that the different nations will curse you, blame you, bear animosity toward you and harm you.

They will even act in such a way as to shed your blood. Beware not to cause any sorrow to them, not even to injure the feelings of anyone with a word. Do nothing to cause any sorrow within any heart. These are the qualities of the Bahá'í people.[44]

The next morning, the pilgrims left for Haifa and then to Beirut.

Juliet was almost distraught at being away from 'Abdu'l-Bahá, so she was overjoyed when she received permission on 7 August to return to Haifa from Beirut. She arrived in Haifa on the 10th, but then waited for three days without word from the Master. At dawn on the 13th, she had prayed and finally felt a 'wonderful peace'. Soon she was again in the Master's presence.[45]

By 21 August the Kinneys and Alice Beede had also returned to Haifa, and that day 'Abdu'l-Bahá spoke of the harrowing journey from Tehran to Baghdad during the January of 1853. The translator said:

'the family was pillaged, for three days and nights they were left absolutely foodless, and with not a mat to lie on. In such condition, in mid-winter, amid the cold and frost, they were banished . . . The Master . . . did not have but one pair of stockings, which He was wearing, and that had a big hole in it, so that His foot was bitten by the frost; He feels it now. On the way from Teheran to Bagdad there is a stage called Saadabad, where it is intensely cold. It was thirty below zero, and as the foot was already bitten by the frost and they were all terribly tired and unable to go on any farther, they decided to stop there, have a little supper and try to get warm. For supper they were to have bread and pudding; there was no tea. It was night and no light could be had. However they got some molasses, some butter and some flour to make the pudding. It being so dark that they could see nothing, by mistake a handful of pepper was put in; image the pudding! But as there was nothing else, they had to eat it – and it burned to the inmost part! Notwithstanding this, they were in a condition of utmost joy.' (While the Master was recounting these misfortunes, He laughed heartily.) 'The purpose in telling this is to show that whosoever enters the Kingdom must not be joyous because of wealth and home, nor sorrowing when indigent, destitute and homeless.'[46]

Finally, after 12 more days in Haifa, 'Abdu'l-Bahá again told Juliet it was time to go. On her last day, 22 August, 'Abdu'l-Bahá invited her to lunch. She went back to her room and decided to prepare herself especially for Him:

> I wanted to make myself as beautiful as I could! And everything went wrong; it was like a nightmare! I chose an elaborate white lace dress, fastened in the back with hooks-and-eyes and my fingers couldn't find the right hooks. I tried to put on my veil, a rose-coloured one with a border, in the most becoming way, and couldn't arrange it becomingly enough! And before I was through adorning myself, Khusraw ran in with an appalling message: the Master and the Holy Household were already at the table!
>
> By the time I reached the House and the dining room, the Master had risen from His seat and was washing His hands in a basin near the window. He asked me to please excuse Him for leaving so soon, He had only taken a little soup.
>
> I sat stricken with an awful shame: speechless with shame, as I realized overwhelmingly the disrespect I had shown to our Lord in keeping Him waiting – and all because of my vanity![47]

But in the afternoon he called her to Him again. She had had 12 days in 'Akká and now 12 days in Haifa. He told her return to America and be a force for unity, to never speak unkindly of anyone, and to anyone else who spoke unkindly of another, to stop them and tell them it is against the command of Bahá'u'lláh. That night she sailed away from Haifa and her heart's desire.[48]

Valíyu'lláh Varqá

Valíyu'lláh Varqá (1884–1955) spent several years studying in Beirut and every summer 'Abdu'l-Bahá summoned Him to 'Akká where he would advance his Bahá'í education with Hájí Mírzá Haydar-'Alí. It was Varqá's plan was to finish in Beirut, then to continue his education at a university in England, but in the summer of 1909, 'Abdu'l-Bahá gave him a mission to Tehran. Completing the mission, Varqá then married Bahíyyih Khánum and began work at the Russian Legation. In 1912 he had the bounty of travelling with the Master in the West before returning to Tehran where he worked at the Turkish Embassy and served on both the Local Spiritual Assembly of Tehran and the National Spiritual Assembly from its inception in 1934. Varqá served for twelve years as the Trustee of Huqúqu'lláh for Shoghi Effendi and was appointed a Hand of the Cause of God in 1951.[49]

Susan Moody and Louise Waite

In about 1908, a group of American Bahá'ís travel teaching in Persia learned about the need for a woman doctor there. Since men doctors could not treat women, women were deprived of good care. When this group, which may have included Mason Remey and Sydney Sprague, returned to 'Akká, they told this to 'Abdu'l-Bahá, and He asked if they knew of such a doctor. Dr Susan Moody's name was brought up. 'Abdu'l-Bahá sent her a message saying that she had been chosen for this medical work in Persia. 'I knew then', Dr Moody later said, 'why I had felt the urge so strongly to study medicine; I was obliged to study medicine in order to come to Iran.' When Dr Moody received the Master's call, she left immediately, stopping to see 'Abdu'l-Bahá enroute.[50]

On 8 October, the group composed of Dr Susan Moody, Sydney Sprague, Cecilia Harrison, and Louise Waite arrived in Haifa. Susan vividly remembered their arrival at 7:30 in the evening, 'landing by small boat – the uproar – the rearing and tearing of the lawless native – and we are glad to come out of it with our lives. I am mourning the loss of my black bag which I gave to Cook's man.' The bag contained a large number of letters and supplications from American believers.[51]

The group went to the Shrine of the Báb on the 10th and Susan wrote about the visit to her friend Eva:

> A silence fell on us as we neared the building. An old man was heating coffee or water over a little fire out doors. The flowers in front were four-o'clocks, roses, jessamine and still a few orange blossoms. After greeting the keeper we took off our shoes and entered the carpeted (rugs) vestibule. Mirza Assad Ullah advanced to the door, knelt and bowed his head to the threshold, touching with his lips three times. Each followed in turn while the holy solemnity intensified and soon Mirza Assad Ullah began a beautiful chant. The Tomb vibrated until every atom of our bodies responded. Dear Eva, no word can give you the rest of it.[52]

On the 11th, the group went to 'Akká, arriving at 10:30 in the morning. The ladies spent the rest of the morning with Munavvar Khánum, Rúhá Khánum and the Greatest Holy Leaf. Susan remembered the Greatest Holy Leaf, whom she had met earlier in Haifa where she described her as 'dressed in white, a light wool princess dress with a delicate soft veil, bordered with tatting, neatly drawn back under her hair which is plainly combed back. The strong face is full of love, and so strongly marked by suffering that it is touching in the extreme.' Now, she wrote, she 'impresses one most powerfully . . . Last night as we sat in a dimly lighted room, talking with her and the mother [Munírih Khánum], she really resembled pictures of the agony on the cross.'

Towards noon, Louise had an unexpected but memorable encounter with 'Abdu'l-Bahá:

> To describe Abdul Baha so as to form any mental picture of Him that would in any way do Him justice, is as impossible as to try to paint a sunbeam. The artist may put the ray of yellow light in exactly the right place and with most beautiful effect; but, no matter how great his skill, he cannot catch the real essence of the sunbeam – that

golden luminosity, which is like an elixir of life, is uncatchable, unpaintable. So it is with the likeness of Abdul Baha. His expression is ever changing; each thought and emotion is mirrored forth and the face becomes so illumined that words are but as the dull, lifeless paint which cannot reproduce the sunbeam – yet some idea can be gathered from them.

When I first saw Abdul Baha I was alone and I came face to face with Him all unexpectedly. He stood not over four feet from me . . . It might have been anyone else . . . but every atom of my being, my heart and my soul cried out: 'It is He.' The face of my dream of Him stood before me with that same heavenly smile of welcome. The light of Infinite Love was radiating from His countenance. Majestic and yet sublimely tender, He was looking right into my eyes. I gave a start as if I had suddenly plunged into an ocean – then stood transfixed. It seemed as if I had come upon Him unawares and saw the 'Glory of the Lord' shining forth around Him . . . He motioned me to pass on. I could not. A sense of my great unworthiness made me bow my head – then He passed by me. He was dressed all in white. His hair fell in soft waves about His shoulders and His head was crowned with a white turban bound with a white cloth. His step was firm and kingly. When He reached His door He turned and motioned me again to pass on. I came toward Him and when I reached His door, I looked up into those marvelous eyes. I knew that every thought every act of mine was known to Him. Yet, knowing this I could look fearlessly, unwaveringly at Him, realizing all my sins and weaknesses, yet knowing He understood me as I could never understand myself, and that He was indeed 'Infinite Love Incarnate'. I could not pass until He turned and entered His room – then, nearly overcome by the vibrations which thrilled me thru and thru, I passed on. Later He came to greet us and I was fully confirmed – it was truly Abdul Baha, but a very different one, I now felt, from the one I had first seen. As he firmly grasped my hand with that welcoming pressure that comes deep from the heart, a hand-shake that warms you thru and thru, I saw the Divinely human man, the personification of my highest ideal of an earthly father. I never again, while in Acca, saw Him as I had in that first meeting. It was then as if I had seen the Reality of His being, with the shades of flesh all raised that the Light of Spirit might stream forth.

... His voice is full, and vibrant, each word uttered with marked distinctness and with that tone quality that leaves a faint echo, as it were, or wave vibrations such as come from a beautifully toned bell. All thru the day it rings out, first in one place, then another, for with astonishing rapidity Abdul Baha seems to be everywhere – now in the garden, now in the room close beside the entrance, now in a guest's room – or you may hear Him calling some one in the 'family section' of the 'prison home' . . . Like His face, His voice expresses every emotion, from tones that are stern and emphatic to those as tender and loving as the cooing of a dove.

His eyes defy description. I only know that to me they seemed gray, with a circle of white around the iris, which at times became luminous. Sometimes in the light I caught a shade of blue, and again by lamp light they seemed almost brown – ever changing were they and wonderful . . .

I was deeply impressed by His perfect naturalness, His lack of conventionality and set form, and His refreshing simplicity. Divinely simple is He and simply Divine.[53]

At 2 o'clock, 'Abdu'l-Bahá met the women who had gathered in Susan Moody's room. He greeted them, saying 'I am happy that you are here. Did you have a good journey? How are the believers? When one has so great an aim for a journey as this, the little losses and trials you have on the way should not upset you.' This was an obvious reference to Susan's lost bag which she had not told Him about. 'When you have the ocean, you do not need the river. When you have the sun, you do not need the lamp.' After taking each of their hands, the Master left to greet Sydney Sprague in his room. The three women sat in silence until someone finally spoke of the great privilege they had. Munavvar Khánum said,

> Yes, it means much, but if you treat it as a child does a toy, it is worth nothing. If it does not benefit our lives, if we do not live the teaching, all is lost . . . Is it not strange that little Acca should be the place of this light? Think how many beautiful cities there are in the world, and yet little Acca is the place! Many have not even heard of Acca, and many right here do not know Him. They realize that He is a great and good man, but they are indifferent. They will not even stop to inquire why it is that He is different from other men.[54]

Susan was up at 5:45 the next morning. Before she had finished dressing, she heard voices in the courtyard and soon a girl rapped at the door and told her to be ready in 20 minutes. At the appointed time, Susan, Cecilia and Louise were taken to where the women were to meet the Master. 'Abdu'l-Bahá was already there 'sitting in Oriental fashion in the corner of the divan'. As one of the women chanted, He continued sorting and addressing Tablets.

At the Master's dining table during this visit Louise Waite had another interesting moment. She was listening to Him talk, when she looked at her full water glass and then suddenly thought:

> 'Oh! if only Abdu'l-Bahá would take my heart and empty it of every preconceived idea and earthly desire, just as one would take this glass and empty it, and then refill it with divine Love and understanding.' It was just a flash of consciousness, yet 'Abdu'l-Bahá seemed to read it. He was in the midst of His discourse; He stopped abruptly . . . and addressed His attendant who served the friends. He said but a few words in Persian to him, then continued His conversation . . . The attendant came quietly up behind the writer [Louise], reached over and removed her glass from the table and taking it over to the corner of the room, emptied its contents of water into the waterbasin, then returned the empty glass to its former place. Still no one noticed what had happened. 'Abdu'l-Bahá continued to speak, the while reaching over and taking the water-bottle on the table in His hand, and in the most casual manner, still talking on the subject of His discourse, refilled her empty glass . . . Her heart was filled with unspeakable joy. This proved conclusively that the innermost thoughts and innermost desires of the hearts of all present were an open book to 'Abdu'l-Bahá, and that His love encompassed all.[55]

Louise was a self-trained musician and composer who started the first North American Bahá'í Choir. 'Abdu'l-Bahá gave her the name 'Shahnaz' and said of her composition 'Benediction': 'Sing this melody in all gatherings of Love and Harmony of the beloved of God.'

On the morning of 12 October, Susan from her high perch of a room watched 'Abdu'l-Bahá walking about in the garden, talking with some people and calling others. Sydney Sprague was called for an interview and when it was done, he went to see Susan with instructions from the Master for them to leave the next day for Constantinople (Istanbul) and Iran saying, 'This is for your own good. If you delay, the weather will be cold and the journey will be much more difficult.'[56]

At 10:45 that morning, 'Abdu'l-Bahá sent for Susan and seated her beside Himself.

> You are to go to Persia. At first you will find things difficult, – the conveniences are not the same. Many of the people are poor and sleep on the floor, as they have no beds. You must not look at their circumstances, but at their hearts. They will love you very much and I want you to be happy there. You must have much patience and try very hard to be faithful; lose sight of yourself entirely; work only for the love of God and you will succeed. You will find much love there – all will love you.[57]

In the afternoon, Susan twisted her ankle. At first she tried to hide the injury, but soon the pain forced her to confess. Miss Gamblin, who was teaching English in the household, helped her bandage it and Susan managed to keep the injury secret until the next morning when she went with the other women into the presence of 'Abdu'l-Bahá. When they sat, 'Abdu'l-Bahá looked at Susan:

> He looked me through and through very searchingly. I did not know it, but this accounts for the instant consciousness I had of being absolutely nothing, weak, ashamed of my former self, and as Zeah Khanum . . . chanted the first prayers, I felt myself melt and melt until the tears rained down my face. I realized my unworthiness and His great love. When I tho't that this was my last day, I had to exert myself to restrain my longing to kneel at His feet.
>
> Gradually my horizon cleared and, through the chanting of Monever Khanum and two other maid-servants, I became tranquil again.[58]

Susan vowed, 'All that I am and have, and all that I hope to be and have, I dedicate to Thee, O God.' She served the medical needs of Iranian women for 15 years before being forced to leave Tehran. When conditions improved three years later, Susan returned at the age of 77, to continue her work until her death, still at her post.[59]

Other pilgrims and visitors

Four American women, Isabella Brittingham, Maria Wilson, Miss Englehorn, and Elizabeth Stewart (a niece of Mrs Brittingham), reached 'Akká and the Master's presence on 23 October. At their first meal together, 'Abdu'l-Bahá told the visitors that women had made great progress, surpassing, in fact, the men. He said that He was receiving ten supplications from American women to every one from American men. He then called them to 'Come and assist to elevate woman to her true dignity and station.' On another day, the Master offered them honey, saying, 'I hope, when you go back to America, that you will be transformed like this honey, you will be so sweet. Some people are very bitter, while others are sweet. Those spiritual souls and divine persons are very sweet.'[60]

Isabella Brittingham noted that 'Abdu'l-Bahá was busy day and night. After dinner with the pilgrims, he went to His public reception room to meet 'men of importance'. In addition to the Western pilgrims, there were also five Zoroastrian pilgrims from India and others from Egypt. Isabella also recorded that on Saturdays and Sundays, the holy days of the Muslims and Christians, respectively, 'Abdu'l-Bahá entertained many visitors from those Faiths.[61]

1910–1911

Howard Struven and Mason Remey

On 8 May 1910, Howard Struven and Mason Remey arrived from India, three-quarters of the way through a momentous globe-circling teaching trip. The pair left America in November 1909 and visited Hawaii, Japan, China, Burma and India before reaching Haifa seven months later.[1]

When the two men arrived in Haifa, the Master greeted them with:

> Welcome! You are blessed in making such a world pilgrimage and by being allowed to serve in so many countries. Many tourists travel around the globe visiting places and cities, but their tours have no lasting effect and are soon forgotten. The effect of your tour will be eternal. Its effect will be seen during the ensuing centuries.[2]

'Abdu'l-Bahá told Howard and Mason to tell the American believers that great results would occur if some of them would go to Japan. He also said, 'Encourage the Bahais to hasten to India, both men and women teachers. In India, in particular, women teachers are needed. Delay not! Now is the time to travel there, and in Persia, too.'[3] Four years later, He repeated the call to Japan to Agnes Alexander, who promptly arose and opened Japan to the Faith.[4]

The next morning, Howard and Mason took a long walk up Mount Carmel, through the German Colony and up to the monastery. A monk gave them a tour of Elijah's cave. As they continued toward the top of the mountain, they passed a convent where, they had been told, the nuns were constantly looking out of a window that faced the Tomb of the Báb awaiting the return of Christ.[5] After the passing of Bahá'u'lláh, 'Abdu'l-Bahá had retreated for three weeks to a cave near the Cave of Elijah. While there, He one day went to visit the nearby convent and asked admission, saying He had 'a message of importance to deliver to the Sisters of the order.' But the Mother Superior would not allow it, saying that rules of their order prohibited His entering. 'Abdu'l-Bahá returned a second time and was again refused entry. He left unable to tell them that the Man Whose return they were constantly watching for had come and gone.⁶

Howard and Mason went to 'Akká on 13 May where they were shown the photograph of Bahá'u'lláh. Howard was struck by the great similarity between Bahá'u'lláh and 'Abdu'l-Bahá. Some of the older believers added that their ways and voices were also very similar. After viewing the photo, they went with 'Abdu'l-Bahá to His Father's Tomb. As they entered, 'Abdu'l-Bahá gave them rose water, saying in English, 'Come in, my sons.' Inside the building were 50 or 60 other believers sitting in complete silence. The Master chanted two prayers, then the Persians and the other believers left the two Americans alone with 'Abdu'l-Bahá. Howard and Mason knelt side by side at the threshold of Bahá'u'lláh's room. After losing himself in his prayers and supplications, Howard rose to find himself alone.⁷

One day, Howard wrote that he had 'witnessed for the first time in my life what the Divine Wrath is'. One of the Covenant-breakers had been bragging of the 'great services he had rendered to the Blessed Perfection'. 'Abdu'l-Bahá took vigorous exception and, as He spoke,

> his voice became like thunder and his face like lightning, and I trembled and felt that the pillars of the world must be shaken. We have heard how the meek and gentle Christ spoke in His Wrath and denounced the Pharisees. So did 'Abdu'l-Baha speak of this traitor to the Cause. 'How dare he speak of serving the Blessed Perfection,' 'Abdu'l-Baha cried, 'That Holy One Who served us, Who lay in chains in a dungeon for us, Who was crucified every day of His life for us. When I was a child I entered the dungeon – how dark and terrible it was and how the chains cut into the Blessed neck.'
>
> 'Abdu'l-Baha said these last words with a sob in his voice that made our hearts break. Then he continued in a voice of thunder. 'If the Blessed Perfection were present could this man stand before Him and say that he had served Him? The Blessed Perfection would have driven him from His presence at once. Serve Him! If we sacrifice a thousand lives in his path it is not enough.'⁸

On 15 May, Howard and Mason attended a feast hosted by 'Abdu'l-Bahá near the Tomb of the Báb. Mason wrote:

> When the feast was prepared Abdul-Baha served us as we were seated about the table which had twenty-four places. There was a second service and also a third, there being between sixty and seventy present. After all had been served then he, himself, partook of food. As Abdul-Baha gave the material food he made [a] brief but soul sustaining address. It was the most impressive meal that one could possibly imagine . . . Not only were there the many . . . pilgrims present, but also a number of those old and faithful servants of the Cause – men who have done pioneer work in Persia and in neighboring lands – men who have suffered for the faith in prisons and in exile, and who now are spending the evening of life serving in the shadow of Abdul-Baha. In the late afternoon the friends assembled before the door of the Tomb. Abdul-Baha was there. All entered the outer chamber and stood facing the door of the inner chamber while he chanted two tablets. All stood save one, for whom a chair had been placed, Aga Seyed Taghi, the aged Afnan who was assisted into the building, tenderly supported upon one side by Abdul-Baha and upon the other by our good brother, Howard Struven.
>
> Directly over the Tomb hangs a nine-branched candelabra and in this we were permitted to place lighted candles. In the night Howard and I again climbed the mountain a second time. The candles were still burning, and we had a quiet hour of prayer there together, remembering in our supplications the friends in the many assemblies and lands visited on our long journey and thanking God for His wonderful bounties and blessings.[9]

Mason saw that 'Abdu'l-Bahá looked beneath the surface of each person and saw the reality of his heart. He recounted the story of an American Bahá'í who had arrived unannounced:

> One of 'Abdu'l-Baha's interpreters was telling the story of a certain young American lad who blew in one day to see the Master . . . His steamer was in port . . . He blew in to the house at Akka while 'Abdu'l-Baha was still living in the fortress. He asked if he could see the Master.

'Abdu'l-Baha came in. A number of Orientals were in the room. 'Abdu'l-Baha began to speak some words of welcome to be translated by the interpreter. The young man said, 'Tell Him I am very glad to see Him.' 'Abdu'l-Baha said, 'I am very glad to see you.' This boy was just bubbling over. The young man said, 'Tell Him I heard of His Cause in the West, and I believe and I want to devote myself to His service.' 'Abdu'l-Baha said, 'Very good' . . .

The young man took his watch out and pried off the back. He said, 'I am very much in love with a girl and here's her photograph.'

The interpreter demurred a little bit at translating this because in the Orient they do not usually speak of these things before strangers . . . The Master asked the interpreter to translate it, and he did so. The Master looked at the photograph. The young fellow said, 'I pray that she may become a worker in your Cause.' 'Abdu'l-Baha said, 'she will be accepted. Her service will be acceptable.'

The young man said to the interpreter, 'Ask Him if He doesn't think she is very beautiful?'

The interpreter simply could not interpret that before all those people, but the Master insisted upon knowing, and then he said, 'Yes, she is very beautiful. She has the smile of the Kingdom on her face.'

The young man was very pleased. 'Abdu'l-Baha started to say something again. Then the young man opened the other side of his watch and said, 'Well, I am in a great hurry. My ship is sailing. Tell Him Good-bye.'

The old [Persians] there were simply paralyzed. But the Master said afterward, 'I look below the surface. That young man's heart is very pure. I wish that I had more friends of that type.'[10]

At one point, Mason was kneeling before 'Abdu'l-Bahá and the Master put His hands on Mason's shoulders. Mason remembered that he started to 'move several times, and He held me down tightly until I thought my knees would break upon the marble floor. And after He had held me thus for some time He bade me rise and I parted from Him.'[11]

On the day of their departure for America, 17 May, 'Abdu'l-Bahá told Howard and Mason that 'when you go back to America you must circulate in detail all the incidents and news about your vast trip and inform them fully of the works achieved successfully throughout the different countries'.[12] Then hopefully, the Bahá'ís would arise and teach around the world. To Mason, He said, 'Your body is tired and you must return to America to rest and regain your strength. Study Persian with Mírzá Ahmed and after a while I will send you out again to fight.' To Howard He said, 'You are strong, you have great strength, and as you are not worn out you must go to Cairo, Stuttgart, Paris and London, and travel in some cities of the United States. You must tell the glad tidings. You must become a column of fire.'[13]

Grace Crockett

Grace Crockett also came to Haifa in May to see 'Abdu'l-Bahá. She was not a believer, but had come at the suggestion of a Bahá'í friend in Hawaii, Frances Johnson. She went simply because she was travelling in the area and her friend said she should. She left feeling a bit changed. In a letter to Frances, she wrote:

> I know you will be eager to hear of my interview with the one in Palestine whose teaching means so much to you, the Prophet, or Abbas Effendi, as he is generally called.
>
> I found that he is not now kept a prisoner at Acca, but since the order of constitutional government in Turkey he is free to live in his home at Haifa (near by) and go and come as he will.
>
> I planned my trip so that I could stop and see him, for I remember when you gave me some of the literature to read you said: 'If you go to Egypt, Palestine is not far away and you will surely want to see him.' So I planned for the interview with him when the others of the party went to Acca for a drive. (Perhaps you know that Haifa is a pretty little town right at the foot of Mt. Carmel.)
>
> Well, I sent word to him of my wish to see him and he replied that he would see me in the afternoon, as his time was taken up that morning in seeing some people from India. So I went to his house at the time appointed and was shown into the presence of an old man, clothed in the flowing robe of a Persian, with white hair and a long white beard, with eyes that seemed to look me through and yet were most friendly, too. It was the Prophet! He received me most graciously, and his interpreter, a young Syrian, a student at the American Missionary College at Beyrout.

I told him first about the little circle of his friends in far off Honolulu – you who meet together to discuss his teachings – and I told him of your love and loyalty. He seemed very happy at this and his faced lighted up as he asked for the names of those who knew and loved him . . . He sent you all his love and blessing and said he would pray for each one of you, and he added: 'Tell them that they have a great mission – to make the blind eyes see, to make the deaf ears hear and to shed the light of knowledge where the darkness of ignorance prevails.' That was his message for you. He talked with me for some time, first telling me of his country, Persia, of his life and then of his teachings.

As he talked with me I felt my heart soften under the influence of his goodness and kindness, and the tears came to my eyes. He asked me about myself, if I were well and if I were happy. I replied to the latter question: 'I have had many sorrows.' 'Forget them!' he answered. 'When your heart is filled with the love of God there will be no room for sorrow. There will only be love and happiness.' I cannot tell you the sweet sympathy of his voice as he said these beautiful and comforting words.

Then he had the attendant bring in tea, a cup for him and a cup for me. We drank together wishing each other health and happiness, and then he told me that he hoped he should take tea with me in the Kingdom of Heaven!

When I praised the tea he said it was real Persian tea and presented me with a package to take away with me . . .

. . . I went away feeling softened, uplifted and blessed. I am so glad you told me of him and urged me to see him. He wrote his name in my book for me and told me always to remember it.[14]

Stanwood Cobb returns

At the Master's own invitation, Stanwood Cobb arrived on pilgrimage for a week in the summer of 1910. It was his second visit, having been there in 1908 through the invitation of Lua Getsinger. This time, 'Abdu'l-Bahá was living in freedom in the house built for Him by Edith Jackson. Stanwood wrote: 'The oppressive and cruel governor who had in vain sought graft from Him and had threatened to send Him to the malign dungeons of Tunis, had himself met the fate he had designed for

'Abdu'l-Bahá – the fate of death . . . And 'Abdu'l-Bahá was enjoying, for the first time since His boyhood, the luxury of freedom.'[15]

He thought that the Master seemed 'more noble in countenance, more regal in bearing, more potent in the power of His presence' than before. Each evening, 'Abdu'l-Bahá met with the pilgrims. One afternoon, Stanwood found a group of pilgrims waiting for 'Abdu'l-Bahá and joined them. When the Master's carriage arrived at the foot of the hill, 'Abdu'l-Bahá walked up in order to get a little exercise. Stanwood noted the reverential attitude of his fellow pilgrims:

> All of the Persian pilgrims stood in their customary reverential attitude, awaiting His approach with bowed heads and arms crossed upon their breasts. I alone, as an American, took the privilege of watching Him as He approached, enjoying the majesty of His movements and the nobility of His whole appearance. But as He neared me I involuntarily also bowed my head. Some power emanating from Him seemed to obligate this attitude. So had Professor E. G. Browne, the only Occidental ever to visit Bahá'u'lláh, felt obligated to bow his head in the presence of the Prophet.
>
> This power emanating from 'Abdu'l-Baha was not expressed for the purpose of producing submission. It was a power which He never expressed to non-Baha'is. Let us say, rather, that it was a privilege He gave us, of seeing a little behind the veil; of experiencing the direct effect of that Cosmic Power which in this early period of our development seems supernormal, however normal it may become to us at some distant future stage of our soul's development.
>
> No, 'Abdu'l-Baha never put forth any of His spiritual power to dazzle, persuade or overawe sceptics or unbelievers.[16]

This power was shown forth on other occasions as well. In 1911, 'Abdu'l-Bahá invited Friedrich and Annemarie Schweizer, from Stuttgart, to meet Him in Paris. Both were very anxious to meet the Master and prayed that their hearts would be purified. They arrived in the presence of 'Abdu'l-Bahá with Lady Blomfield and she stepped forward first, bending her knees before the Master. Friedrich stated flatly, 'That I cannot do – kneel down before a man!' But when the Schweizers entered, as recounted by Mrs Schweizer, 'the first one to kneel down was Friedrich, so greatly was he overwhelmed by the majesty and glory of His sanctity'.[17]

When Stanwood arrived in Haifa he was suffering from dysentery. 'Abdu'l-Bahá sent his own physician to help him recover. It was three days before he was well again. Stanwood later remarked that it seemed a little strange that 'Abdu'l-Bahá didn't use His healing power on him as He had done in 1908.

> Why did He not restore me directly to health by means of spiritual healing? There is some deep spiritual lesson here. It was not 'Abdu'l-Baha's province to go about healing physical diseases. It was His mission to expound the Teachings and express the spiritual potency of the world's Divine Physician. Physical events and conditions are of less importance in our lives than the development of our spiritual nature.
>
> In regard to health in general, I will quote here a statement which 'Abdu'l-Baha had made to me on my previous visit: that health is the expression of equilibrium; that the body is composed of certain elements, and that when these elements are in the right proportion, health results; and that if there is any lack or preponderance in these elements, sickness results.[18]

The mouse and the sugar

At some time, a pilgrim brought the Master a cone of rock sugar. 'Abdu'l-Bahá promptly told his servant Khalíl to break up the cone and distribute it among the servants, which he did. When he returned, 'Abdu'l-Bahá asked where His portion was. The embarrassed Khalíl had to go to each of the servants and retrieve a small portion, the total of which he offered to the Master. 'Abdu'l-Bahá directed him to split His portion into four parts, saying 'Khalíl, there is a mouse in this room. I want these pieces for the mouse . . . It is a pretty white mouse.'

'Abdu'l-Bahá then placed one portion on His desk and very quickly the white mouse appeared, climbed up onto the desk and ate the sugar. Khalíl was very uncomfortable having a mouse in the house, but 'Abdu'l-Bahá told him, 'You must not harm or kill any animal around here. This mouse harms no one.' Both the mouse and Khalíl then left. The Master soon recalled Khalíl and told him to capture the mouse without hurting it and to let it go at the gate. When the confused Khalíl asked why, the Master replied: 'This mouse is pregnant and this room is not suitable for such developments.'[19]

Agnes Parsons

Agnes Parsons made her first pilgrimage in 1910. She was a very wealthy socialite from Washington DC and had learned of the Bahá'í Faith two years earlier, but could not accept that 'anyone of His description could be "real". She determined that she must see Him with her own eyes and that she would judge the Faith by what she found in Him.' Agnes was worried that the Faith would 'set upside down her engrained values. She fortified herself for the meeting. She would challenge the claims of 'Abdu'l-Bahá and then decide.'

When she arrived at the Master's home, no one seemed aware of her high social position and she was kept waiting for an 'insultingly long period' of time. Finally summoned by the Master, she entered His room full of her own dignity:

> He looked at her. The first thing she knew He was courteously raising her to her feet. She had fallen flat on the floor. Why had she been overcome? Because a blinding ray of light had passed from His eyes into hers.
>
> This meeting, notwithstanding, Mrs. Parsons was still doubtful. The next morning she visited the tomb of Baha'u'llah and asked for a sign. She said that not a breeze was blowing but, when she asked for her sign, the flowers at the entrance of the tomb blew vigorously back and forth as if in a gale, and a little bird flew into the bosom of her dress and nestled there for a moment. She accepted this as Baha'u'llah's answer.[20]

While on pilgrimage, Mrs Parsons asked the Master if He would stay in her home if He went to America and He said He would. It was a promise He kept in 1912. Agnes Parsons became a stalwart of the Faith.

Sydney Sprague gets married and sets the stage for conflict

Sydney Sprague was in Haifa for several months during the summer and autumn, primarily to marry Farahangiz Khánum, the sister of Dr Amín Fareed. The wedding was timed so that Stanwood Cobb could be present. On 3 August, Sprague wrote:

On that day all the pilgrims and the Bahais of Haifa gathered in the home of Mirza Assad Ullah, and Abdul-Baha was present . . . A wonderful Tablet, which he had revealed especially for our marriage, was chanted, and after the special prayers revealed by Baha'o'llah for such occasions were chanted, Abdul-Baha gave a long, beautiful talk, dwelling on the great significance of this union and calling down the blessing of God upon it. Then I had the great joy of pouring rose water, which I had brought from the garden of Kurat-ul-Ayn [Tahireh] in Kazvin, on the hands of Abdul-Baha and all the guests and of serving them shereeni (sweets), tea, etc. In another place Farahangiz was holding a meeting for women. These meetings took place a little before sunset. Four days later a Mulla came and married us according to the laws of Islam, Abdul-Baha also being present. Then that same night he called Farahangiz and me to him, and as we knelt before him, he took from his hand two rings and gave them to us, anointed our heads with oil and sent us forth hand in hand from his presence, uplifted with pure and holy joy. Oh! I am sure no wedding was ever more sacred, more pure, more beautiful . . . The Greatest Holy Leaf has given me a ring she used to wear and she, herself, prepared Farahangiz for the wedding – a thing she has never done before, saying that Farahangiz was her own daughter. She and the holy mother and all sent us beautiful presents. Abdul-Baha presented us each with our wedding clothes . . .

There were several pilgrims here from Eschkabad, Baghdad and Kazvin, and I entertained them and the Bahais of Haifa at a dinner. Farahangiz entertaining the women.[21]

Unfortunately, this marriage ended up creating a huge dilemma for Sprague when, just a few years later, he had to choose between his new wife and 'Abdu'l-Bahá. Sprague had been very active in the Faith, making a long travel-teaching trip to India and Burma with Mason Remey in 1904–1905 and a year-long trip to Iran in 1908–1909.[22] When Amín Fareed became a Covenant-breaker in 1914, Farahangiz stayed loyal to her brother. Sprague had to choose and he chose to stay with his wife. This made him a Covenant-breaker by association. But 'Abdu'l-Bahá wrote a Tablet to Thornton Chase in which he said that Sprague would come back to the Faith. In 1931, Sprague began his return and ten years later, Shoghi Effendi declared him to be faithful a Bahá'í once again.[23]

The future Guardian through the eyes of a Westerner

Dr Josephina Fallscheer was the Swiss doctor in Haifa who took care of the women of 'Abdu'l-Bahá's family. On 6 August, she had attended an injured member of the family in the House of the Master, after which she sat with the Greatest Holy Leaf. And as they talked, they saw 13-year-old Shoghi Effendi:

> the son-in-law (the husband of the eldest daughter of Abbas Effendi), entered the room, evidently for the purpose of taking leave of the Master. At first I did not notice that behind the tall, dignified man his eldest son, Shoghi Effendi, had entered the room and greeted his venerable grandfather with the oriental kiss on the hand. I had already seen the child fleetingly on a few other occasions. Behia Khanum had recently informed me that this young boy of perhaps twelve years of age was the oldest direct male descendant of the family of the Prophet and destined to be the only successor and representative (vazir) of the Master. As Abbas Effendi spoke in Persian regarding some matter to Abu Shoghi (the father of Shoghi Effendi), who was standing in front of Him, the grandson, after greeting us politely and also kissing the hand of his great aunt, remained near the door in a most respectful attitude. At this moment a number of Persian gentlemen entered the room and greetings and leave-takings, comings and goings, took place for a quarter of an hour. Behia Khanum and I withdrew to the right near the window and in lowered voices continued our conversation in Turkish. However, I never removed my eyes from the still very youthful grandson of Abbas Effendi. He was dressed in European summer clothes, with short pants but long stockings that came up above his knees and a short jacket. From his height and build one would have taken him to be thirteen or fourteen . . . In the still childish face the dark, already mature, melancholy eyes struck me at once. The boy remained motionless in his place and submissive in his attitude. After his father and the man with him had taken their leave of the Master, his father whispered something to him as he went out, whereupon the youth, in a slow and measured manner, like a grown up person, approached his beloved grandfather, waited to be addressed, answered distinctly in Persian and was laughingly

dismissed, not however, without being first permitted the respectful kiss on the hand. I was impressed by the way the youth walked backwards as he left the room, and how his dark, true-hearted eyes never for a moment wavered from the blue, magical glance of his grandfather.

Abbas Effendi rose and came over to us and we immediately stood up, but the Master urged us to take our seats again and Himself sat down informally on a stool near us, or rather facing us. As usual in silence we waited for Him to speak to us, which He did shortly: 'Now my daughter,' He began, 'How do you like my future Elisha?' 'Master, if I may speak openly, I must say that in his boy's face are the dark eyes of a sufferer, one who will suffer a great deal!' Thoughtfully the Master looked beyond us into space and after a long time turned His gaze back to us and said: 'My grandson does not have the eyes of a trailblazer, a fighter or a victor, but in his eyes one sees deep loyalty, perseverance and conscientiousness. And do you know why, my daughter, he will fall heir to the heavy inheritance of being my Vazir (Minister, occupant of a high post)?' Without waiting for my reply, looking more at His dear sister than at me, as if He had forgotten my presence, He went on: 'Bahá'u'lláh, the Great Perfection – blessed be His words – in the past, the present and forever – chose this insignificant one to be His successor, not because I was the first born, but because His inner eye had already discerned on my brow the seal of God.

'Before His ascension into eternal Light the blessed Manifestation reminded me that I too – irrespective of primogeniture or age – must observe among my sons and grandsons whom God would indicate for His office. My sons passed to eternity in their tenderest years, in my line, among my relatives, only little Shoghi has the shadow of a great calling in the depths of his eyes.' There followed another long pause, then the Master turned again to me and said: 'At the present time the British Empire is the greatest and is still expanding and its language is a world language. My future Vazir shall receive the preparation for his weighty office in England itself, after he has obtained here in Palestine a fundamental knowledge of the oriental languages and the wisdom of the East.' Whereupon I ventured to interject: 'Will not the western education, the English training, remould his nature, confine his versatile mind in the rigid bonds of intellectualism, stifle through dogma and convention his oriental irrationality and intuition so that he will no longer be a servant of the Almighty but rather a slave to the rationality of western opportunism and the shallowness of every day life?' Long pause! Then Abbas Effendi 'Abdu'l-Bahá rose and in a strong and solemn voice said: 'I am not giving my Elisha to the British to educate. I dedicate and give him to the Almighty. God's eyes watch over my child in Oxford as well - Inshallah!'[24]

While most people only saw a junior youth, 'Abdu'l-Bahá visualized the future Guardian.

Ethel Stefana Stevens

Sometime before 'Abdu'l-Bahá's departure for the West, American Ethel Stefana Stevens came to see Him. Ethel was not a Bahá'í at that time, but she was very taken both with Him and His Message:

> Regard him well, my friends, for in him you behold one of the most significant figures in the religious world to-day; one who is perhaps doing more for the uplifting of the Oriental than any other force; one who has actually suffered for his faith; one whom nearly two millions of people hold in greatest reverence as the Light in the Lantern, the Knowledge within the Gate.
>
> Come with me now to the Master's home in Haifa, that you may hear from his own lips the simple tenets of the Baha faith. We shall have scant trouble in finding it, for every dragoman, cab-driver, and street urchin in the town will vociferously urge his services as guide to the residence of the Persian Prophet, as Abbas Effendi is locally called. The hour when the sun sinks behind the Samarian hills is his time for receiving visitors; and, however long and tiring his day's work has been, he never refuses to admit and talk with those who have any just claim upon his time, though no Bahai would presume to visit Haifa without first obtaining his permission.
>
> His white-walled, red-roofed, rose-smothered house, different in no respect from the dwellings of the Saviour's day, is as simple within as without, for he lives, though wholly without affectation, in the utmost plainness. Leaving our shoes without the door, after

the Oriental fashion, we enter a reception room, spacious, airy, and spotless, its woodwork and undecorated walls painted white, and the low divans that encircle it covered in unpretentious linen. It is a room with many windows, and jars of blushing roses stand on every table, for, as a result of his long imprisonment, perhaps, Abbas Effendi requires a wealth of light and flowers.

Just at sunset, the pilgrims and disciples enter with bent heads and folded hands and seat themselves silently about the room. For each man as he enters, Abbas Effendi has a kindly greeting, a tactful remark, a personal inquiry, or sometimes a humorous sally, which brings a flittering smile to the grave faces – for with these pilgrims this is a solemn and impressive moment. Most of them have suffered for their faith, and many of them have traveled far for this meeting with the Master.

This lean-faced convert at our right is a Fire-Worshipper from the shores of the Caspian; beyond him, he of the yellow skin and silken coat is a Sart from Samarkand; over there is a hungry-looking Parsee from the Punjab, and, in the corner, a keen-faced Japanese. And for each of them the Baha has ready sympathy and sound, comprehensible advice. And therein lies his power. He possesses to a positively miraculous degree the faculty of interesting himself in every human soul that asks his spiritual or material aid, and it is this very power which has made him so passionately beloved by his disciples. But above all, he possesses that subtler quality of spirituality which is felt rather than understood by those with whom he comes in contact. Gentle, genial, and courteous always, he receives, instructs, advises, and assists with unfailing tact and understanding the cosmopolitan stream of pilgrims which flows so steadily and so increasingly toward this little Syrian coast town.

The charities of Abbas are bounded by no horizon of race or creed. The thirty-odd Persian families who followed Baha Ullah into exile have more than once had his son to thank for the clothes they wore and for their daily bread. 'Not a year passes,' a Roman Catholic remarked not long ago, 'that Abbas Effendi does not help our work among the poor, and' – she paused, for his charities are never open – 'if I were only permitted to tell you of the secret good that he has done!' Question them, and the imams of the Haifa mosques and the pastor of the German Lutheran Church, the foreign consular agents and the resident manager of the Hedjaz Railway, will tell you the same . . .

The aim of the Bahais, briefly put, is to establish an earthly kingdom of Love; a kingdom whose only law shall be the Golden Rule. 'The religionists of the world,' Abbas Effendi remarked one day, 'have abandoned the essence of their faiths and hold only to the letter. Picture the students in a university wrangling and disputing with each other as to which professor was the best, instead of attending to the lessons given them by those professors, and you have a parallel of the conditions which prevail in the world to-day . . .

'Such, then, is our message and our mission. Day and night we must labor to establish community, unity, and harmony among mankind. The world has had enough and to spare of quarrels, backbitings, and criticisms. See how the Catholics disparage the Protestants and the Protestants the Catholics, and both of them the Jews. See how, here in this Syrian land, the adherents of Moses, Christ, and Mohammed are always at each other's throat. Do the Catholics and the Protestants, Christians both, love each other as Christ commanded? Have they a brotherly feeling toward each other? And as it is with one religion, so it is with all. But we Bahais hope that these obstacles to a mutual love and understanding may eventually be removed; that the followers of each belief may respect and admire the others; until the Word of God, with all its perfections, brings them all unto His kingdom'.

'What is the true definition, Effendi,' I asked, of a Bahai?'

Standing there in his spotless robes, amid the fragrances of his quiet garden, on his kind old face the serenity which comes only from faith and love, he made an answer which I like to remember. 'To be a Bahai,' he said, 'means to love humanity and try to serve it; to work for the universal peace and the universal brotherhood of mankind.'[25]

Becoming a Bahá'í, she wrote this magazine article that so attracted Howard Colby Ives in New York and began his journey towards the Bahá'í Faith and his fateful meeting with 'Abdu'l-Bahá.

The Master's departure for the West

One day in mid-August 1910, 'Abdu'l-Bahá summoned Mírzá Jalál, his son-in-law, and asked him to 'perform an important mission, provided no one must know anything about it'. Mírzá Jalál later related that the Master said:

'You go now to the steamship agency and get for me one first class ticket, without giving my name.' Without asking him any question, I left his Presence and came into the street. I searched my pockets and found no money wherewith to buy the ticket, but knowing the Agent it was a simple matter to pay him to-morrow. When I arrived at the Agent's Office, I was shaking with apprehension. I asked him to give me a ticket for a first class passenger. Laughingly he told me he would not sell [it to] me. I told him 'Please, do not joke. I am in a hurry.' 'Well, for whom do you want the ticket?' For an instant I did not know what to say. Then I gave him a name which I don't remember; he handed me the ticket, and putting it into my pocket, I said: 'Good Bye. To-morrow I will pay you for it' and hastened away. I came to the Master and gave him the ticket.

Then he said, 'You must now transfer my satchels from my room to your home without a single soul seeing them', which I did with the utmost circumspection. I returned again to receive further orders. He said: 'Tell the driver to make ready my carriage. I will go to the Tomb of the Bab to meet the friends. From there I will go direct to the steamer; you also by some roundabout way bring my baggage. Send word to Mírzá Noureddin, to be ready to accompany me, and send Khosro by the next steamer.' When night time came, I hired a carriage and for the sake of precaution took two of the believers with me, Ustád Mohammad Ali and Abdor-Rasoul, on the condition they must not ask any questions. Realizing that Mírzá Noureddin was not ready to depart, I took with me Mírzá Moneer [Zayn].

When we reached the steamer, I saw the Beloved walking on the deck. He was there ahead of it. There were many people on board. I told the Master what I had done, and how I had brought with me these two believers and Mírzá Moneer, the latter to accompany him to Port Said. He called the other two, and they were surprised and wonderstruck, because I had not told them anything, neither did they see him on the deck.

He asked for a steamer chair, but there were none to be had. One of the rowers, a big fellow, told me he would bring one, and after a few minutes he came back with one. In the Master's cabin there was an Englishman. We did our utmost to find a cabin all to himself, but there was no use. The first class was full. The Beloved said: 'Never mind.' He could get along very well with the Englishman. While he was giving us his last instructions, the steamer's whistle blew and we all had to hurry out. In the darkness of the night, we could see the outline of the Kossier [the ship's name was actually Khedivial] making for the sea, carrying away the Lord of Love out into the world after forty years of prison life. He was going to teach mankind how to love, how to live and how to embody the virtues of God. But at that time we could never dream of the triumphs achieved, of the victories won, of the great and tumultuous meetings arranged for him all over Europe and America.

When we reached land, I asked the rower how he got the steamer chair for the Beloved. He said: 'I searched and searched, but could not find any. Finally went to the third class. I saw two old Arabs were sitting on steamer chairs. Somehow I made them quarrel with each other, and after a few minutes they arose to make the quarrel more strenuous and demonstrative with their fists. When I saw them so nobly engaged, I took one of the chairs and ran away with it!'[26]

'Abdu'l Bahá told no one, not even His sister, the Greatest Holy Leaf, of His departure. He wrote to her, probably from the ship as He sailed away. The reason for the secrecy quickly became apparent. The Covenant-breakers rapidly spread the idea that 'Abdu'l-Bahá was afraid of the members of a committee of investigation. Then they said that He had committed treason and, fearing the consequences of His actions, had fled the country.[27]

For the next three years, until December 1913, pilgrims didn't go to visit 'Abdu'l-Bahá. 'Abdu'l-Bahá went to visit them.

Egypt

One pilgrim tried to visit 'Abdu'l Bahá in 1911, not realizing that He was not in 'Akká. F. Carl Smith was on a Mediterranean cruise that year and spent a day in Haifa. Carl greatly wished to visit the Master, but did not have the time for the journey to 'Akká. Instead, he climbed Mount Carmel and looked across the bay at 'Akká, then went to the beach, from which he, being an artist, made a sketch of Mount Carmel which he took home to Washington DC and put in his studio. In April 1912, when 'Abdu'l Bahá went to America, Carl asked if he could sketch Him, but was told that there would be no time. 'Abdu'l-Bahá did visit Carl's studio, though, where He saw the drawing of Mount Carmel, exclaiming 'My beloved Mount Carmel! That was the view I had of it for many years in Akka!' Carl immediately began sketching and 'Abdu'l Bahá spent most of the morning sitting in Carl's studio speaking about the Teachings of the Faith while Carl completed his sketch.[28]

When 'Abdu'l-Bahá arrived in Egypt, He hadn't planned on staying, but His health forced Him to spend almost a year there. Initially, the Egyptian newspapers were not friendly and raised a 'great cry and clamor . . . All were expressing opinions of Abdu'l-Baha. No one could form a just and impartial view of him. Facts were exaggerated and misrepresentations abounded in every paper. One writer expressed the opinion that Abdu'l-Baha hates all religions . . .'[29] Some of the more incendiary news companies would send their papers where Bahá'í visitors would see them. At first, a few of the Bahá'ís wanted to respond and correct the lies, but 'Abdu'l-Bahá simply said, 'These are the heralds of the Kingdom. God is using them to inform the people of our arrival. Let them write anything they like. They will come to investigate, realize the truth and themselves make answer.'[30]

Things happened just as the Master had predicted. The editor of a Persian newspaper in Cairo wrote defamatory articles about 'Abdu'l-Bahá and the Master subsequently summoned him to His presence. When the editor left the meeting, he was a changed man and in his next article wrote:

> I was very much benefited in meeting Abdul-Bahá. The Arabic newspapers are now anxiously waiting to read my comment upon the matter. You shall read my paper No. 20 and believe you will

prize it very highly. There is no doubt that some people will slander and accuse me of being bought, but I do not care. I have seen the Truth, and I will write the truth, no matter what may happen.[31]

'Abdu'l-Bahá Himself noted that the editor of the Arabic newspaper *Moaid*, who had written a defamatory article, was 'well known throughout the country for his learning . . . But when Abdul-Baha arrived in this country, with one interview he was completely changed and contradicted his former articles with this one. This is the type of the just man!'[32]

On 28 November, the *Moggatam*, one of the most influential Arabic newspapers, contained a long article that defended

> in most eloquent terms the Teachings of Abdul-Baha. Not being satisfied with this, the editor quotes from the Book of Akdas . . . He even upbraids in the strongest terms the other newspaper writers, calling attention to the responsibilities and duties of their position – that is, to mirror forth facts and realities and not falsehoods and accusations. He says that every writer has been reveling in a riotous feast of exaggeration and derision; that they have gone beyond the limit of politeness and courtesy, which attributes differentiate man from beast.[33]

In March 1911, a daily newspaper called *The Valley of the Nile* contained a full-page article about 'Abdu'l-Bahá, describing His life and His teachings. The report on this noted that 'all the prominent people of Egypt are beginning to feel his spiritual presence and call upon him to receive instruction'.[34] A Persian weekly called *Chihrih-Nimá*, whose editor had previously been distinctly unfriendly towards 'Abdu'l-Bahá and the Bahá'ís, changed its attitude and began reporting on 'Abdu'l-Bahá's travels and showed great respect and admiration.[35]

The Master's Western journey

All through His journey, 'Abdu'l-Bahá met and changed those who came into His presence. In France, Ẓillu's-Sulṭán, grandson of Náṣiri-Dín Sháh who had martyred the Báb and imprisoned Bahá'u'lláh, and who himself had been involved in the martyrdoms of Bahá'ís in Iran, came into 'Abdu'l-Bahá's presence and, shorn of power, abjectly begged the Master's forgiveness. Rashíd Pasha, who had rapaciously abused his authority as the Governor of Beirut and tried to extort money from 'Abdu'l-Bahá when He was his prisoner, came to the Master in Paris and departed humble and contrite.

'Abdu'l-Bahá's journey touched Egypt, Switzerland, France, Britain, Germany, Austria, Hungary, the United States and Canada. By the time it was over, tens of thousands of people had come into contact with the spiritual power of the Centre of the Covenant of God and had been changed. One man, a new student at Stanford University, heard 'Abdu'l-Bahá speak there just a month after enrolling. Seventy years later, he started up a group called Beyond War, based generally on what he had heard at the Master's talk and whose motto was 'Mankind is One'. Louis Gregory, a black American, and Louisa Mathew, a white English woman, were brought together and married at 'Abdu'l-Bahá's instigation to show the true meaning of racial unity. A thief who 'rode the rails' like a hobo to meet 'Abdu'l-Bahá, became a symbol of purity when Shoghi Effendi chose to use the story of Fred Mortenson in *God Passes By*. Martha Root was so inspired by the Master that she circled the globe four times, spreading the message of 'Abdu'l-Bahá's Father to paupers and queens. But He met no world leaders. The President of the United States, William Howard Taft, had the opportunity, but when 'Abdu'l-Bahá arrived at the White House for an appointed meeting, the President sent word he had no time for him.[36]

The full story of 'Abdu'l-Bahá's Western journeys can be found in the book, *'Abdu'l-Bahá in Their Midst*, previously published by George Ronald. The second volume of *Visiting 'Abdu'l-Bahá* will take up the story from the Master's return to Haifa in December 1913.

BIBLIOGRAPHY

'Abdu'l-Bahá. *Memorials of the Faithful.* Trans. M. Gail. Wilmette, IL: Bahá'í Publishing Trust, 1971.

— *Selections from the Writings of 'Abdu'l-Bahá.* Comp. Research Department of the Universal House of Justice. Haifa: Bahá'í World Centre, 1978. Wilmette, IL: Bahá'í Publishing Trust, 1997.

— *Tablets of 'Abdu'l-Bahá* (originally published as *Tablets of Abdul-Baha Abbas.* 3 vols. Chicago: Bahá'í Publishing Society, 1909–1916). Wilmette, IL: National Spiritual Assembly of the Bahá'ís of the United States, 1980. Also available at http://reference.bahai.org/en/t/ab/TAB/tab-489.html.

Afnán, Mírzá Habíbu'lláh. *Memories of the Báb, Bahá'u'lláh and 'Abdu'l-Bahá.* Los Angeles, CA: Kalimat Press, 2005.

Afroukhteh, Youness. *Memories of Nine Years in 'Akká.* Oxford: George Ronald, 2003.

Agnew, Mrs Arthur. United States Bahá'í National Archives, George Latimer Papers, 1907.

Albertson, Alma. United States Bahá'í National Archives, Albert Vail Papers, 1900.

Alexander, Agnes. *Forty Years of a Bahá'í Life in the Hawaiian Islands.* Honolulu: National Spiritual Assembly of the Bahá'ís of the Hawaiian Islands, 1974.

Alkan, Necati. *Dissent and Herodoxy in Late Ottoman Empire,* Analecta Isisina: Ottoman and Turkish Studies. Piscataway, NJ: Gorglas Press, 2009.

Allen-Dyar, Aseyeh. United States Bahá'í National Archives, Thornton Chase Papers, 1907.

Azizi, Jinab-i-Aziz'u'llah. *Crown of Glory.* Teheran: Baha'i Publishing Trust of Iran, English translation 1991.

Badí'u'lláh. *An Epistle to the Bahá'í World.* Chicago: Baha'i Publishing Society, 1907. Available at http://bahai-library.com/badiullah_epistle_bahai_world.

Bagdadi, Zia. *History of the Violation of I. Khairallah.* United States Bahá'í National Archives, Emogene Hoagg Papers, 1920.

Bahá'í Holy Places at the World Centre. Haifa: Bahá'í World Centre, 1968.

Bahá'í News. Periodical. National Spiritual Assembly of the Bahá'ís of the United States and Canada, 1924–.

The Bahá'í World: An International Record. Vol. IV (1930–1932), Wilmette, IL: Bahá'í Publishing Committee, 1934; vol. V (1932-1934), Wilmette, IL: Bahá'í Publishing Trust, 1936; vol. VI (1934–1936), Wilmette, IL: Bahá'í Publishing Trust, 1937; vol. VII (1936–1938), Wilmette, IL: Bahá'í Publishing Trust, 1940; vol. VIII (1938-1940), Wilmette, IL: Bahá'í Publishing Trust, 1942; vol. IX (1940–1944), Wilmette, Bahá'í Publishing Trust, 1945; vol. X (1944-1946), Wilmette, IL: Bahá'í Publishing Trust, 1949; vol. XI (1946–1950), vol. XII (1950-1954), Wilmette, IL: Bahá'í Publishing Trust, 1956; vol. XIII (1954-1963), Haifa, The Universal House of Justice, 1970; vol. XIV (1963-1968), Haifa: The Universal House of Justice, 1974; vol. XVIII (1979-1983), Haifa: Bahá'í World Centre, 1986.

Bahá'u'lláh. *The Kitáb-i-Aqdas: The Most Holy Book.* Haifa: Bahá'í World Centre, 1992.

— *The Summons of the Lord of Hosts: Tablets of Bahá'u'lláh.* Haifa: Bahá'í World Centre, 2002.

— *Tablets of Bahá'u'lláh Revealed after the Kitáb-i-Aqdas.* Comp. Research Department of the Universal House of Justice. Haifa: Bahá'í World Centre, 1978. Wilmette: Bahá'í Publishing Trust, 1988.

Balyuzi, H. M. *'Abdu'l-Bahá.* Oxford: George Ronald, 1971.

Barney, Elsa (Laura) Clifford. United States Bahá'í National Archives, Ahmad Sohrab Papers, 1901.

Beasley, Elmer and Gladys. *Our Pilgrimage to Haifa.* http://bahai-library.com/beasley_pilgrimage_haifa, 1957.

Blomfield, Lady. *The Chosen Highway.* London: Bahá'í Publishing Trust, 1940. RP Oxford: George Ronald, 2007.

Bosch, Louise. United States Bahá'í National Archives, Bosch Papers, 1921.

Brittingham, Isabella D. Talk Given by Mrs. Brittingham of New York. United States National Bahá'í Archives. Thornton Chase Papers, 1901.
— United States Bahá'í National Archives, Agnes Parsons Papers, 1901.
— United States Bahá'í National Archives, Albert Vail Papers, 1901.
— and others. United States Bahá'í National Archives, Mary Rabb Papers, 1909.

Brooks, Richard. 'We visit the prison-home of 'Abdu'l-Bahá'. Marion Hofman Papers.

Bryan, William Jennings. 'Queer customs of the land of the Moslem are described by William Jennings Bryan', in *The Constitution* (Atlanta, Georgia, 26 August 1906), p. 4.

Cameron, Glenn, with Wendi Momen. *A Basic Bahá'í Chronology.* Oxford: George Ronald, 1996.

Cardell, Ted (Edward). United States National Bahá'í Archives, Nancy Bowditch Papers, Ted Cardell, 1952.

Chase, Thornton. *In Galilee.* Chicago, IL: Bahai Publishing Society, 1921. RP Los Angeles: Kalimát Press, 1985.

Cobb, Stanwood. *Memories of 'Abdu'l-Bahá*. Avalon Press, 1962.

Cole, Juan Ricardo, and Moojan Momen. *From Iran East and West*, Bahá'í Studies, vol. 1. Los Angeles: Kalimát Press, 1984.

The Compilation of Compilations. Prepared by the Universal House of Justice 1963–1990. 2 vols. Sydney: Bahá'í Publications Australia, 1991.

Cooper, Ella G. United States Bahá'í National Archives, Hannen-Knobloch Papers, 1908.

Cowles, Josephine C. United States Bahá'í National Archives, Albert Vail Papers, 1901.

Day, Michael. *Journey to a Mountain: The Story of the Shrine of the Báb*. Vol. 1: 1850–1921. Oxford: George Ronald, 2017.

Devine, Aline Shane. United States Bahá'í National Archive, Mary Rabb Papers, 1906.

Dixon, Emily. United States Bahá'í National Archives, Albert Vail Papers 1900.

Dodge, Wendell P. and William C. United States Bahá'í National Archives, Wendell Phillips Dodge Papers, 1901.

Dodge, William. Audio recording. http://bahai-library.com/audio/d/dodge_recollection_visits_abdulbaha.mp3.

— United States Bahá'í National Archives, Wendell Phillips Dodge Papers, 1901.

Finch, Ida, Fanny Alma Knobloch and Alma S. Knobloch. *Flowers Culled from the Rose Garden of Acca*, 1908. Available at http://bahai-library.com/finch_knobloch_flowers_acca, 1908.

Ford, Bahiyyih Randall. *Notes from Bahiyyih Ford's visit to Madrid after being in Haifa and visiting 14 European countries*. The Heritage Project of the National Spiritual Assembly of the United States, 1952.

— (Margaret Randall Ford). *Sarah J. Farmer*. Unpublished manuscript, United States Bahá'í National Archives, 1947.

Ford, Mary Hanford. 'An interview with 'Abdu'l-Bahá', in *The Bahá'í Magazine*, vol. 24, no. 4 (July 1933), pp. 103–7.

— *The Oriental Rose*. New York: Broadway Publishing Co., 1910.

Gail, Marzieh. *Arches of the Years*. Oxford: George Ronald, 1991.

— *Summon Up Remembrance*. Oxford: George Ronald, 1987.

Getsinger, Edward and Lua. United States Bahá'í National Archives, Thornton Chase Papers, 1900.

Getsinger, Lua. United States Bahá'í National Archives, Agnes Parsons Papers, 1898.

— United States Bahá'í National Archives. Anna Beach Papers, 1899.

Goodall, Helen S. and Ella Goodall Cooper. *Daily Lessons Received at Acca, January 1908*. Chicago: Bahai Publishing Society, 1908. RP Wilmette, IL: Bahá'í Publishing Trust, 1979.

Grundy, Julia. *Ten Days in the Light of Acca*. Chicago: Bahai Publishing Society, n.d. RP Wilmette, IL: Bahá'í Publishing Trust, 1979.

Hannen, Joseph. United States Bahá'í National Archives, Hannen-Knobloch Family Papers, 1909.

Hannen, Pauline. United States Bahá'í National Archives, Hannen-Knobloch Family Papers, 1909.

Hannen, Joseph and Pauline, *'Akká Light*, The Heritage Project of the National Spiritual Assembly of the United States, 1909.

Harper, Barron. *Lights of Fortitude: Glimpses into the Lives of the Hands of the Cause of God*. Oxford: George Ronald, rev. ed. 2007.

Harris, Hooper. United States Bahá'í National Archives, Thornton Chase Papers, 1906.

Hearst, Phoebe. United States Bahá'í National Archives, Thornton Chase Papers, 1899.

Herron, Sarah. United States Bahá'í National Archives, Thornton Chase Papers, 1900.

Hoagg, Emogene. United States Bahá'í National Archives, Hoagg Papers, 1920.
— United States Bahá'í National Archives, Mary Rabb Papers, 1913–14.
— 'Letter from Haifa in the Time of Mourning, 1922': from Emogene Hoagg to Nelly French, in *World Order*, vol. 6, no. 2 (Winter 1971–72). 1972.

Hoar, Anna. United States Bahá'í National Archives, Revell Papers, 1900.

Hoar, William H. United States Bahá'í National Archives, Marie Bohmann Papers, 1900.
— United States Bahá'í National Archives. Ahmad Sohrab Papers, 1910.

Hofman, Marion. Marion Hofman Papers, private collection.

Hogenson, Kathryn Jewett. *Lighting the Western Sky*. Oxford: George Ronald, 2010.

Hollinger, Richard. 'Some new notes on Ibrahim Kheiralla', in *Bahá'í Studies Bulletin*, vol. 2, no. 3, December 1983.

Jasion, Jan Teofil. *Never Be Afraid to Dare*. Oxford: George Ronald, 2001.

Jessup, H. H. *Fifty-Three Years in Syria*. New York: Fleming H. Revell Company, 1910.

Khademi, Mona. 'Glimpse into the life of Laura Dreyfus-Barney', in *Lights of Irfán*, vol. 10 (2009), pp. 71–106.

Latimer, George. United States Bahá'í National Archives, George Latimer Papers, 1914 and 1919.

Lucas, Mary L. United States Bahá'í National Archives, Thornton Chase Papers, 1905.
— *A Brief Account of My Visit to Acca*. Chicago: Bahá'í Publishing Society, 1905.

MacNutts. United States Bahá'í National Archives, Mary Rabb Papers, 1905.

MacNutt, Mary. United States Bahá'í National Archives, MacNutts Papers, 1905.

Maxwell, May. *An Early Pilgrimage*. Oxford: George Ronald, 1953.

McKay, Doris. *Fires in Many Hearts*. Canada: Nine Pines Publishers, 1993.

Metelmann, Velda Piff. *Lua Getsinger*. Oxford: George Ronald, 1997.

Moe, Judy. *The Story of the Hannens and Knoblochs*. Unpublished manuscript.

Momen, Moojan, *Dr. J. E. Esslemont*, London: Bahá'í Publishing Trust, 1975.
— (ed). *The Bábí and Bahá'í Religions, 1844–1944: Some Contemporary Western Accounts*. Oxford: George Ronald, 1981.

Moody, Susan. United States Bahá'í National Archives, Mary Rabb Papers, 1909.

Nakhjavani, Violette. *The Maxwells of Montreal*, vol 1. Oxford: George Ronald, 2011.

Nourse, Catharine. Audio recording, 1963. Bahá'í Heritage Project, National Spiritual Assembly of the United States.

Osborne, Mr & Mrs. United States Bahá'í National Archives, Grace Weiss Papers, 1906.

Peeke, Margaret B. *My Visit to Abbas-Effendi in 1899*. Cleveland, OH: Dr Pauline Barton-Peeke, 1911.

Phelps, Frances J. United States Bahá'í National Archives, Frances J. Phelps Papers, 1907.

Phelps, Myron H. *The Master in 'Akká*. Los Angeles: Kalimát Press, 1985.

Rabbani, Ahang. "Abdu'l-Baha in Abu-Sinan: September 1914–May 1915', in *Bahá'í Studies Review*, no. 13 (Association for Bahá'í Studies, English-Speaking Europe, 2005).

Rabbani, Rúḥíyyih. *The Priceless Pearl*. Rutland, UK: Bahá'í Publishing Trust, 2000.

Redman, Earl. *'Abdu'l-Bahá in Their Midst*. Oxford: George Ronald, 2011.
— and Duane Troxel, *Agnes Alexander, Hand of the Cause of God*, forthcoming from George Ronald 2019.

Remey, Charles Mason. *A Comprehensive History of the Bahá'í Movement*. United States Bahá'í National Archives, 1927.
— *Observations of a Bahai Traveller*, 1908. Washington, DC: J. D. Milans & Sons, 1915. Available at http://www.archive.org/details/observationsaba01remegoog.
— United States Bahá'í National Archives, Thornton Chase Papers, 1901.
— United States Bahá'í National Archives, Charles Mason Remey Papers, 1921.

Revell, Jessie E. 'A Bahá'í pioneer of East and West – Doctor Susan I. Moody', in *The Bahá'í World* (1934–1936), vol. VI, p. 484.

Rohani, Aziz. *Sweet and Enchanting Stories*. Hong Kong: Juxta Publishing Co., 2005.

Root, Martha. United States Bahá'í National Archives, Mary Lucas Papers, 1921.
— Martha Root, *Herald of the Kingdom*. Comp. Kay Zinky. New Delhi: Bahá'í Publishing Trust, 1983.

Ruhe, David. *Door of Hope*. Oxford: George Ronald, 2001.

Russell, Sigurd. United States Bahá'í National Archives, Mary Rabb Papers, 1904.

Rutstein, Nathan. *Corinne True: Faithful Handmaid of 'Abdu'l-Bahá*. Oxford: George Ronald, 1987.

Scaramucci, Mary. United States Bahá'í National Archives, Thornton Chase Papers, 1907.

Shoghi Effendi. *Directives from the Guardian*. Comp. Gertrude Garrida. New Delhi: Bahá'í Publishing Trust, 1973.
— *God Passes By* (1944). Wilmette, IL: Bahá'í Publishing Trust, rev. ed. 1974.
— *The World Order of Bahá'u'lláh: Selected Letters by Shoghi Effendi* (1938). Wilmette, IL: Bahá'í Publishing Trust, 2nd rev. ed. 1974, 1991.

Sohrab, Ahmad. *Ahmad Sohrab's Diary*. United States Bahá'í National Archives, 1913–1914.
— European diary letters. Courtesy of Chad Jones, Granite Bay, CA.

Sprague, Sydney. *A Year with the Bahá'ís in India and Burma*. Los Angeles: Kalimát Press, 1986.

Star of the West: The Bahai Magazine. Periodical, 25 vols. 1910–1935. Vols. 1–14 RP Oxford: George Ronald, 1978. Complete CD-ROM version: Talisman Educational Software/Special Ideas, 2001.

Stevens, Ethel Stefana. 'The light in the lantern', in *Everybody's Magazine* (New York), 1 December 1911.

Stockman, Robert. *The Bahá'í Faith in America*. Vol. 1: *Origins, 1892–1900*. Wilmette: Bahá'í Publishing Trust, 1985; vol. 2: *Early Expansion, 1900–1912*. Oxford: George Ronald, 1995.

Struven, Howard. United States Bahá'í National Archives, Revells Papers, 1910.

Taherzadeh, Adib. *The Covenant of Bahá'u'lláh*. Oxford: George Ronald, 1992.
— *The Child of the Covenant: A Study Guide to the Will and Testament of 'Abdu'l-Bahá*. Oxford: George Ronald, 2000.

Thompson, Juliet. *The Diary of Juliet Thompson*. Los Angeles, CA: Kalimát Press, 1995.

Tooba Khanum. United States Bahá'í National Archives, Mary Rabb Papers, UD.

Troxel, Duane. *The Life of Agnes Alexander*. Available at: http://bahai-library.com/troxel_life_agnes_alexander, 1998.

True, Corinne. United States Bahá'í National Archives, George Windust Papers. 1907.
— 'In Memory of Munírih K͟hánum', in *The Bahá'í World*, vol. VIII, p. 265.

Waite, Louise R. United States Bahá'í National Archives, Albert Vail Papers, 1909, 1919.
— United States Bahá'í National Archives. Thornton Chase Papers, 1909.

Watson, Anna. United States Bahá'í National Archives, Mary Rabb Papers, 1904.

Weinberg, Robert. *Ethel Jenner Rosenberg*. Oxford: George Ronald, 1995.

Whitehead, O. Z. *Portraits of Some Bahá'í Women*. Oxford: George Ronald, 1996.
— Some Bahá'ís to Remember. Oxford: George Ronald, 1983.

Whitmore, Bruce. *The Dawning Place*. Wilmette, IL: Bahá'í Publishing Trust, 1984.

Whyte, Jane. 'A visit to 'Akká', in *The Bahá'í World*, vol. IV (1930–1932), pp. 396–7.

Wilhelm, Roy. 'Two glimpses of 'Abdu'l-Bahá', in *The Bahá'í World*, vol. IX, pp. 804–7.

Winterburn, George T. and Rosa V. *Table Talks with Abdul-Baha*. Chicago: Bahai Publishing Society, 1904.

Winterburn, George. United States Bahá'í National Archives, Helen Moss Papers, 1904.

Woodcock, Edwin W. United States Bahá'í National Archives, Thornton Chase Papers, 1907.

Woodcock, May and A. M. Bryant. Hawaiian Bahá'í National Archives. Available at http://bahai-library.com/woodcock_bryant_letter, 1909.

Zaine, Moneer. United States Bahá'í National Archives, Elizabeth Bowen Papers, 1909.

NOTES AND REFERENCES

Preface
1 'Abdu'l-Bahá, *Selections from the Writings of Abdu'l-Bahá*, no. 163, p. 195.
2 Bahá'í World News Service, 30 August 2010.
3 Afroukhteh, *Memories of Nine Years in 'Akká*, pp. 193–4.
4 Metelmann, *Lua Getsinger*, pp. 198–9.
5 Shoghi Effendi, *The World Order of Bahá'u'lláh*, p. 5.
6 Shoghi Effendi, *Directives from the Guardian*, no. 147, p. 54.
7 Momen, *Dr J. E. Esslemont*, p. 16.
8 USBNA, Chase Papers, Box 9: Edwin W. Woodcock, pp. 1–2.
9 USBNA, Windust Papers, Box 31: Corinne True, p. 14.
10 USBNA, Chase Papers, Box 9: Louise R. Waite, p. 7.
11 USBNA, Chase Papers, Box 9 F11: Isabella Brittingham, p. 6.
12 USBNA, Chase Papers, Box 9: Aseyeh Allen-Dyar, p. 4.
13 USBNA, Latimer Papers, Box 11, 1919: George Latimer, p. 43.

Who is 'Abdu'l-Bahá
1 USBNA, Chase Papers, Box 9: Hooper Harris (1906), p. 3.
2 Bahá'u'lláh, *Tablets of Bahá'u'lláh Revealed after the Kitáb-i-Aqdas*, pp. 219–20.
3 Quoted in Shoghi Effendi, *The World Order of Bahá'u'lláh*, p. 135.
4 Bahá'u'lláh, *The Kitáb-i-Aqdas*, p. 82.
5 Quoted in Shoghi Effendi, *The World Order of Bahá'u'lláh*, p. 134.

1897–1898
1 Afnán, *Memories of the Báb, Bahá'u'lláh, and 'Abdu'l-Bahá*, p. 67.
2 ibid. p. 147.
3 Bahá'u'lláh, Súriy-i-Haykal, in Bahá'u'lláh, *The Summons of the Lord of Hosts*, p. 68.
4 Bahá'u'lláh, Lawḥ-i-Aqdas (Tablet to the Christians), in Bahá'u'lláh, *Tablets of Bahá'u'lláh Revealed after the Kitáb-i-Aqdas*, p. 13.
5 Quoted in Shoghi Effendi, *The World Order of Bahá'u'lláh*, p. 135.
6 Afnán, *Memories of the Báb, Bahá'u'lláh, and 'Abdu'l-Bahá*, p. 69.
7 ibid. p. 70.
8 ibid. p. 74.
9 ibid. pp. 81–90 passim.
10 Quoted in Stockman, *The Bahá'í Faith in America*, vol. 1: *Origins 1892–1900*, pp. 136–7.
11 Hogenson, *Lighting the Western Sky*, pp. 10–11.
12 USBNA, Latimer Papers, Box 11: George Latimer, p. 85.

13 Afnán, *Memories of the Báb, Bahá'u'lláh, and 'Abdu'l-Bahá*, pp. 148–9.
14 Quoted ibid. pp. 149–50.
15 Hogenson, *Lighting the Western Sky*, pp. 61–74.
16 ibid. p. 95.
17 USBNA, Chase Papers, Box 9: Edward and Lua Getsinger, p. 1.
18 Hogenson, *Lighting the Western Sky*, pp. 192–3; Stockman, *The Bahá'í Faith in America*, vol. 1: *Origins 1892–1900*, pp. 149–50.
19 Metelmann, *Lua Getsinger*, p. 23.
20 Stockman, *The Bahá'í Faith in America*, vol. 1: *Origins 1892–1900*, pp. 151, 153–4;
21 ibid. p. 155.
22 Hogenson, *Lighting the Western Sky*, pp. 148–9.
23 USBNA, Hoagg Papers, Box 7: Zia Bagdadi, p. 7.
24 Letter from Lua Getsinger to the Assembly in Chicago, USBNA, Parsons, Box 20: Lua Getsinger, p. 1.
25 ibid. pp. 1–2.
26 Nourse, audio recording, Bahá'í Heritage Project.
27 Letter from Lua Getsinger to the Assembly in Chicago, USBNA, Parsons, Box 20: Lua Getsinger, p. 2.
28 ibid. p. 3.
29 Hogenson, *Lighting the Western Sky*, pp. 107–8.
30 ibid. p. 101.
31 Letter from Mrs Thornburgh-Cropper to Lady Blomfield, in Blomfield, *The Chosen Highway*, pp. 235–6; also quoted in Hogenson, *Lighting the Western Sky*, p. 98.
32 Letter from Phoebe Hearst to Isaiah N. Bradford, 19 November 1899, USBNA, Chase, Box 9: Phoebe Hearst, p. 1.
33 Letter from Phoebe Hearst to O. M. Babcock, 5 December 1899, in *The Bahá'í World*, vol. VII (1936–1938), pp. 801–2; also quoted in Balyuzi, *'Abdu'l-Bahá*, pp. 70–71.
34 Hogenson, *Lighting the Western Sky*, p. 98.

1899

1 Nakhjavani, *The Maxwells of Montreal*, vol. 1, pp. 50, 68.
2 Maxwell, *An Early Pilgrimage*, p. 9.
3 ibid. p. 11.
4 ibid. pp. 12–13.
5 ibid. pp. 15–16.
6 Hogenson, *Lighting the Western Sky*, p. 49.
7 Maxwell, *An Early Pilgrimage*, p. 17.
8 ibid. pp. 19–20.
9 ibid. pp. 25–6.
10 ibid. pp. 29–30.
11 ibid. pp. 34–5.
12 Ruhe, *Door of Hope*, pp. 110–13.
13 Maxwell, *An Early Pilgrimage*, pp. 35–8.
14 Hogenson, *Lighting the Western Sky*, p. 130.
15 Maxwell, *An Early Pilgrimage*, pp. 39–42.
16 Peeke, *My Visit to Abbas-Effendi in 1899*, p. 5.

17 ibid. pp. 9–10.
18 ibid. p. 12.
19 ibid. pp. 12–14.
20 ibid. p. 15.
21 ibid. pp. 16–19.
22 Brown, *For My Children and Grandchildren*, p. 36; quoted in Hogenson, *Lighting the Western Sky*, pp. 104–5.
23 Letter from Ella Goodall to Helen Goodall, quoted in Stockman, *The Bahá'í Faith in America*, vol. 1: *Origins 1892–1900*, pp. 151–2.
24 USBNA, Goodall Papers, quoted in Hogenson, *Lighting the Western Sky*, pp. 108–9.
25 Rabbaní, *The Priceless Pearl*, pp. 5–6.
26 ibid. p. 7.
27 Goodall and Cooper, *Lessons Received in Acca*, p. 16 (p. 13 in 1979 reprint).
28 USBNA, Anna Beach Papers, Box 3: Lua Getsinger, pp. 7–8.
29 Hollinger, 'Some new notes on Ibrahim Kheiralla', in *Bahá'í Studies Bulletin*, vol. 2, no. 3, p. 28.
30 USBNA, Anna Beach Papers, Box 3: Lua Getsinger, pp. 12–14.
31 Gail, *Summon Up Remembrance*, p. 98.
32 ibid. p. 100.
33 ibid. p. 101.
34 ibid. p. 105.
35 ibid. pp. 107–9.
36 ibid. p. 109.
37 ibid. pp. 109–10.
38 ibid. p. 120.
39 Tablet from 'Abdu'l-Bahá to O. Wolcott, 4 June 1920, USBNA, Translation of Tablets of 'Abdu'l-Bahá Collection.
40 Hogenson, *Lighting the Western Sky*, pp. 199–200.
41 ibid. p. 204.
42 Haddad, *An Outline of the Bahai Movement in the United States*, p. 14, quoted ibid.
43 Hogenson, *Lighting the Western Sky*, pp. 204–5.

1900

1 Gail, *Summon Up Remembrance*, pp. 110–11, 115.
2 Afroukhteh, *Memories of Nine Years in 'Akká*, p. 113.
3 ibid. pp. 123–4.
4 ibid. p. 124.
5 Margaret Randall Ford, *Sarah J. Farmer*, pp. 12–13.
6 ibid. pp. 2–3.
7 *The Bahá'í World*, vol. VII (1936–1938), p. 84.
8 Redman, *'Abdu'l-Bahá in Their Midst*, p. 173.
9 It was formerly thought that William Hoar made the pilgrimage with his wife, but later evidence, including his own accounts, show that he came later, alone, in May 1901.
10 USBNA, Revells Papers, Box 7: Mrs Hoar, p. 1.
11 *Star of the West*, vol. VI, no. 19 (2 March 1916), p. 166.
12 USBNA, Revells Papers, Box 7: Mrs Hoar, pp. 1–2.

13　ibid. p. 2.
14　*Star of the West*, vol. VI, no. 19 (2 March 1916), p. 166.
15　ibid.
16　Metelmann, *Lua Getsinger*, pp. 38–9.
17　Afroukhteh, *Memories of Nine Years in 'Akká*, p. 21.
18　ibid. pp. 21–2.
19　USBNA, Vail Papers, Box 8, Emily Dixon, p. 1, arrival date is given as 30 October and the departure date given twice as 8 October, which is probably a mistake since they met Agnes Alexander in Rome on 24 November; Gail, *Summon Up Remembrance*, p. 118.
20　Gail, *Summon Up Remembrance*, p. 118.
21　USBNA, Vail Papers, Box 8: Emily Dixon, p. 1.
22　ibid. pp. 1–2.
23　ibid. p. 2.
24　ibid. p. 3.
25　ibid.
26　Alexander, *Forty Years of a Bahá'í Life in the Hawaiian Islands*, p. 7.
27　Laura Clifford Barney, letter to Mírzá Abu'l-Faḍl, USBNA, Ahmad Sohrab, Box 17: Elsa (Laura) Clifford Barney, p. 7.
28　ibid. pp. 7–8.
29　Gail, *Summon Up Remembrance*, p. 145.
30　ibid. p. 215.
31　USBNA, Ahmad Sohrab Papers, Box 17: Elsa (Laura) Clifford Barney, pp. 9–12.
32　ibid. pp. 13–15.
33　ibid. pp. 15–16.
34　ibid. pp. 17–18.
35　Whitehead, *Portraits of Some Bahá'í Women*, pp. 3–4; USBNA, Vail, Box 8: Alma Albertson, p. 7.
36　De Mille, 'Emogene Hoagg: Exemplary pioneer', in *Bahá'í News*, no. 511 (October 1973), p. 6.
37　ibid. p. 7.
38　Cooper, 'Henrietta Emogene Martin Hoagg', in *The Bahá'í World*, vol. X (1944–1946), p. 520.
39　De Mille, 'Emogene Hoagg: Exemplary pioneer', in *Bahá'í News*, no. 511 (October 1973), p. 7.
40　*Star of the West*, vol. VIII, no. 4 (17 May 1917), p. 43.
41　USBNA, Vail Papers, Box 8: Alma Albertson, p. 20.
42　Cooper, 'Henrietta Emogene Martin Hoagg', in *The Bahá'í World*, vol. X (1944–1946), pp. 520–21.
43　Balyuzi, *'Abdu'l-Bahá*, p. 64.
44　Remey, *A Comprehensive History of the Bahá'í Movement*, USBNA, Charles Mason Remey Papers, Box 16, vol. 75, p. 154.
45　Jessup, *Fifty-Three Years in Syria*, p. 687.
46　ibid.
47　ibid. p. 688.
48　ibid. p. 687–8.
49　ibid. p. 637.
50　USBNA, Chase Papers, Box 9: Sarah Herron, p. 35.

1901

1. Hogenson, *Lighting the Western Sky*, p. 183.
2. Nakhjavani, *The Maxwells of Montreal*, p. 131.
3. Gail, *Summon Up Remembrance*, p. 137.
4. *The Bahá'í World*, vol. XIII (1954–1963), p. 879.
5. ibid. pp. 879–80.
6. Gail, *Arches of the Years*, p. 297.
7. USBNA, Sohrab Papers, Box 17: Elsa (Laura) Clifford Barney, pp. 19–20.
8. Afroukhteh, *Memories of Nine Years in 'Akká*, pp. 301–2.
9. Momen, *The Bábí and Bahá'í Religions, 1844–1944*, p. 319.
10. Rohani, *Sweet and Enchanting Stories*, p. 79.
11. ibid. pp. 79–80.
12. *Bahá'í Holy Places*, pp. 54–5; Ruhe, *Door of Hope*, p. 141.
13. Afnán, *Memories of the Báb, Bahá'u'lláh, and 'Abdu'l-Bahá*, p. 125.
14. ibid. p. 154.
15. ibid. p. 159.
16. Taherzadeh, *Child of the Covenant*, pp. 348–50.
17. Balyuzi, *'Abdu'l-Bahá*, p. 51.
18. Taherzadeh, *Child of the Covenant*, p. 350.
19. USBNA, Sohrab Papers, Box 17: Elsa (Laura) Clifford Barney, p. 22.
20. ibid. p. 29.
21. USBNA, Chase Papers, Box 9: Charles Mason Remey, pp. 1–2.
22. Afroukhteh, *Memories of Nine Years in 'Akká*, Chapter 1.
23. ibid. pp. 103–4.
24. For 'Abdu'l-Bahá's account of his life, see 'Muḥammad-Muṣṭafá Baghdádí', in 'Abdu'l-Bahá, *Memorials of the Faithful*, pp. 131–4.
25. USBNA, Sohrab Papers, Box 17: William H. Hoar, pp. 2–3.
26. ibid. p. 4.
27. ibid. p. 5.
28. Redman, *'Abdu'l-Bahá in Their Midst*, p. 23.
29. USBNA, Sohrab Papers, Box 17: William H. Hoar, pp. 7–8.
30. ibid. pp. 8–9.
31. Afroukhteh, *Memories of Nine Years in 'Akká*, p. 106.
32. ibid. p. 105.
33. ibid. p. 107.
34. Afroukhteh, *Memories of Nine Years in 'Akká*, p. 107.
35. USBNA, Sohrab Papers, Box 17: William H. Hoar, p. 10.
36. ibid. pp. 12–13.
37. ibid. pp. 15–16.
38. ibid. pp. 16–17.
39. ibid. pp. 21–2.
40. ibid. pp. 18–21; also in USBNA, Marie Bohmann Papers: William H. Hoar, pp. 1–2.
41. Afroukhteh, *Memories of Nine Years in 'Akká*, p. 108.
42. Stockman, *The Bahá'í Faith in America*, vol. 2: *Early Expansion, 1900–1912*, p. 51.
43. Gail, *Summon Up Remembrance*, pp. 137–8.
44. Badí'u'lláh, *An Epistle to the Bahá'í World*, pp. 13–14.
45. Shoghi Effendi, *God Passes By*, pp. 264–5.

46 Balyuzi, *'Abdu'l-Bahá*, p. 95.
47 Momen, *The Bábí and Bahá'í Religions, 1844–1944*, p. 319.
48 Badí'u'lláh, *An Epistle to the Bahá'í World*, p. 18.
49 ibid. pp. 19–20.
50 Afroukhteh, *Memories of Nine Years in 'Akká*, p. 125.
51 Momen, *The Bábí and Bahá'í Religions, 1844–1944*, pp. 319–20.
52 USBNA, Vail Papers, Box 8: Isabella D. Brittingham, p. 1.
53 Talk given by Isabella Brittingham in Chicago, 10 November 1901, in USBNA, Chase Papers, Box 9 F11: Isabella Brittingham, p. 1.
54 ibid. p. 2.
55 USBNA, Vail Papers, Box 8: Isabella D. Brittingham, pp. 2–5.
56 *The Bahá'í World*, vol. VII (1936–1938), p. 709.
57 USBNA, Agnes Parsons Papers, Box 20: Isabella D. Brittingham, pp. 1–2.
58 USBNA, Vail Papers, Box 8: Isabella D. Brittingham, pp. 5–6.
59 Afroukhteh, *Memories of Nine Years in 'Akká*, p. 138.
60 ibid. p. 138.
61 ibid. pp. 139–41.
62 ibid. p. 141.
63 'Abdu'l-Bahá, *Tablets of Abdul-Baha Abbas*, pp. 452–3.
64 Afroukhteh, *Memories of Nine Years in 'Akká*, pp. 142–2.
65 Hogenson, *Lighting the Western Sky*, p. 189.
66 USBNA, Wendell Phillips Dodge Papers, Box 1: William Copeland Dodge, p. 1.
67 ibid. p. 3.
68 ibid.
69 USBNA, Wendell Phillips Dodge Papers, Box 1: Wendell P. and William C. Dodge, p. 20.
70 ibid. Box 1: William Copeland Dodge, p. 5.
71 ibid. Box 1: Wendell P. and William C. Dodge, pp. 28–9.
72 ibid. Box 1: William Copeland Dodge, pp. 5a–6.
73 Momen, *The Bábí and Bahá'í Religions, 1844–1944*, p. 320.

1902–1903

1 Afroukhteh, *Memories of Nine Years in 'Akká*, pp. 143–4.
2 *Star of the West*, vol. V, no. 5 (5 June 1914), p. 68.
3 Afroukhteh, *Memories of Nine Years in 'Akká*, p. 145.
4 ibid. p. 146.
5 ibid. p. 147.
6 ibid. pp. 147–8.
7 Phelps, *The Master in 'Akká*, pp. 1–10.
8 *The Bahá'í World*, vol. V (1932–1934), p. 415.
9 Afroukhteh, *Memories of Nine Years in 'Akká*, p. 148
10 ibid. p. 149.
11 USBNA, Rabb Papers, Box 7: Tooba Khanum, p. 1.
12 Letter from Ahmad Sohrab to Harriet Magee, 6 January 1913, pp. 5–6, in *Ahmad Sohrab's Diary*.
13 ibid. p. 7, and Afroukhteh, *Memories of Nine Years in 'Akká*, pp. 305–6.

1904

1 Afroukhteh, *Memories of Nine Years in 'Akká*, p. 215.

NOTES AND REFERENCES

2   Winterburn and Winterburn, *Table Talks with Abdul-Baha*, p. 25.
3   ibid. p. 29.
4   ibid. p. 26.
5   ibid. pp. 29–30.
6   Afroukhteh, *Memories of Nine Years in 'Akká*, p. 216.
7   Winterburn and Winterburn, *Table Talks with Abdul-Baha*, p. 27.
8   Afroukhteh, *Memories of Nine Years in 'Akká*, pp. 216–17.
9   USBNA, Helen Moss Papers, Box 1: George Winterburn, p. 2.
10 Winterburn and Winterburn, *Table Talks with Abdul-Baha*, p. 26.
11 Afroukhteh *Memories of Nine Years in 'Akká*, p. 216.
12 Winterburn and Winterburn, *Table Talks with Abdul-Baha*, pp. 28–9.
13 ibid. p. 30–31.
14 ibid. p. 32.
15 Afroukhteh, *Memories of Nine Years in 'Akká*, pp. 217–18.
16 ibid. pp. 218–19.
17 ibid. p. 219.
18 ibid. p. 220.
19 ibid.
20 ibid.
21 ibid. p. 221.
22 The location of Badkubih is uncertain, but possibly could have been Baku, a port on the Caspian Sea, through which Persian pilgrims commonly passed, and would have been the port of entry into Russia. In *Crown of Glory*, Azizi wrote that after their release, they tried to sail across the Black Sea, but gave no time frame between release and sailing. There is a port town on the Black Sea called Batumi, but in 1904, it was under the Ottoman government, not the Russian.
23 Azizi, *Crown of Glory*, pp. 68–9.
24 ibid. p. 70.
25 ibid. p. 69.
26 ibid. pp. 70–71.
27 ibid. p. 79.
28 ibid. p. 82.
29 Afroukhteh, *Memories of Nine Years in 'Akká*, pp. 349–50.
30 Shoghi Effendi, *God Passes By*, pp. 265–66.
31 Day, *Journey to a Mountain*, p. 53.
32 Afroukhteh, *Memories of Nine Years in 'Akká*, pp. 346, 350; Balyuzi, *'Abdu'l-Bahá*, p. 112.
33 Balyuzi, *'Abdu'l-Bahá*, p. 114.
34 Shoghi Effendi, *God Passes By*, p. 269.
35 Afroukhteh, *Memories of Nine Years in 'Akká*, pp. 346–47.
36 USBNA, Rabb Papers, Box 7: Sigurd Russell, p. 1.
37 ibid. pp. 1–2.
38 Weinberg, *Ethel Jenner Rosenberg*, p. 73.
39 Khademi, 'Glimpse into the life of Laura Dreyfus-Barney', pp. 71–106.
40 Letter from Laura Dreyfus-Barney to Yúnis Khán, 7 August 1937, quoted in Afroukhteh, *Memories of Nine Years in 'Akká*, pp. 343–4.
41 *Star of the West*, vol. VII, no. 11 (27 September 1916), pp. 108.
42 Weinberg, *Ethel Jenner Rosenberg*, p. 73.
43 Afroukhteh, *Memories of Nine Years in 'Akká*, pp. 314–15.

44 Balyuzi, *Abdu'l-Bahá*, p. 82.
45 Afroukhteh, *Memories of Nine Years in 'Akká*, pp. 315–16.
46 ibid. pp. 316–17.
47 ibid. p. 318.
48 ibid. p. 317.
49 ibid. p. 318.
50 ibid. p. 319.
51 Sprague, *A Year with the Bahá'ís in India and Burma*, pp. 2, 4–5.
52 ibid. pp. 5–7.
53 ibid. p. 8.
54 Afroukhteh, *Memories of Nine Years in 'Akká*, p. 199.
55 ibid. pp. 199–201.
56 ibid. pp. 201–2.
57 Rohani, *Sweet and Enchanting Stories*, no. 27, p. 64.
58 Afroukhteh, *Memories of Nine Years in 'Akká*, pp. 239–42.
59 USBNA, Rabb Papers, Box 7: Anna Watson.
60 ibid. Box 7: MacNutts, p. 1.

1905

1 USBNA, MacNutt Papers, Box 9: Mary MacNutt, pp. 6–7.
2 ibid. pp. 7–8.
3 ibid. pp. 13–14, 18–19.
4 ibid. pp. 22–5.
5 ibid. pp. 26–7.
6 ibid. pp. 1–2.
7 ibid. pp. 31–5.
8 ibid. p. 2.
9 ibid. pp. 58–9.
10 ibid. pp. 2–3.
11 Grundy, *Ten Days in the Light of Acca*, pp. 38–40. The quotations are as in the original edition of 1907.
12 ibid. p. 72.
13 ibid. pp. 73–4.
14 ibid. p. 74–5.
15 ibid. pp. 74–5.
16 Lucas, *A Brief Account of My Visit to Acca*, pp. 4–5. (This account also draws on USBNA, Chase, Box 9: Mary L. Lucas).
17 ibid. pp. 7–10.
18 ibid. pp. 12–13. See *The Compilation of Compilations*, vol. II, no. 1422, for the complete account of the Master's talk.
19 ibid. pp. 16, 19–20.
20 ibid. p. 23.
21 ibid. pp. 26–7.
22 ibid. pp. 33, 36.
23 ibid. pp. 37–8, 42.
24 *The Bahá'í World*, vol. V (1936–1938), p. 419.
25 Josephine Cowles Lagnel, USBNA, Ahmad Sohrab Papers, Box 17, 1905.
26 As recorded in Gail, *Summon Up Remembrance*, p. 226.
27 Alkan, *Dissent and Herodoxy in Late Ottoman Empire*, pp. 154–7.

28 Shoghi Effendi, *God Passes By*, p. 270.
29 Quoted in Momen, *The Bábí and Bahá'í Religions, 1844–1944*, p. 322.
30 Goodall and Cooper, *Daily Lessons Received at Acca: January 1908*, p. 23.
31 ibid. pp. 24–5.
32 Quoted in Momen, *The Bábí and Bahá'í Religions, 1844–1944*, p. 321.
33 Shoghi Effendi, *God Passes By*, pp. 270–71.
34 USBNA, Latimer Papers, Box 11: George Latimer, diary pp. 93–7.
35 Afroukhteh, *Memories of Nine Years in 'Akká*, p. 346; Balyuzi,*'Abdu'l-Bahá*, p. 121.
36 Afroukhteh, *Memories of Nine Years in 'Akká*, pp. 254–5.
37 ibid. p. 255.
38 ibid.
39 Quoted in Momen, *The Bábí and Bahá'í Religions, 1844–1944*, p. 323.
40 Afroukhteh, *Memories of Nine Years in 'Akká*, pp. 346–7.
41 Shoghi Effendi, *God Passes By*, p. 270.
42 See http://yomi.mobi/egate/Yildiz_Attempt.
43 USBNA, Latimer Papers, Box 11: George Latimer, diary p. 98.
44 Afroukhteh, *Memories of Nine Years in 'Akká*, pp. 379–80.
45 Shoghi Effendi, *God Passes By*, pp. 317–18.
46 Afroukhteh, *Memories of Nine Years in 'Akká*, pp. 379–80.
47 Quoted in Momen, *The Bábí and Bahá'í Religions, 1844–1944*, p. 321.
48 ibid.
49 'Abdu'l-Bahá, *Selections from the Writings of 'Abdu'l-Bahá*, no. 188, p. 219.
50 *Baha'i News Letter*, vol. 46 (November 1930), p. 12.

1906

1 Whyte, 'A visit to 'Akká', in *The Bahá'í World*, vol. IV (1930–1932), pp. 396–7.
2 Bryan, 'Queer customs of the land of the Moslem are described by William Jennings Bryan', in *The Constitution* (26 August 1906), p. 4.
3 *Star of the West*, vol. V, no. 8 (1 August 1914), p. 119.
4 Gail, *Summon Up Remembrance*, pp. 222–4.
5 ibid. p. 226.
6 ibid. p. 235.
7 ibid. pp. 226–7.
8 ibid. pp. 237–8.
9 ibid. p. 242.
10 ibid. p. 243.
11 ibid, pp. 260–61.
12 ibid. p. 262.
13 ibid. p. 263.
14 ibid. p. 272.
15 ibid. p. 277.
16 ibid. pp. 282–3.
17 ibid. p. 284.
18 ibid.
19 *The Bahá'í World*, vol. XII (1950–1954), pp. 703–4.
20 *The Bahá'í World*, vol. XIV (1963–1968), p. 352.
21 Azízí, *Crown of Glory*, p. 95.
22 ibid. p. 96.

23 ibid.
24 ibid. p. 99.
25 ibid. pp. 99–100.
26 ibid. pp. 116–143.
27 USBNA, Rabb Papers, Box 6: Aline Shane Devine, p. 1.
28 Quoted in Whitehead, *Some Bahá'ís to Remember*, p. 122, from a talk by Harlan Ober and unpublished notes of Dr Elizabeth Kidder Ober.
29 ibid. pp. 123–4.
30 USBNA, Chase Papers, Box 9: Hooper Harris, p. 1.
31 ibid. pp. 4–5.
32 ibid. pp. 5–6.
33 ibid. pp. 1–3.
34 Whitehead, *Some Bahá'ís to Remember*, pp. 125–6.
35 *The Bahá'í World*, vol. XIII (1954–1963), p. 869.
36 *The Bahá'í World*, vol. VI (1934–1936), p. 488.
37 *The Bahá'í World*, vol. XIII (1954–1963), p. 869.
38 USBNA, Grace Weiss Papers, Box 1: Mr & Mrs Osborne, pp. 1–2, 4, 6.

1907

1 USBNA, Chase Papers, Box 9: Edwin W. Woodcock, pp. 4, 6.
2 ibid. pp. 6–7.
3 *The Bahá'í World*, vol. XIII (1954–1963), p. 880.
4 USBNA, Chase Papers, Box 9: Edwin W. Woodcock, pp. 9–10.
5 Rutstein, *Corinne True*, p. 51.
6 ibid. p. 69.
7 ibid. p. 53.
8 Corinne True, 'In Memory of Muním̲ih K̲h̲ánum', in *The Bahá'í World*, vol. VIII, p. 265.
9 USBNA, Windust Papers, Box 31: Corinne True, p. 3.
10 Corinne True, 'In Memory of Muním̲ih K̲h̲ánum', in *The Bahá'í World*, vol. VIII, p. 265.
11 USBNA, Windust Papers, Box 31: Corinne True, p. 4.
12 ibid. p. 5.
13 Rutstein, *Corinne True*, p. 58.
14 USBNA, Chase Papers, Box 9: Mary Scaramucci, p. 1.
15 Rutstein, *Corinne True*, pp. 60–61.
16 ibid. p. 61.
17 Whitmore, *The Dawning Place*, p. 31.
18 Redman, *'Abdu'l-Bahá in Their Midst*, p. 111.
19 Rutstein, *Corinne True*, p. 62.
20 USBNA, Windust Papers, Box 31: Corinne True, p. 11.
21 Rutstein, *Corinne True*, p. 65.
22 ibid. pp. 65–6.
23 Corinne True, 'In Memory of Muním̲ih K̲h̲ánum', in *The Bahá'í World*, vol. VIII, p. 265.
24 Rutstein, *Corinne True*, p. 69.
25 Corinne True, 'In Memory of Muním̲ih K̲h̲ánum', in *The Bahá'í World*, vol. VIII, p. 265.

26 Rutstein, *Corinne True*, p. 69.
27 USBNA, Windust Papers, Box 31: Corinne True, p. 18.
28 Richard Brooks, 'We visit the prison-home of 'Abdu'l-Bahá', Marion Hofman Papers.
29 USBNA, Windust Papers, Box 31: Corinne True, p. 19.
30 Chase, *In Galilee*, pp. 6–7.
31 ibid. pp. 9–11.
32 ibid. p. 13.
33 ibid. pp. 15–16.
34 ibid. pp. 19–23.
35 ibid. pp. 23–4.
36 ibid. pp. 26–7.
37 ibid. pp. 28–30.
38 USBNA, Latimer Papers, Box 1: Mrs Arthur Agnew, pp. 1–2.
39 Arthur Agnew, 'In Wonderland', in Chase, *In Galilee*, p. 75.
40 Chase, *In Galilee*, pp. 32–3, 35.
41 Arthur Agnew, 'In Wonderland', in Chase, *In Galilee*, p. 83.
42 Chase, *In Galilee*, pp. 36–9.
43 ibid. pp. 58–60.
44 ibid. p. 63.
45 ibid. p. 62.
46 USBNA, Latimer Papers, Box 1: Mrs Arthur Agnew, p. 4.
47 Chase, *In Galilee*, pp. 66–8.
48 ibid. pp. 68–9.
49 ibid. p. ix (1985 edition).
50 USBNA, Latimer, Box 1: Mrs Arthur Agnew, pp. 4–5.
51 Cole and Momen, *From Iran East and West*, p. 145.
52 USBNA, Chase Papers, Box 9: Aseyeh Allen-Dyar, p. 4.
53 ibid. p. 4.
54 ibid. pp. 2 3.
55 ibid. p. 7.
56 Wilhelm, 'Two glimpses of 'Abdu'l-Bahá', in *The Bahá'í World*, vol. IX, p. 804.
57 ibid. pp. 804–5.
58 ibid.
59 ibid.
60 ibid..
61 ibid. pp. 802–3.
62 ibid. p. 807.
63 USBNA, Frances J. Phelps Papers: Frances J. Phelps, p. 29.
64 ibid. pp. 30–31.
65 ibid. p. 33.
66 ibid. pp. 33–4.
67 Remey, *A Comprehensive History of the Bahá'í Movement*, p. 56.
68 USBNA, Frances J. Phelps Papers: Frances J. Phelps, p. 37.
69 Remey, *A Comprehensive History of the Bahá'í Movement*, p. 90.
70 Ford, 'An interview with 'Abdu'l-Baha', p. 104.
71 ibid. p. 105.
72 ibid. pp. 104–5.

73   Ford, *The Oriental Rose*, pp. 162–3.
74   ibid. pp. 172–3.
75   Ford, 'An interview with 'Abdu'l-Baha', pp. 106–7.
76   ibid. p. 107.
77   ibid.
78   Ford, *The Oriental Rose*, p. 6.
79   Quoted in Remey, *A Comprehensive History of the Bahá'í Movement*, p. 59–60.
80   ibid. pp. 61–2.
81   Sohrab, USBNA, *Ahmad Sohrab's Diary*, 20 July 1914, pp. 1147–8.
82   Jasion, *Never Be Afraid to Dare*, pp. 34–5.
83   Chicago House of Spirituality notes, https://www.h-net.org/~bahai/notes/vol2/chs.1908.html.
84   Jasion, *Never Be Afraid to Dare*, p. 35.
85   Ford, 'An interview with 'Abdu'l-Bahá', p. 103.
86   Ahang Rabbani, "Abdu'l-Baha in Abu-Sinan: September 1914–May 1915'.
87   ibid.
88   Sohrab, USBNA, *Ahmad Sohrab's Diary*, 14 March 1914, p. 791.
89   Remey, *A Comprehensive History of the Bahá'í Movement*, p. 114.

1908

1   Goodall and Cooper, *Daily Lessons Received at Acca: January 1908*, pp. 8–9.
2   ibid. pp. 10–14.
3   USBNA, Hannen-Knobloch Papers, Box 28: Ella G. Cooper, p. 2.
4   Goodall and Cooper, *Daily Lessons Received at Acca: January 1908*, pp. 10–11.
5   ibid. p. 15.
6   ibid. pp. 39–40.
7   Jasion, *Never Be Afraid to Dare*, p. 20.
8   ibid. p. 27.
9   USBNA, Hannen-Knobloch Papers, Box 28: Ella G. Cooper, p. 7.
10   Jasion, *Never Be Afraid to Dare*, pp. 28–31.
11   Goodall and Cooper, *Daily Lessons Received at Acca: January 1908*, p. 19.
12   USBNA, Hannen-Knobloch Papers, Box 28: Ella G. Cooper, p. 8.
13   Jasion, *Never Be Afraid to Dare*, p. 32.
14   ibid. pp. 39–40.
15   ibid. pp. 37–8.
16   ibid. p. 38.
17   *The Bahá'í World*, vol. XVIII (1979–1983), p. 815.
18   Cobb, *Memories of 'Abdu'l-Bahá*, p. 4.
19   ibid. p. 5.
20   ibid. pp. 5–6.
21   ibid. pp. 6–7.
22   ibid. p. 7.
23   *The Bahá'í World*, vol. XVIII (1979–1983), p. 816.
24   USBNA, Nancy Bowditch Papers, Ted Cardell, pp. 1–2.
25   Remey, *Observations of a Bahai Traveller*, p. 24.
26   USBNA, Remey, *A Comprehensive History of the Bahá'í Movement*, p. 64.
27   Remey, *Observations of a Bahai Traveller*, p. 25.
28   ibid. p. 26.
29   *Bahá'í News (Star of the West)*, vol. 1, no. 9 (20 August 1910), p. 2.

30 Remey, *Observations of a Bahai Traveller*, p. 30.
31 ibid. pp. 32–3.
32 Cameron, *A Basic Bahá'í Chronology*, p. 168.
33 Remey, *Observations of a Bahai Traveller*, pp. 126–7.
34 'Abdu'l-Bahá, *Selections from the Writings of 'Abdu'l-Bahá*, no. 190, pp. 225–7.
35 Remey, *Observations of a Bahai Traveller*, pp. 127–8.
36 Tuttle, 'Fanny A. Knobloch', in *The Bahá'í World*, vol. XI (1946–1950), p. 473.
37 Judy Hannen Moe, manuscript about Alma and Fanny Knobloch with material from the Washington DC Archives, Chapter 9, 'Fanny and Alma meet the Master', p. 24.
38 Tuttle, 'Fanny A. Knobloch', in *The Bahá'í World*, vol. XI (1946–1950), p. 474.
39 ibid.
40 Finch, Knobloch and Knobloch, *Flowers Culled from the Rose Garden of Acca*, pp. 6–7.
41 ibid. p. 12.
42 ibid. pp. 17–18.
43 ibid. pp. 21–2.
44 Tuttle, 'Fanny A. Knobloch', in *The Bahá'í World*, vol. XI (1946–1950), pp. 474–5.
45 ibid. p. 75.

1909

1 *Star of the West*, vol. VII, no. 11 (27 September 1916), p. 107.
2 Remey, *A Comprehensive History of the Bahá'í Movement*, p. 116.
3 Nakhjavani, *The Maxwells of Montreal*, vol. 1, p. 250.
4 ibid. pp. 251–2.
5 USBNA, Hannen-Knobloch Papers, Box 29: Pauline Hannen.
6 ibid. Box 29: Joseph Hannen, p. 1.
7 ibid. pp. 2–3.
8 ibid. Box 29: Pauline Hannen.
9 ibid. Box 29: Joseph Hannen, p. 3.
10 ibid. Box 29: Pauline Hannen.
11 ibid.
12 Joseph and Pauline Hannen, *'Akká Light*, The Heritage Project of the National Spiritual Assembly of the United States.
13 USBNA, Hannen-Knobloch Papers, Box 29: Pauline Hannen.
14 Redman, *'Abdu'l-Bahá in Their Midst*, p. 92.
15 USBNA, Hannen-Knobloch Papers, Box 29: Pauline Hannen.
16 ibid. Box 29: Joseph Hannen, p. 23.
17 Shoghi Effendi, *God Passes By*, pp. 275–6.
18 USBNA, Elizabeth Bowen Papers, Box 4: Moneer Zaine.
19 ibid.
20 Hawaiian Bahá'í National Archive, May Woodcock and A.M. Bryant, http://bahai-library.com/woodcock_bryant_letter.
21 Elmer and Gladys Beasley, *Our Pilgrimage to Haifa*, p. 11.
22 USBNA, Elizabeth Bowen Papers, Box 4: Moneer Zaine.
23 Wikipedia, http://en.wikipedia.org/wiki/Caliphate.
24 Thompson, *The Diary of Juliet Thompson*, pp. 5–6.
25 ibid. pp. 10, 12.

26 ibid. pp. 13–14.
27 ibid. pp. 14–15.
28 ibid. pp. 15–16.
29 ibid. pp. 16–20.
30 ibid. p. 21.
31 ibid. p. 22.
32 ibid. p. 23.
33 ibid. pp. 27–33.
34 ibid. pp. 40–41.
35 ibid. p. 43.
36 ibid. pp. 44–5.
37 ibid. pp. 49–50.
38 ibid. pp. 75–6.
39 ibid. p. 86.
40 ibid. pp. 83–4; *Star of the West*, vol. VIII, no. 17 (19 January 1918), p 226.
41 Thompson, *The Diary of Juliet Thompson*, pp. 93–4.
42 ibid. pp. 94–5.
43 ibid. p. 96.
44 ibid. pp. 108–10.
45 ibid. pp. 113–14.
46 Notes taken by Saffa Kinney, USBNA, Bosch Papers, Box 12: Louise Bosch.
47 Thompson, *The Diary of Juliet Thompson*, pp. 141–2.
48 ibid. pp. 144–6.
49 *The Baháʾí World*, vol. XIII (1954–1963), p. 832. For more about his life, see Harper, *Lights of Fortitude*, pp. 249–52
50 Revell, 'A Baháʾí pioneer of East and West – Doctor Susan I. Moody . . .', in *The Baháʾí World*, vol. VI (1934–1936), p. 483.
51 USBNA, Mary Rabb Papers, Box 7: Susan I. Moody, p. 1.
52 ibid. p. 2.
53 USBNA, Vail Papers, Box 8: Louise R. Waite, pp. 1–2.
54 USBNA, Mary Rabb Papers, Box 7: Susan I. Moody.
55 *Star of the West*, vol. XVIII, no. 9 (December 1927), pp. 285–6.
56 ibid. pp. 3–5.
57 ibid. p. 8.
58 ibid. p. 9.
59 *The Baháʾí World*, vol. VI (1934–1936), pp. 484–6.
60 USBNA, Mary Rabb Papers, Box 7: Misses Wilson/Englehorn/Stewart/Mrs Brittingham, 1909, pp. 1, 4.
61 Remey, *A Comprehensive History of the Baháʾí Movement*, p. 117.

1910–1911
1 Stockman, *The Baháʾí Faith in America*, vol. 2, pp. 348–9.
2 *Star of the West*, vol. 1, no. 11 (27 September 1910), p. 5.
3 ibid. p. 7.
4 Troxel, *Life of Agnes Alexander*, http://bahai-library.com/troxel_life_agnes_alexander; Redman and Troxel, *Agnes Alexander, Hand of the Cause of God*, forthcoming from George Ronald.
5 USBNA, Revells Papers, Box 7: Howard Struven, p. 4.
6 USBNA, Remey Papers, Box 2 [v.2]: Charles Mason Remey, p. 45.

7   USBNA, Revells Papers, Box 7: Howard Struven, p. 10.
8   Remey, *A Comprehensive History of the Bahá'í Movement*, p. 120–21.
9   *Star of the West*, vol. I, no. 8 (1 August 1910), p. 2.
10 Remey, *A Comprehensive History of the Bahá'í Movement*, pp. 71–3.
11 ibid. p. 70.
12 *Star of the West*, vol. I, no. 8 (1 August 1910), pp. 7–8.
13 USBNA, Revells Papers, Box 7: Howard Struven, p. 15.
14 *Star of the West*, vol. 1, no. 9 (20 August 1910), pp. 5–6.
15 Cobb, *Memories of 'Abdu'l-Bahá*, p. 8.
16 ibid. p. 9.
17 *The Bahá'í World*, vol. XI (1946–1950), p. 487.
18 Cobb, *Memories of 'Abdu'l-Bahá*, p. 10.
19 Rohani, *The Sweet and Enchanting Stories*, pp. 23–4.
20 McKay, *Fires in Many Hearts*, pp. 49–50; USBNA, Lucas, Box 1: Martha Root, p. 2.
21 *Star of the West*, vol. 1, no. 12, p. 7.
22 Stockman, *The Bahá'í Faith in America*, vol. 2, pp. 258, 289.
23 *The Bahá'í World*, vol. IX (1940–1944) pp. 633–5.
24 Rabbani, *The Priceless Pearl*, pp. 11–13.
25 Stevens, *Everybody's Magazine*, 1 December 1911.
26 Sohrab, *Ahmad Sohrab's Diary*, 30 November 1913, pp. 524–5.
27 ibid. 28 June 1913, pp. 1090–93.
28 *Star of the West*, vol. XIV, no. 4 (July 1923), pp. 118–19.
29 ibid. vol. I, no. 17 (19 January 1911), p. 5.
30 ibid. vol. XV, no. 4 (July 1924), p. 108.
31 ibid. vol. I, no. 14 (23 November 1910), p. 3.
32 ibid. vol. I, no. 15 (12 December 1910), p. 3.
33 ibid. vol. I, no. 17 (19 January 1911), p. 5.
34 ibid. vol. II, no. 3 (28 April 1911), p. 5.
35 Balyuzi, *'Abdu'l-Bahá*, p. 137.
36 USBNA, Remey Papers, Box 10 [v.10]: Charles Mason Remey.

INDEX

'Abdu'l-Bahá
    conversations and talks on most
        pages of the book
    and Covenant-breakers 4-7, 12, 36,
        67-70, 80, 98-100, 126, 130, 131
    descriptions by pilgrims and others
        on most pages of the book
    general effect on pilgrims viii, xiii,
        151, 153, 155, 201-2, 245, 252
    and Shrine of the Báb 53-5, 98, 127,
        214-16
    station 1-2, 57, 78, 97, 120, 146-7
'Abdu'l-Karím 12, 31
Abdu'r-Raḥman Páshá 182
Abdu'r Rasúl (Abdor Rasoul) 254
Abela, Pietro 126, 130
Abu'l-Faḍl (Gulpaygání) 31, 39-40,
    47-9, 53, 59, 102, 110, 143, 207
Abu'l-Qásim (gardener), 73-4, 169, 174
Afnán, the 1, 2, 241
Afnán, Aqay-i (Mírzá Núri'd-Dín) 3, 8
Afnán, Habíbu'lláh, 3-7, 55-6
Afnán, Muḥammad-Alí 3
Afroukhteh, Dr Youness (Yúnis Khán)
    viii, ix, 4, 58-60, 66, 67, 70, 74-6,
    82-3, 86, 88, 90-91, 93-4, 98, 103,
    106-7, 130
Aghsán, the 1-2
Agnew, Arthur 151, 159-60, 165-9
Agnew, Mary 159, 164-9
Agnew, Ruhullah 159
Albertson, Alma 46
Alexander, Agnes 43, 239
Allen-Dyar, Aseyeh (Wellesca) xiii,
    170-71
Apperson, Anne 9, 19
Áqá Ján, Mírzá 4-7, 36

Aref Bey 130
Asadu'lláh, Mírzá 119, 125-6, 153, 160,
    167, 187, 218
Asadu'lláh, Siyyid 220
Azízí, Azíz'u'lláh 95-8, 141-3, 273

Bachrodt, Emily (Amelia) 15
Badí'u'lláh 4, 50, 67-9, 139, 185
Badrí Beg, General 77, 99, 130
Bagdadi, Mustapha 58-9
Bagdadi, Zia 49, 59, 175
Bahá'u'lláh
    commemoration of Ascension 64-6,
        123-4
    Covenant of, Covenant-breaking 1-2,
        4-6, 20-21, 33, 67-8, 99-100, 250
    first mention in the West 48-9
    photograph 17, 22, 33, 79, 94, 167,
        240
    pilgrims to and contemporaries of
        viii, 3, 58, 198, 200, 245
    power of His Revelation 9, 37, 44,
        48, 119, 125, 138, 195, 211,
        229-30, 252
    and Shrine of the Báb 53, 214
    and story of locusts 43, 73-4
Ballora, Edna 218, 221
Barney, Alice 123
Barney, Laura 44-6, 53, 55, 57, 98,
    102-4, 110, 121, 123, 143, 147, 224
Bashír 136, 137, 192
Beede, Alice 217, 224, 230
Bingham, Charlotte 143
Blomfield, Lady 102, 143, 245
Bolles, May (Maxwell) 9, 17-23, 46, 52,
    71, 73, 208-9, 224
Bray, Rev Mr 50

Breakwell, Thomas 71-7
Breed, Florence (Khan) 44, 135-40
Brittingham, Isabella xiii, 10, 71-4, 238
Brooks, Richard 159
Browne, Edward Granville 49, 245
Bryan, William Jennings 133-4
Bryant, A. M. 215

Chapman, Mrs J. C. 149
Chase, Thornton 10, 14, 32, 159-70, 184, 248
Cobb, Stanwood 195-7, 244-6, 247
Cole, Helen Ellis 46, 52
Coles, Claudia, 224
Cooper, Ella (Goodall) 9, 11, 27-30, 187-93
Cowles, Josephine (de Lagnel) 123-4
Crockett, Grace 243-4
Curtis, William E. 79

d'Ange d'Astre, Madame 131
de Bons, Dr Joseph 52-3, 149-50
de Bons, Edith (McKay) 52-3, 149-50
De Canavarro, Madame 80, 82-3, 85-6
de Lagnel, Josephine (Cowles) 123-4
Devine, Aline Shane 143
Dixon, Charlotte 41-3
Dixon, Eleanor 41-3
Dixon, Louise 41-3
Ḍíyá'iyyih Khánum 46, 189
Dodge, Arthur, 10, 39-40, 77
Dodge, Elizabeth 39-40, 77
Dodge, Wendell 70, 77-9
Dodge, William 70, 77-9
Dreyfus, Hippolyte 86, 102

Escobino 128
Englehorn, Miss 238
Esslemont, Dr John xi

Fá'izih Khánum 56-7
Fallscheer, Dr Josephina 249-51
Farahangiz Khánum 247-8
Fareed, Amín ix, 59-60, 64, 66, 77, 218, 247-8
Faríq Pasha 99
Farmer, Sarah 37-9

Finch, Ida 202-7
Ford, Mary Hanford 176-81, 184
Ford, Rev. George 48
Frank, Frank 93-5

Getsinger, Edward x, 9, 10-15, 19, 31, 39-40, 43, 46, 52
Getsinger, Lua 9, 10, 12-15, 19, 30-32, 39-40, 46, 52, 170, 196-7, 224, 244
Goin, Ellen 44
Goodall, Helen 10, 27, 187-93
Grant, Percy 226-7
Greatest Holy Leaf (Bahíyyih Khánum) 3, 14, 19, 28-9, 30, 42, 46, 121, 135, 157, 171, 178, 184, 187, 189, 192, 193, 203, 214, 218, 233, 248, 249, 255
Green Acre, Maine 37-8, 196
Gregory, Louis 258
Grossmann, Hermann 34
Grundy, Julia 112-18, 144

Haddad, Anton 7-8, 11, 31, 34-5, 39, 48
Hakím, Alfátún 85-6
Hakím, Arastú Khán 82, 85-6
Hakím, Lotfullah ix
Hannen, Joseph 202, 210-13
Hannen, Pauline 202, 210-13
Harris, Hooper 143-5, 147
Hashimi-Zadeh, Siyyid Hasan 95
Hay, Drummond 130
Ḥaydar-'Alí, Mírzá 32, 49, 56-7, 106-7, 140, 168, 185, 232
Hearst, Phoebe ix, 8-12, 15-17, 19, 27, 34, 46, 143
Herron, Sara G. 50
Hillyer, Helen (Nell) 9, 11, 27, 30
Hoagg, Emogene 46-8, 194
Hoar, Anna 39
Hoar, William 58-66
Holbach, M. M. 80
Hopper, Herbert 71-7
Ḥusayn Effendi 33

Ibn-i-Aṣdaq 95
Ibtiháju'l-Mulk 36-7

INDEX

Isfandíyár 46
Ives, Howard Colby 253

Jack, Marion 48, 184, 190-95
Jackson, Edith 53, 55, 101, 124, 218, 244
Jalál, Mírzá 254
Jessup, Rev. Henry H. 48-50

Kaiser Wilhelm II 8
Keating, Mrs 37
Kerif Pasha, General 62
Khabiri, Ustad Mahmud 95
Khalíl (servant to 'Abdu'l-Bahá) 246
Khan, Ali-Kuli ix, 32-4, 36-7, 41, 43, 44-5, 52-3, 59, 135-41
Khan, Florence 44, 135-40
Khan, Rahim 135
Kheiralla, Ibrahim ix, 7, 9-13, 31, 34-5, 37, 40, 46, 53, 66, 110
Kheiralla, Marian (Miller) 9, 11, 16, 31, 37
Kermani 64
Khusraw 231
Kinney, Carrie 217-20, 224, 225, 227-8, 230
Kinney, Edward 217-20, 222, 225, 230
Kinney, Howard 217, 224
Kinney, Sandy (Sanford) 217, 224
Kishani, Asadu'lláh 166
Knobloch, Alma, 202-3, 206-7, 210
Knobloch, Fanny 202-3, 206-7, 210
Knudson, Elizabeth 37
Koropatkan, General 81

Lachenay, Madame 102
Latimer, George xiii, 126
Lává Páshá 62-3, 99, 106
Letitia, Mademoiselle 86-7
Locke, Josephine 37
Lucas, Mary 110, 120-23, 196

MacNutt, Howard 10, 98, 109, 110-20, 224
MacNutt, Mary 98, 109, 110-20
Majdu'd-Dín 4, 7, 67
Man<u>sh</u>ádí, Siyyid Taqí 36, 59-60, 78

Mathew, Louisa, 258
Maxwell, Mary 210
Maxwell, May (Bolles) 9, 17-23, 46, 52, 71, 73, 208-9, 224
Maxwell, Sutherland 208-9
McKay, Edith (de Bons) 52-3, 149-50
McKay, Marie-Louise 52-3
Miller, Marian (Kheiralla) 9, 11, 16, 31, 37
Mírzá Amín see Fareed
Mi<u>sh</u>kín-Qalam 6, 89, 141-2, 215
Momen, Moojan 125
Monahan, James H. 54, 68, 70-71
Moody, Dr Susan 232-3, 235-7
Moore, Louisa see Getsinger, Lua
Mortenson, Fred 258
Muḥammad-'Alí, Mírzá 4-5, 7, 20-21, 36, 50, 53, 66-9, 80, 99, 127, 129, 131, 214
Muḥammad-'Alí, Ustád 34, 254
Muḥammad-Ḥasan, Mírzá 186
Muḥammad-Husayn, Mírzá 186
Muḥammad-Sadiq, Áqá Siyyid 56
Muḥammad-Taqí, Ḥájí Mírzá 198
Munavvar <u>Kh</u>ánum 42, 154, 189, 195, 218, 218-19, 221, 224, 233, 235
Munír, Mírzá (Zayn) 140, 184, 187, 213-15, 254
Muníriḥ <u>Kh</u>ánum 19, 71, 121, 153, 157-8, 189, 203-4, 233

Náṣiri-Dín <u>Sh</u>áh 257
Nuru'lláh Effendi 17, 48, 60
Núru'd-Dín, Mírzá 94, 106, 149, 175

Ober, Harlan 143, 146-7
Osborne, Mr and Mrs 147

Parsons, Agnes 224, 247
Pearson, Julia 9, 19
Peeke, Margaret 23-7
Phelps, Frances 174-6
Phelps, Myron 80, 82-6

Ramsey, Mrs 87-8, 139
Ra<u>sh</u>íd Pasha 258
Remey, Mason 52, 57-8, 126, 131,

174-6, 182, 190, 198-201, 226-7, 232, 239-43, 248
Rodgers, Caroline 219, 224-6
Rosenberg, Ethel 52, 102-3, 208
Rúhá Khánum 30, 42-3, 140, 152-3, 189, 191, 209, 233
Rúhí Effendi 224
Rúḥíyyih Khánum (Mary Maxwell) 29, 208, 210
Russell, Sigurd 53, 101

Ṣádiq Páshá 54
Sanderson, Edith 86, 143, 170-71, 190
Scaramucci, Mary 151-3, 155, 159
Scheffler, Carl 159-61, 170
Schushtari, Muḥammad 161
Schweizer, Annemarie 245
Schweizer, Friedrich 245
Shoghi Effendi ix, 46, 66, 74, 174, 189, 194, 109-10, 232, 248, 258
   childhood and youth 21, 29, 42, 140, 153, 157, 193, 216, 224, 249
   writings x, 2, 99-100, 124-5, 129, 214
Shrine of the Báb 18, 39, 43, 53-5, 56, 74, 79, 98, 111, 113-14, 135, 140, 153-4, 160-61, 171, 172, 175, 211, 214-16, 218, 233, 239, 241, 254
Shrine of Bahá'u'lláh 3, 6, 7, 14, 20-22, 28, 30, 37, 43, 46, 50, 62, 64-6, 68, 79, 98, 99, 123-4, 131, 132, 147, 169, 174, 176, 191, 224-5, 240, 247
Shu'á'u'lláh 67, 139
Smith, F. Carl 256
Sohrab, Ahmad ix
Sprague, Sydney 104-6, 200, 227, 232, 235-6, 247-8
Stannard, Jean 194-5
Stapfer, Louise 208
Stevens, Ethel Stefana 251-3
Stewart, Elizabeth 238
Struven, Howard 32, 239-43
Sulṭán 'Abdu'l-Ḥamíd II 68, 125-6, 129, 133, 185, 200, 216-17

Taft, President William Howard 258
Taliqani, Ḥájí Mírzá (Ḥasan-i-Adíb) 97

Thompson, Juliet 217-32
Thornburgh, Harriet 9, 17, 19-20, 41, 52
Thornburgh-Cropper, Mary Virginia (Maryam) 9, 15-16, 132, 143
Townshend, George 197
Tronvé, Emma 44-5
True, Arna 155-7
True, Corinne xii, 155-8, 164
Túbá Khánum 86-7, 189, 218-19
Turner, Robert 9, 19

Varqá, Mírzá 'Abdu'lláh Khán 4
Varqá, Mírzá 'Alí-Muḥammad 4
Varqá, Valíyu'lláh 232

Waite, Louise xii, 232-6
Watson, Anna 108
Wells, Captain 49
Wells, Mr 175
Whyte, Alexander, Rev. Dr 132-3
Whyte, Jane 132-3
Wilberforce, Archdeacon 39
Wilhelm, Laurie 170-74
Wilhelm, Roy 170-74,
Wilson, Maria P. 37-9, 238
Wilson, President Woodrow 133, 134, 180
Winterburn, George 89-93, 98, 144, 163
Winterburn, Rosa 89-93, 98, 144
Wolcott, O. 34
Woodcock, Aloysis 110
Woodcock, Edwin 13, 149-50, 152
Woodcock, Eva 110
Woodcock, May 110, 215
Woodcock, Percy 110

Yaḥyá, Mírzá 68
Yazdí, Aḥmad 17, 48, 58, 149, 152
Yazdí, Muḥammad 'Alí 58, 161, 202
Youseff, Sheikh 200
Yúnis Khán *see* Afroukhteh

Zayn, Munír 140, 184, 187, 213-15, 254
Zillu's-Sulṭán 257

ABOUT THE AUTHOR

Earl Redman is a geologist who worked in Alaska and Chile for two decades. One job was for the US Bureau of Mines, studying mineral deposits in the Juneau Gold Belt, Alaska. In 1999 he moved with his wife Sharon to Ireland, where he has researched and written five books, exploring the gold mines of the stories included in *'Abdu'l-Bahá in Their Midst*, the two volumes of *Shoghi Effendi Through the Pilgrim's Eye*, a book on the Knights of Bahá'u'lláh, and this volume on pilgrims who visited 'Abdu'l-Bahá in the Holy Land before His Western journeys. A second volume tells the story of pilgrims to the Holy Land after 'Abdu'l-Bahá's return in 1913.

Earl and Sharon have travelled widely and for long periods in recent years and are much in demand as speakers and storytellers.

www.ingramcontent.com/pod-product-compliance
Lightning Source LLC
Chambersburg PA
CBHW020943230426
43666CB00005B/141